PENGUIN BOOKS

FLOYD ON OZ

Keith Floyd was born in 1943 and educated at Wellington School, Somerset. Since then he has devoted his life to cooking, except for a few brief excursions into the Army, antiques and the wine trade. Happily released from the rigours of running a restaurant by a chance meeting with a television producer, he has presented six television cookery series and written several bestselling books. When he is not hurtling around the world he spends his time in Devon, where he owns a pub.

FLOYD
on
OZ

Keith Floyd

PENGUIN BOOKS

With special thanks to Anne Barclay for making me sit down at the typewriter when I wanted to go to the pub. And to the whole Australian film crew, but especially Paul Shire for the photographs and Maggie for the cucumber sandwiches.

Thanks to all the Aussies who were so co-operative while we were filming. And to the cooks, wine growers, cheesemakers and *bon viveurs* of Australia, who helped us on our way.

PENGUIN BOOKS

Published by the Penguin Group
Penguin Books Ltd, 27 Wrights Lane, London W8 5TZ, England
Penguin Books USA Inc., 375 Hudson Street, New York, New York 10014, USA
Penguin Books Australia Ltd, Ringwood, Victoria, Australia
Penguin Books Canada Ltd, 10 Alcorn Avenue, Toronto, Ontario, Canada M4V 3B2
Penguin Books (NZ) Ltd, 182–190 Wairau Road, Auckland 10, New Zealand

Penguin Books Ltd, Registered Offices: Harmondsworth, Middlesex, England

First published by Michael Joseph 1991
Published in Penguin Books 1992
10 9 8 7 6 5 4 3 2 1

Recipe photographer: Laurie Evans
Home economist: Berit Vinegrad
Stylist: Leslie Richardson
Cookery adviser: Sue Ashworth

Printed and bound in Singapore by Kyodo Printing Co.

CONTENTS

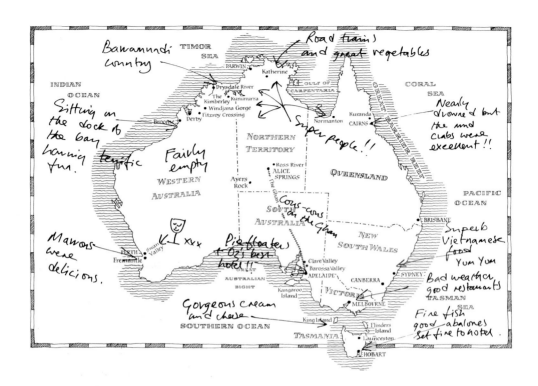

Barramundi country

TIMOR SEA

Road trains and great vegetables

INDIAN OCEAN

Sitting on the dock of the bay having terrific fun.

Drysdale River
The Kimberley
Kununurra
Windjana Gorge
Fitzroy Crossing
Broome
Derby

DARWIN
Katherine

GULF OF CARPENTARIA

CORAL SEA

Nearly drowned but the mud crabs were excellent !!

Super people !!

Normanton
Kuranda
CAIRNS

Fairly empty

WESTERN AUSTRALIA

NORTHERN TERRITORY

Ross River
ALICE SPRINGS

QUEENSLAND

PACIFIC OCEAN

Ayers Rock

Couscous on the Ghan

SOUTH AUSTRALIA

Mawsons were delicious.

K I xxx
PERTH
Swan Valley
Fremantle

Pie-floater + Oz's best hotel !!

GREAT AUSTRALIAN BIGHT

Clare Valley
Barossa Valley
ADELAIDE
Kangaroo Island

NEW SOUTH WALES

BRISBANE

Superb Vietnamese food Yum Yum

CANBERRA
VICTORIA
MELBOURNE

SYDNEY

Bad weather good restaurants

TASMAN SEA

Gorgeous cream and cheese

King Island
SOUTHERN OCEAN

Flinders Island
Launceston
TASMANIA
HOBART

Fine fish good abalone set fire to hotel.

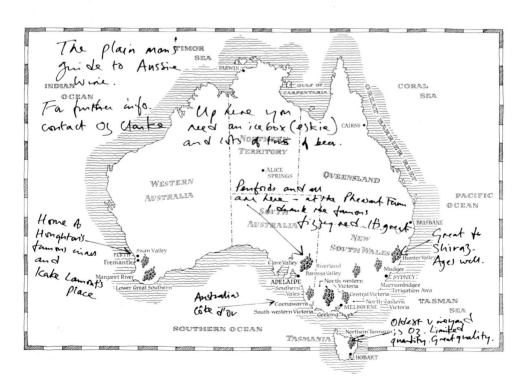

The plain man's guide to Aussie wine.

TIMOR SEA

INDIAN OCEAN

For further info. contact Oz Clarke

DARWIN

Up here you need an icebox (eskie) and lots of tins of beer.

GULF OF CARPENTARIA

CORAL SEA

NORTHERN TERRITORY

CAIRNS

WESTERN AUSTRALIA

ALICE SPRINGS

QUEENSLAND

PACIFIC OCEAN

Home of Houghton's famous wines and Jake Lamont's place

PERTH
Swan Valley
Fremantle
Margaret River
Lower Great Southern

Penfolds and all are here — at the Pheasant Farm South of the famous AUSTRALIA fizzy red. It's great

Clare Valley
Riverland
Barossa Valley
ADELAIDE
Southern Vales

BRISBANE

Great for Shiraz. Ages well.

Mudgee
Hunter Valley
NEW SOUTH WALES
SYDNEY

Australian Côte d'Or

North western Victoria
Murrumbidgee Irrigation Area
Central Victoria
North-eastern Victoria
Coonawarra
South-western Victoria
Geelong
MELBOURNE

TASMAN SEA

SOUTHERN OCEAN

Northern Tasmania
TASMANIA
HOBART

Oldest vineyard in Oz. Limited quantity. Great quality.

Cooks, convicts and Kangaroos

Captain Cook drained his glass of madeira and stretched back contentedly in the polished comfort of his cabin. He stood up to yawn and bumped his head on the low ceiling. Something he often did when he had had too many glasses of sercial. But so what, if he was a little tired and emotional, it had been one hell of a voyage.

Pall Mall, the Naval Club, London, and home were a long way away. He remembered the day sitting in his club, glass in hand, having been inactive for several months, and on half-pay to boot, when a breathless messenger arrived at his table and said: 'Begging your pardon, sir. A very important message from the Admiralty.'

'Then read it to me, my good man,' said Cook, cursing the interruption to his claret drinking. The messenger shook himself and tried to pose his stance, fumbled open the sealed scroll, cleared his throat and hesitantly began to read:

'Their Lordships hereby request and require that their trusted servant, Captain James Horatio Hornblower, whoops I mean Captain James Cook, do make utmost dispatch to prepare two or three vessels, suitably victualled and manned (by the way, their Lordships advise you to take an artist, a botanist, a surveyor and a diarist), and proceed immediately to go and discover something.

'You will be aware that petty crime among the working classes is on the increase. Indeed, had you heard the Home Secretary on this morning's "Yesterday In Parliament" on the subject of prison overcrowding, you would realise that we need somewhere to put these pestilent vagabonds.

'An informed intelligence source, whom one of their Lordships overheard in the Drunken Admiral, reports that according to some Dutch guy called Van Diemen, about 12,000 miles away there is a very big island, called New Holland. It is their Lordships' wish that you should go immediately and colonise New Holland, call it Australia and fill it up with convicts. Apparently there are quite a lot of trees there and this could be really useful for building boats and warships, just in case the French or somebody else tries to take over Indonesia.

'Signed and sealed by their Lordships, in this year of Christ 1770 [or thereabouts].'

Cook rubbed the bump on his head. 'Oh dearie me,' he said, and rang the little bell for his steward. 'Pass me my frock coat, I am going on deck to look at our landfall.'

As he leaned over the taff rail, looking at the uncompromising coastline, he wondered what he was going to do with the country now he had arrived. He didn't have a phone, so he couldn't ring up and say, 'I've got here, what shall I do with it?'

But being of firm British resolve, he lowered his barge and with a small escort of Marines he, the botanist, the artist and the surveyor made speed for the shore. Bearing in mind they'd all had a few, they really did quite well.

Joseph, for that was the botanist's name, was in raptures because of all the little wild flowers that grew just above the beach. There were nasturtiums, daisies, buttercups, coolabahs, prickly wattle, beefwood, tea trees and witchetty bushes.

He could not contain his excitement at this splendid plethora of flora and, unheeding of his fresh white breeches, was soon on his hands and knees gathering a bouquet of flowers. Only slightly slurring his words, he said: 'I say, James, I have got a capital idea. I mean, you know this place has got lots of flowers, so why not let's call it Botany Bay, the convicts will adore it.'

'Good idea, old bean. Make a note of that, Mr Surveyor,' said Captain Cook. 'It's going to be really good fun, working out names for all these places. Look at that promontory over there, for example. What does that remind you of?'

'Well, now you come to mention it,' giggled Joseph, 'it reminds me of the coxswain.'

'Splendid, let's call it Yorkies Knob.'

And so it came to be, dear reader, that most of Australia was named at whim by a bunch of drunken sailors. Typically, they disregarded the Aboriginal names, names going back for forty-thousand years, and typically when they did meet some Aboriginals they used the old British trick of just shouting louder.

Consequently, one of the great historical misnomers of all time occurred when they saw this large animal, with a long tail, hopping through the undergrowth. To a man they reached for their hip flasks, but Cook steadied himself after a hearty swig. 'Ask one of our black friends the name of that thing.'

The Aboriginal shook his sad old head and said, 'Kangaroo'. And so it was that this jumping, leaping animal obtained its English name. In fact, as any student of the Aboriginal languages will tell you, kangaroo means: 'Sorry, John, I haven't got a clue.'

And I assure you that every preceding word has been hammered on the anvil of truth.

One

"Hot town - Summer in the city"

I don't know what sort of food Captain Cook had on his ship out to Australia, probably salt beef and bread and pretty stale potatoes. And if it had been one of the young chefs at my pub's restaurant working for him, no matter how good the beef was, I bet he would have been served with cold potatoes.

I, on the other hand, travelled on a huge jumbo jet, first-class naturally, and what took Captain Cook several months, took me a mere thirty hours in the comfort of a Qantas 747. I must say, given the constraints of in-flight catering, the food was jolly good, except that it's a bit like being in an expensive hospital. They keep waking you up and pouring champagne and caviar down your throat instead of pills and medicaments.

But they were a charming lot and the Captain regaled us for most of the journey with the news that England was being absolutely wiped out by the Aussies in a series of cricket tests. In fact, he was so full of this that he seldom got round to the usual in-flight information, like how high we were, where we were going and stuff like that.

Anyway, I am not a cricket fan, so I wiped a little bit of bread across my plate of grilled chicken and *sauce diable*, plugged in the headset and enjoyed an excellent Cabernet Sauvignon from Coonawarra called Rouge-Homme as I settled back to watch *My Mother Is An Alien* for the second time in three months. This was my third trip to Australia in as many months and I was beginning to feel a bit of an old hand.

But I was glad when the plane finally landed in Sydney and, after a cursory customs check, I was met by my producer, Pam Stockley, poured into the back of a white Rolls-Royce and driven to my hotel, the Regent, with a suite overlooking Sydney Harbour, the Bridge and the Opera House. It has to be one of the most spectacular sights.

I showered and changed and went up about 500 floors to the bar to meet the crew who were going to participate in this odd little journey round Australia. Just so that you know as you will see their names throughout the book, I will tell you that Steve is the cameraman (but we call him Bruce), Tim is the sound recordist, Helen is a production assistant, Pies did everything, Barbara is a production assistant, John Chase and Pam Stockley are the producers, Paul is the stills photographer, David Pritchard is the director, Maggie is supposed to be a driver and my assistant.

So after a few nervous G'days, we settled down to the serious business of having a few drinks and getting to know each other before the great adventure started tomorrow.

The crew in Broome. From left to right, standing: John 'No Worries' Chase; Pritchard, D.; Mark, who joined us for a day only; me; 'Bruce'; Tim on sound. Sitting: Helen; Maggie; Pies; Alison. Missing are Paul Shire (who took the picture) and Pam Stockley

Sydney, Day 1

Up early to rendezvous on Number 5 wharf for a quick sail around Sydney Harbour, in a twelve-metre ex-Americas Cup yacht called *Vim*. The idea is to shoot the opening scene of the series with me mixing a non-alcoholic cocktail while at the helm of this magnificent craft, sailing full pelt under Sydney Harbour Bridge.

As usual there are no rehearsals. Once all the equipment is plugged in, David sort of looks at me and says, 'Are you ready?' and I say, 'I think so' and he says, 'Okay. Quiet please, off you pop.'

So struggling with the helm, a rising wind, a stiff breeze and a battery-operated cocktail mixer, I said this little piece to camera. 'In my unceasing quest to find an Australian heiress, I've borrowed this modest ex-Americas Cup yacht, the *Vim*. And with my trusty crew, we've been thirty days and nights at sea. Waves with teeth like bananas and a hell of a white water. But after the unrelenting battle, we find ourselves here in Sydney, capital of New South Wales, and the home of the most wonderful and, I hasten to add, alcohol-free cocktails in the world.

'Now, Bruce; this is Bruce, my new man. We couldn't get Clive, he's still in the Home. Just a quick spin round the ingredients. We've got some gum tree honey, some freshly-squeezed oranges, some eggs, lime juice – squeeze some of that into the glass. Not all that easy to steer a yacht and make cocktails at the same time, but I can do it. There's only an American warship to hit if we get in the way of anything.

'That goes into there, an egg into there like that, eggshells are biodegradable so they can go overboard, fresh orange juice into there and then with my trusty little toy just mix that up.

'Notice, my nautical friends, there isn't a flap of sail to be heard even though I'm holding us tight – I think it's on a broad reach we call this. There we are. Cinnamon over the frothy top. G'day, welcome to Sydney.'

Although that's a bit out of context in this book, I include it because it was a nerve-racking moment to deliver your first piece to camera with a brand new crew. I mean, I have got so used to working with Clive North, Andy, Tim, Steve and Frances that I find working before strangers makes me strangely nervous and I am anxious not to fluff my lines or to give them the chance to say David and I are a pair of wimpy Poms. But as luck would have it, I delivered it fluently and mixed up the drink correctly at the same time and, although nobody said anything, David winked at me and I knew we were going to be okay.

It was an exhilarating sail and although it only lasted for an hour or two I could have happily spent a week on board the thing. As it was, we turned back to the wharf and had a little picnic.

As picnics go, it was pretty good. We had blue swimmer crabs, Balmain bugs – sort of piscatorial flying saucers that look like huge woodlice, and they taste of shrimps or prawns. Then we had a plate of huge raw New Zealand mussels, big, green-shelled things, a great deal of sushi made with raw ling, tuna, squid, salmon, prawns and so on and washed down with some rather Chablis-like Hardy white wine.

It was a very promising start, I felt. Needless to say, delicious as it all was, I was already too stuffed to be able to eat yet another plate of seafood. On the plane over I had had more crayfish, smoked salmon, caviar, lobster and prawns than I ever want to see again. So I just had a couple of cucumber sandwiches with the crusts off.

That night we were invited to a reception sponsored by the Sydney Fish Market, where I fell for the first of many prepared PR traps. I actually thought the party was for us, and I tucked into tray upon tray of little Sydney rock oysters with gay abandon, posing here and there for photographs, grinning behind a glass of wine, signing the odd autograph, chatting up a boatload of Australian foodies and beauties and feeling good in my white tuxedo and red carnation.

What I didn't know was that the famous Sydney rock oyster had recently been severely polluted after three very severe storms had flooded several thousand square miles of farmland, which overflowed with silage and farming waste into the oyster beds. So when next day I opened the papers to see myself printed large in the centre pages, grinning from ear to ear and holding a tray of oysters under a headline that said, 'Floyd says Sydney oysters are okay', I realised I had unwittingly been endorsing oysters.

Never mind, it was one hell of a good party, and the oysters didn't do me any harm even though they're not as good as my favourites from County Cork and from the Helford River.

The round of receptions, press, radio and TV interviews, visitations from the Tourist Board and the Fishing Authority, went on apace. The drinks flowed and the questions were unceasing and by midnight on Day Two the jetlag that I hoped I'd overcome hit me like a wall of treacle and I passed out into a deep and untroubled twelve-hour sleep.

When you go to a foreign country you often meet someone who has turned their passion for the countryside, history and geology that surrounds them into some kind of commercial enterprise. One such person is my latest chum, Libby Buhrich, who was born and raised in Cabbage Palm Road (now there's a nice thing, only Australians would blend the normality of cabbages and palm trees and would be so honest as to describe the sole indigenous Australian palm tree as a cabbage palm, because it actually looks like a cabbage). Anyway, Libby, who loves this area and this vast Ku-ring-gai Chase National Park, a staggering expanse of natural beauty with Aboriginal rock carvings on tessellated pavements, earns a few dollars and satisfies herself by taking tourists or even journalists and television presenters on gastronomic safaris. But there is no such thing as a free lunch and before Libby would take me on her bush picnic in Ku-ring-gai, before she would show me the odd plants and the strange trees and the whole thing I, of course, would have to cook for her.

It is a bright and sunny day. I am standing on a promontory looking over Broken Bay and the Hawkesbury River. Over to the East is an outcrop of rock that looks like a sleeping lion. Above that a strip of sandy beach, with a timber jetty. Even from a mile away you can hear a De Havilland Beaver float plane grinding its way out of the water and into the sky. Tall pine trees full of ravens, magpies, kookaburras and lyrebirds. The lyrebird earns its living as an impressionist, and can imitate perfectly the calls of other birds from seagulls to parrots. There is a flotilla of small boats tacking in from behind the promontory. In these clear and untainted waters green turtles still thrive. On an outcrop of desolate rock a colony of fairy penguins splash and play. Tall pine trees give way to cabbage palms. It was probably Admiral Hawkesbury who named this idyllic spot when he landed here in eighteen-whateveritwas.

Aboriginals fished and speared their food and for ever kept a small fire on red clay burning in their canoes. You can find evidence of all this by walking a few hundred yards to the exposed plateaus of sandstone where scenes from their daily lives are etched into the rock.

But, of course, the British, when they arrived, couldn't really handle fishing or collecting berries or wild mushrooms. So ingrained were they in their diet of meat that they damned nearly starved waiting for the supply ships with salted beef and mutton.

It's a funny old scene. I am leaning against one of these circular bronze mushrooms that appear in National Parks, with the pointers engraved and little compasses pointing to far-distant places. And John 'No Worries' Chase, one of my producers, is trying to assemble 'Clive'. Steve the cameraman, whom as I mentioned, we have purely for fifth-form sense of humour reasons, decided to call Bruce, is unpacking his gear. Barbara, Maggie and Helen are rummaging through plastic bags of food. David is impatient to film. Me, I'm just enjoying the view.

John Chase, a sturdy, thickset, practical and quietly-spoken Australian gentleman of some forty summers, has designed this wonderful stove, so I am free to cook anything, anywhere. It's a portable contraption, on legs. It folds up and it folds out. It has built-in chopping boards, it can take a wok. It can griddle a steak, it can simmer a stew. Or at least that's what he told me when we met in England, but today it's like Monsieur Hulot's Holiday. The portable stove, which we have decided to christen Clive in honour of our usual cameraman Clive North who cannot be with us, is an absolute nightmare. Pop one leg in, and the shelf falls off. Balance the shelf, and the gas bottle topples over. Finally, John Chase said, 'She's a Jake (an expression meaning that things are all right, which they are not).' I think this is all quite funny, until David decides that I should be the one made to look a prat, but on film. So he says, 'You assemble it, and we can do this wonderful scene of you bristling with confidence and enthusiasm at the start of your Australian tour, but absolutely unable to assemble the cooker.'

He thinks it's hysterical, but I don't want to be seen in this light of incompetence. I make enough mistakes as it is, without deliberately setting up a scene like that. Anyway, I agree, of course, because I suppose it will be funny. After a few rubbed ankles and pinched fingers in the metalwork of this monstrous machine, I assemble the ingredients for the little snack I am going to cook Libby.

I have got the bits spread round when the mobile phone rings. It is some radio station who want to do a live interview with me. I am happy to do it but it would have been nice if they had told me so I could prepare myself. So with the telephone in one hand and a frying pan in the other, I attempt to give a little Cooking on Radio programme. I am so caught on the hop that all I can do is chatter away down the line to the radio station as if we were filming, which, in fact, we were. I am hoping that David will actually use it so that we can have the funny situation of doing a live radio interview and a TV cooking sketch at the same time. It went something like this.

'Right, Bruce, a quick spin around the ingredients. Down here we have superbly fresh large prawns, some simple spring onions, very fresh coriander, lemon, lime, ginger and garlic. I've also got a bit of sesame oil to cook in, some pepper and salt.

'The very important thing about fresh prawns is you must run a knife down the back of them to take out that little intestinal tube. This is why these things taste delicious in foreign countries and at home very often taste disappointing, because we haven't taken the trouble to remove that little bit of nastiness in there.

'Anyway, now with any luck – I have to say this is the first time I've actually used this stove – we'll pop the prawns in, sizzle, sizzle.

'It's quite interesting – while they sizzle away and I chop this coriander – when the Brits came to this wonderful National Park outside of Sydney about 200 years ago it used to be inhabited by Aboriginals who fished and enjoyed all the fragrant, wonderful resources of the sea here. But what the Brits did was, they came with barrels of salt beef and pickled lamb and nearly starved because the boats didn't come all that often and they were too idle and too arrogant to fish. So rather than be a silly Pom I'm going to try and take some inspiration from the indigenous Australian people and ignore things like beef and stuff and cook seafood.

'These are sizzling away and are practically cooked now, I expect, so we'll add a couple of bits of spring onion like that, some finely-chopped zest of lemon, a little bit of ginger, and a tiny bit of garlic, which I'm chopping over here.

'The Director really likes these chopping bits, it's part of making the film. You'll soon get the hang of it. That goes in there like that. Add a few more spring onions or scallions.

'One thing they haven't done, they haven't brought me any wine and here we are in one of the richest wine-growing countries in the world. So I don't know if an assistant can suddenly bring some, because if they don't I might go on strike and swim over to Palm Beach over there, which is a fabulous place for lunch.

'Here's my lime juice, a little lime juice in here like that. A fraction of soy sauce, not too much, I put a bit too much in there. Look at that, the wine has come. Very nice indeed. A quick taste of this; I think I'll put a bit more lemon juice into that. There we are.

'I happen to have here one of these neat little side plates. Australia's a big country, big plates, get the joke? That goes on to there. The pot goes there because I haven't got an assistant. And that is a simple Australian-style dish of prawns, spring onions, ginger, lime juice and coriander.'

If all that sounds a little garbled, what I was really doing was stir-frying a few prawns in a bit of oil with ginger, onion and garlic. It's terribly simple, but the prawns here are about nine inches long and are absolutely fabulous. In fact, the actual recipe is on page 175.

Anyway, Libby woofed down the prawns, pronounced them excellent, made me put on a rucksack and marched me off into the park and to her picnic. She strode off like Freya Stark, bouncing over pebbles and sidestepping little outcrops of dark-green moss, pointing out different birds from 160 species, stopping to pick cuttings from bottlebrushes, boronoias, bush rockets, spider flowers, tea trees, Christmas bushes, waratahs, scribbly gums (which is a bit like how this writing is getting), geebungs and God knows what. Libby's output of detailed knowledge of the flora and fauna of this National Park left me breathless, confused and hungry, and I was glad when we sat down on the sandstone and looked at the carvings of whales and green turtles and spears while she unpacked her bush picnic. You'll find one of her recipes on page 198.

And very good it was too. This little holiday is really developing into a sort of Boy's Own adventure. Sea planes and twelve-metre waves and treks across the bush. Jolly exciting, and with a very happy heart I stumbled back into my luxurious seat on board the specially-converted, air-conditioned Greyhound bus that was called the Floydmobile. It has lavatories, televisions and telephones, a kitchen and dining room, hot and cold running gin and tonic. And singing like some crazed rugby club, getting stuck in a few ditches, taking a few wrong turns, we made our way back to Sydney, civilisation, the Regent Hotel, a bath and a reviving drink – before dining at the Bayswater Brasserie where Tony Papas (in conjunction with his partner, Hamish Keith) gave me a couple of super recipes from their repertoire which, by the way, they've published as *The Bayswater Brasserie Book of Food*.

Before dining at the Brasserie, I talked with Tony Papas. His approach to Australian food is full-frontal, fresh and uncomplicated even though it draws upon a reservoir of European influences. I was quite surprised when I discovered he is, in fact, a New Zealander. He told me – well, something like this: 'I remember home cooking was fairly standard New Zealand. But at my grandparents' house, it was different. You see, my grandfather was Greek, and an uncle had travelled extensively in Europe too, so we had exotic things like stuffed aubergines and peppers and courgettes to eat. My Scottish grandmother had a terrific repertoire of hearty puddings and stews.

'Then at home, our Maori neighbours would occasionally give us sacks of fish – crayfish, paua [New Zealand for abalone], giant bivalve toeroa [now a protected species], and sometimes parcels of snapper or kingfish.'

He waxed lyrical over his memories – the unforgettable damp smell of salt and seaweed, the personal influences people bring to their cooking, the virtues of a well-trained nose and a sharp eye (even more vital for today's space-age kitchens). I was fascinated.

It seems that, until after the Second World War, Australian and New Zealand food was a colonial version of working-class English cooking – you know, tons of meat and overcooked vegetables. And did I know that the Scots writer Eric Linklater, visiting Oz in 1951, described the antipodean method of cooking roast mutton as being: 'Something akin to blowing a sheep up with a hand grenade, the fragments being burnt in the resulting fire'?

'But it's not like that now,' Tony Papas assured me, 'our cooking's been transformed by postwar influences, not least by classical and provincial French cuisine, ethnic, other European.'

I asked him about the start of brasserie-style restaurants. He told me that when this type of restaurant arrived in Sydney in the early 1980s, it could well have been just another fashionable variation on a theme – plenty of foodies predicted that. Indeed, some did fail.

And did you know, dear reader, that the original French brasserie served food only as a sideline? Traditionally, they were places in eastern parts of France where beer and cider were made and served along with some pretty basic fare, like *charcuterie* and *choucroute* with garnishes. The Parisians extended them – but there still has to be simplicity in the imaginative and versatile dishes.

Anyway, Tony and two partners opened the present Brasserie in two old terrace buildings on the Bayswater Road. They set out to recapture the ambience of cafés in Europe. The building had to have several different dining areas, such as a conservatory overlooking the street, and the illusion of space. Essential too, a stimulating, friendly atmosphere without rigid timetables, practical surfaces softened by plants, bold colour schemes, heaps of magazines and newspapers, displays of tempting puds and pastries. Bustle and chatter, clatter, speeding waiters, energy, fresh seasonal ingredients, a blackboard of daily specials, hearty fare, informal (and healthy) dining. This also suits the Australian style.

In the seven years that it's been open, the Bayswater Brasserie's unique style has evolved, and it's now run by sixty talented staff, Tony told me proudly. 'Childhood memories, experiences of travelling and living abroad have contributed hugely,' he said.

The trouble with trying to keep a journal is that you have to remember the days and you have to record events as they happen. Otherwise, when you return to the tranquillity of your oak-panelled study and you sit down at the Sheraton desk and tell the servants to walk round in soft shoes so that as they go about their labours polishing your antique silver and dusting the ancestral portraits they don't disturb you, you have completely forgotten the facts. Anyway, such is the case today, as I am trying to reconstruct Day Three, or is it Day Two, of my Sydney sojourn.

I recall leaping from the bed and looking out over Sydney Opera House. A chap I met in the bar told me, 'Needless to say, the man who designed the Opera House went broke in the process.' It's funny, the pain that people have to go through in order to create things of beauty and pleasure for others. You all know what the Opera House looks like – it's like a load of scallop shells on their side.

And my friend Terry Wing, who, like me, has a pub in Tuckenhay, Devon, has his name inscribed on the back of one of the seats. It is seat 769. I spent all morning walking up and down the seats looking for his name! Apparently, years ago, when he was a diplomatic courier, he found himself in Sydney and the developers were desperate for money to complete the building, and since he was at some sort of party to promote the scheme he dipped deep into his pocket.

This, of course, has got nothing to do with the price of fish – which incidentally is not exorbitant in Sydney. There is a terrific fish market, and after one of those really pleasant Australian breakfasts that involves cornflakes and strawberries, fresh fruit, pink grapefruit juice, bacon rashers, eggs, and Rosella tomato ketchup, I decided to take a stroll along the waterfront.

I can't remember if there are any palm trees in front of Sydney's fish market, but if there aren't, there should be, because the façade of the building looks more like a casino than anything else. In fact, in the selling ring there is a huge sort of computerised roulette wheel spinning out the price of fish. Excited merchants haggle, hustle, and shout in what struck me as being about forty different languages ranging from Greek, Spanish and Italian to Thai and Japanese.

Outside the main hall there is an Italian fish merchant, who throws octopus into a cement mixer to tenderise them. A novel idea, almost as good as my friend Jean-Claude who used to have 'The Gourmet' in Whiteladies Road, Bristol, and cleaned his mussels in his wife's washing machine. Needless to say, it was on a cold rinse!

There is a sushi bar for hungry fish porters. There are mountains of mud crabs, pyramids of prawns from little succulent sweet Indian banana ones an inch or so long up to things that would give your average British lobster should they meet in a dark alley one night not only an inferiority complex, but probably a heart attack as well.

I recognised some of the fish. There were many – like mangrove jacks, red emperor, stripey, coral trout, rock cod, goatfish, kingfish, butterfish, pomfret, tuskfish, threadfin salmon. There were tiger prawns, brown and grooved, red endeavour prawns, western king prawns, Indian banana prawns, coral prawns, massive crayfish, eels, squid, shark, tuna – and not a bit of haddock, plaice or cod to be seen, hooray!

Anyway, I bought a basket of fish, slumped back into my club chair in the Floydmobile and trundled off to Watsons Bay to visit my newest chum, called Peter Doyle: fish merchant, restaurateur, raconteur, and a straight up-and-down-the-line fair dinkum Aussie, who among his many enterprises runs a charming wooden-verandahed fish restaurant on the water's edge, which his great-grandparents first established as a tearoom and fish and chip shop in the 1880s. They cook terrific food.

'I am', Peter says, 'living proof that crime really does pay. If my great-grandfather . . .' (or was it his grandfather, I forget, I think I have already alluded to the problems of writing journals when you do not take any notes at the time but, however, I'll save all of that 'Till I paint my masterpiece'). Anyway, if Peter's great-grandfather hadn't stolen half a sheep's head out of the Bishop's larder in Cork, he would never have come to this wonderful country. . . . And as he leaned back in his deckchair on the golden beach at Watsons Bay, silent and strong in his moleskins and R.M. Williams riding boots, telling tales of his Irish heritage, I had this brilliant idea for a feature film. Cooking sketches in which things too frequently go wrong are all very well, but really I would rather be an excellent actor. So if any of you reading this book are talented directors or producers and want to make your name, then you should consider this brilliant idea of mine.

▶PLAY

Even as I speak – as a matter of fact, dictate to one of my minions – I can picture the scene on the day that, disconsolate and alone, he boards the *Three Masters*, which is lying in Cork Harbour. Would he have known that bright-eyed, big, buxom Irish women and black-hearted rabbit thieves were chained in the hold, transportees of a cruel government, condemned to a life of slavery in the Colonies? (Probably not, because he was travelling first-class.)

It's about this lone fisherman who looks a bit like Clint Eastwood and who, back in the 1840s, was a hell-raising, port-swilling young blade. From a terribly good family naturally, our hero had an insatiable predilection for pretty kitchen maids below stairs in the family mansion.

*Peter Doyle (left)
making it clear
that crime does
not pay*

Anyway, let's cut a very long story short – you know, gambling debts, unpaid wine bills, offensive letters from tailors etc, etc, etc. But then, of course, there was that unfortunate incident with the scullery maid. Well, there was a big family meeting and the net result was a one-way ticket to Australia.

Now, this is where the story gets really interesting 'cos our hero, whom we'll call Hector – and you must remember that this is totally fictional, and nothing to do with fishing at all – set off with nothing more than a thoroughbred stallion, a handstitched swag and an AmEx gold card to make his fortune in the inhospitable terrain of New South Wales.

After untold deprivations and misery, lantern-jawed and with an iron resolve, he decided to become a restaurateur and open a fish restaurant and lived happily ever after. In the process of living happily ever after, he became one of the first of the Australian aristocracy, which the Aussies themselves refer to as the 'squatocracy'.

Our hero falls in love with this vibrant, big-boobed, long-legged woman and after a night of passion . . . FADE DOWN SOUND

I think that is enough brilliant ideas for feature films, Ed.

PS I bet Mel Gibson would like a part.   ⏸ PAUSE

According to one of my socialite friends, a rather elegant blonde called Heather, Australians are now very proud of their convict heritage. It is quite the thing to have had a grandmother or a grandfather who was an out-and-out villain – though of course they weren't really villains at all. They were victims of a cruelly oppressive British society.

Anyway, back to reality. The water was still lapping on the beach at Watsons Bay. The sand looked as if it had been recently sifted through fine chiffon. The sun was high and flickered on the wavelets. Clean, crisp white boats bobbed gently at anchor. A steam launch is disgorging happy day-trippers on to the wooden jetty. The float plane grinds laboriously towards its take-off point and a helicopter buzzes overhead like an angry hornet.

It is a perfect day. The spirits are high, the fish is fresh – and I am going to assemble Clive, our portable stove, for what is, in fact, the very first full cooking sketch of the entire trip. (I must point out that I am not keeping this journal or writing this rambling report on my Aussie odyssey in any kind of chronological order.)

John 'No Worries' Chase still reckons his stove is the business and David (Pritchard, of course, my beloved director) thinks it would be marvellous if we could assemble Clive actually in the ocean, and I would stand there in this cool water with a couple of ice buckets containing some wine, a table jammed into the seabed so it doesn't float away groaning with fish and cooking pots.

We were ready to go, I have chopped up my ingredients, I am going to make a fish chowder for Peter Doyle's lunch, when I notice we don't have a gas bottle. So I throw one of my little tantrums. And the phrases that spring easily to memory are 'can't organise a piss-up in a pub', 'you expect me to go into the bush with you', 'what a bunch of prats', and other good-natured jibes – because as you all know, I am a man of infinite patience, tireless tolerance, good humour and munificent good nature. Above all, I am not one to winge, to moan, to complain, to scream, to shout and stomp my foot, but my God, what a bunch of prats!

Watsons Bay, Sydney, ? May

Day One: First cooking sketch. No . . . gas bottle! Off they went. It was a day that developed into Gerard Hoffnungesque insanity – you, of course, remember the bricklayer applying for sick leave. Production assistants, producers, gofers, gaffers, grips shot off in search of a gas bottle.

*Mad cooks and Englishmen out
in the Sydney Sea*

I sat in the shade of the verandah with a pleasantly chilled bottle of Chardonnay, and waited. They returned with a gas bottle – but forgot the tube that connected it to the stove. Off they scurried again. Another bottle went by. Wine, not gas.

They returned with a tube, but the thread didn't fit the union on the stove. I, naturally, am radiating sweetness and light; not a visible sign of frustration, anger, annoyance or rage can be seen on my calm visage.

Off they go again and another bottle passes. They come back with a new tube. It fits the stove perfectly, but sadly, it doesn't fit the gas bottle. I decide it is time I took supreme control of the fiasco and off they go in search of a new burning ring, a new pipe, and a new gas bottle. They do this, they return triumphantly with three items. We connect it up. We light the gas. There is a pathetic flame. You couldn't light a cigarette from it. And yet I have a sort of four-gallon saucepan that has to bubble and boil quickly.

We notice that the tube near the gas bottle is furred up with frost: the gas bottle is leaking. I am still, I assure you, totally calm, unruffled. Peter Doyle wanders over to ask what's for lunch. I tell him he has more chance of being struck by lightning than getting anything to eat. I explained the problem and within thirty seconds he produced a huge gas ring, a tube and another gas bottle. We lit it. It worked, and waist-deep in water, more than slightly tired and emotional after wasting four hours waiting for the stove to work, I set about preparing this delicious little chowder.

It is one of those recipes that does not need quantities. I am not going to say you need four ounces of prawns, you need eight ounces of this or that, you just want a mixture of fish.

I melted a couple of ounces of butter in the pan, put in two chopped onions, a couple of finely-diced carrots, a couple of stalks of celery, finely-chopped, a bit of salt and pepper, and fried them gently till they started to turn golden-brown.

I put in a heaped tablespoon of tomato purée, a can of chopped tomatoes, and a couple of pints of fish stock that I had pinched from Peter's restaurant. I brought it all up to the boil; it had a wonderful

▮▮ PAUSE

Can we have a pause here, for a moment, for postcards? I don't know about you, but I hate receiving flippant letters or postcards from chums on holiday – you know, the sort of thing that says 'Weather here, wish you were fine', or whatever those daft things are that people put on postcards.

So I, when sending letters or cards to friends back home, dig deep into learned books and seek out fascinating pieces of information.

Dear Henry,

Although Australia has been inhabited by Aboriginals for many thousands of years, its modern history is usually taken to have begun only in 1770 with Captain James Cook. Sailing more than 2,000 miles up the immense eastern coast of Australia after his stopover at Botany Bay, the English navigator liked the place so much that he stopped nine times along the coast, including an enforced beaching after the Endeavour *ran aground on the Great Barrier Reef. Cook slapped on the many name tags that are still in use today, like Port Jackson after the Secretary of the Admiralty. Once the* Endeavour *passed Cape York, Cook hoisted a flag on what is now Possession Island and formally claimed in the name of George III the whole coast down to the original landfall at New South Wales.*

Anyway, I am sure that you will find this extremely enlightening and educative and will give you something to talk about when you go down to the Three Ferrets tonight.

Yours ever, Keith!

orangey hue to it. It wasn't as thick as custard, but it was not thin. Then I popped in the fish. I used crayfish cut in half, a few bits of squid, a dozen or so mussels, some cubes of fresh tuna, some fillets of firm-fleshed white fish, a few soft-shelled crabs and some milky-white scallops. I added a little more salt and pepper, a dash – just a dash – of chilli sauce, and let it simmer gently for about twenty minutes.

Of course, by now a crowd had gathered, gazing at us, taking photographs and shaking their heads, wondering what on earth this middle-aged prat with spindly legs (I refer to myself of course) was doing up to his waist in water in Watsons Bay, apparently talking to himself while swigging glasses of Rosemount Chardonnay. When they discovered we were English, they were satisfied. Only a bunch of mad Poms would do such a thing!

By the way, after this fiasco I actually had a spot of lunch at Doyle's and among a selection of pretty dazzling dishes there was one that really stood out. They were deep-fried stuffed green king prawns. You'll see the recipe wot I have nicked from Alice Doyle's cookbook on page 174.

For about forty-thousand years the Aboriginal people have called Australia the 'Land of Dreams', and for the most part it is a timeless land hardly touched by man. But to me, it is the most fabulous place, a journey that takes me to cities, bush, outback, tropical rainforest and desert. It is exciting for a cook because it means new meets old; new ingredients and fresh ideas. A massive melting pot of culinary influences stretching from Europe and all over the Far East.

But most of all it's a land where you are free to experiment without having to worry about breaking weary old rules. You are free to go, free to cook, you are free to make a fool of yourself under the hot sun in Watsons Bay. I did and I was enjoying every second of it.

Somewhere North-East from Sydney, 18 May

A flimsy wooden bridge that wobbled as you walked linked the tiny island to this inland lagoon. It had no trees, but the turf was soft and springy, and the tide was slipping away. A pelican, heavy-jowled, pretended to watch us. It was eleven o'clock in the morning. I had flown in by helicopter along the coast, which was a sandy beach, deserted and white, a lace strip against an ultramarine sea. We flew at about a hundred feet,

Floyd on Oz

against somebody's rules I am sure; every now and again we buzzed a lone fisherman or a group of bronzed surfers wearing violent green swimsuits.

For some reason I was thinking about Malcolm Lowry – there were no volcanoes but this flight reminded me of 'Dark as the grave wherein my friend is laid'. And this is the trouble with journals and cookery books, you get carried away for no apparent reason. I should really be telling you about my journey to Port Stephens, inland from Soldier's Point, to Moffals Barn where they farm oysters in a major way and where I, in the company of Heather Brown, a noted feature writer from *The Australian*, am going to collect oysters, cook oysters, make oyster sausages, barbecue mud crabs, cook bream (which the Australians call brim) and be interviewed by this said Heather.

No problem. Done all that before, know about oysters, know about flat-bottomed aluminium boats that drive between the tramlines on pallets upon which these androgenous little darlings grow. Know all about sarcastic, brittle journalists. Know that at this stage of the narrative too I should insert the recipe about bream – but you'll find that on page 149.

Anyway, that was the plan of things, back on this miniature island with its rickety wooden bridge that reminded me so much of the small ornamental lake with its island and bridge and summer house, which was such a mysterious and forbidden territory when I was twelve years old. It had been built, or created, or scuplted out of the land by the Hancock family just outside Wiveliscombe in Somerset, and as a child I would creep in through the willows and over the wrought-iron fence and watch lazy summer trout bask in the shallow waters. Enough of this nostalgia.

Heather Brown is a sharp cookie; she is very Australian, but dresses like an English lady, and she wants to write a piece on Floyd. And despite my fears of being taken apart by a scalpel-wielding Aussie hack, I was completely wrong – we got on like a house on fire as all of those who have seen the fourteen-page spread from *The Australian* Sunday magazine will realise.

Heather and I were chatting about one of my favourite subjects, slang and the English language. Did you know, said Heather, that 'taking the mickey' – that well-known expression for poking fun at or deflating somebody – originated on the Australian cattle stations? A mickey is a young bullock and, because these tough guys ate only what they could carry, apart from the odd rib of beef from a dead steer, they would at certain times of the year revel in the delights of what they called Prairie Oysters. Prairie Oysters, as you must have guessed by now, are steers'

testicles — stewed, simmered or fried, I know not how, Heather didn't explain. (Although certainly in Lancashire, according to my friend Teddy Cowell, in former times bulls' balls and onions were an esteemed dish. However, I digress, but I do not lie.) Anyway, to get back to 'taking the mickey' it is, as you can see, a euphemism for castrating cattle.

We have gathered the oysters, we have set up Clive, I am wearing my best safari suit and my camel-coloured handmade suede shoes, and I am about to cook and deliver a fluent and meaningful, fruity and passionate piece to camera.

I am trying not to giggle because Heather has just told me a story about the Englishman, the American and the Australian who, taking early morning coffee, are struck by the beauty of the waitress who serves them. When asked what they would like, the American says 'I would like sugar', the Englishman says — well, they all outdo themselves with smug, clichéd compliments to the waitress until it is the turn of the Australian, who says, 'I'll have tea, bag'. Which, on reflection, isn't terribly funny, but it is very Australian!

Things are going absolutely brilliantly. The pot is bubbling, every-thing's perfect, the sun is high, the weather's fine, the camera crew ready and alert. I am bubbling with bright ideas – when a squadron or a flock or a gaggle of whatever you call six bombers flying in formation swooped overhead and discharged their bombs about three miles away.

We are in the middle of nowhere, population seventeen, an area so tranquil that before the arrival of the Royal Australian Air Force you could hear the fish hiccuping, and it has suddenly been turned into a scene from *Apocalypse Now*.

John 'No Worries' Chase decides to ring up the Air Force and ask them to stop bombing because he is trying to make a film about food. The Australian Air Force, very courteously, tell him that much as they would love to stop their bombing exercise unfortunately it is rather too important and the answer is 'No'.

The Royal Australian Air Force, which I thought did not exist anyway, had just sold all of their bombers, it transpired, to Pakistan, and they were training and demonstrating the aircraft to their new owners. And they continued the demonstration, coming back every thirteen minutes, until sunset at about six-thirty. Yesterday was bad enough, with the bloody gas bottle saga, and today we can't do it because the Air Force is playing war games.

But what is even worse, dear reader, is that as I pace the handwoven Turkish carpets in my oak-panelled study, glass of champagne in hand and fluently and articulately dictate to one of my minions these little anecdotes, she says, 'Has it not crossed your mind that you are the kind of person who attracts disasters?' You see, you get it both ways, not only when you are actually doing it do you have all these problems, but even the hired help doubts the veracity of your escapades!

Anyway, on this wet autumn day in Devon, I struggle for inspiration and Port Stephens is not only 12,000 miles away, it is twelve-million light years behind. And because last night I sat too long at the restaurant table, sipping port and telling lies, I am not really up to writing any more today. So I am going to stop now and when I have had a bath, a shave, and got dressed, I am going to take you to a wonderful restaurant called The Last Aussie Fish Caf.

And so we will let the bombers fly off into the sunset, we will leave Heather Brown, we will leave the film crew, we will forget about the oyster sausages, and I shall slump in the luxury of the Floydmobile and head back to town.

Exhaust gases and petrol fumes hang in the hot humid night air. Cars, taxis and pick-up trucks packed with happy Sydneysiders are bumper to bumper in the centre of this Saturday night city.

The pavements are crowded with sailors, sightseers, and backpackers in shorts, with businessmen, couples arm-in-arm and gangs of marauding youths looking for a good time. Bars, restaurants, nightclubs, discos, jazz, rock-'n'-roll, blues, strip shows, live sex shows. Takeaway Japanese, Thai, Vietnamese, Italian, Greek, Spanish, Indian and, of course, the ubiquitous Big Mac all vie for attention with their lurid flashing neon signs.

There are pimps, touts, hookers and whores and it is a good job we have an Australian guide with us, who explains that the most beautiful and scantily-clad of these women are, in fact, men! Not that, of course, any of us in our crew would be tempted by such things in this cheerful Sin City!

Street musicians stroll and play, a lone piper plays a lament, and the traffic nudges forward. Twenty minutes of fighting through the choked streets, the big wheels of my limousine squashing beer cans with the rhythmic regularity of a steam train, clacking along the old fish-plated track.

We are passing through Kings Cross, the Soho of Sydney, the French Quarter of New Orleans, the Sixth Street of Austin. And although it is clear that sex and drugs and rock-'n'-roll are everywhere, it seems a good-natured, cheerful, unmenacing sort of place. I like it, though, and it's better than America.

Oh, by the way, talking about food – which we weren't – I got the chef at my hotel, the Regent, a chap called Serge Dansereau, to prepare me something that epitomised for him Australian cookery. And not unnaturally he looked to the East and to Italy and created a delicate little dish.

He lightly fried some succulent scallops so that they were slightly underdone and juicy. Then using sheets of won ton – that's a sort of Chinese pasta like ravioli – he cut out squares of this stuff, about two and a half inches by two and a half, and on to each square placed a scallop, a teaspoon of diced and fried Chinese mushroom, and a little chopped fresh coriander. He took another square of won ton, painted it with milk and pressed it over the piece with the scallop on so that he ended up with little packages, little parcels, in short, little ravioli.

Meanwhile, into some fish stock he added a cup of wine vinegar and a couple of dashes of thick soy sauce and then a couple of dashes of sweet soy sauce. While that was reducing he sautéed in a little oil some stalks of choy sum (that's a Chinese vegetable similar to chard) for a few seconds.

The sauce was almost reduced to the right consistency but to make it smooth, rich, and also to maintain his European background, he put a little knob of butter into it to thicken it finally.

Meanwhile, he put the ravioli, you know, the little envelopes of scallops and mushrooms, into boiling salted water for about two minutes. He strained them and served them on a plate with some of the sauce and the little cooked and crispy choy sum.

A dead simple dish. But it is worth remembering you really must pinch the edges of the won ton parcels together – having first painted them with milk, that is – or they will separate in the boiling water and leave you with a tasteless mess.

Anyway, I am in my white suit that I bought in Rose Bay from a very upmarket men's shop (and which incidentally cost me even more when I returned to Heathrow some months later, because along with that suit and a few other items of clothing, the odd watch and the odd video camera, I forgot to declare them. And was summarily tried, whipped, executed and fined a couple of grand).

I push open the plate-glass door and stroll into The Last Aussie Fish Caf, which has a long, grown-up, serious, Formica-topped bar and a huge espresso machine, and troughs of crushed ice and a fish tank with plastic fish in it. There are black Formica tables. The colours are pastel – pink, green, blue and grey.

Most of the staff are flying, scurrying with plates of fish and chips or mountains of oysters or plates of sushi. Wearing T-shirts with the phrase 'Lost in the 50s'. Elegant Australian women with long legs are rock-'n'-rolling with Australian men wearing Jonathan Ross-type suits. The music comes from a magnificent Wurlitzer jukebox. Little Richard is belting out 'Good Golly, Miss Molly'.

This is very much my kind of place so I take a stool at the bar and order an alarming concoction of sorbet and vodka – a complete meal in a glass. The noise, the music, were terrific. I had a couple of great fun dishes of barramundi steak with a lime and butter sauce, and then some snapper, with crunchy vegetables, and a chilli and garlic sauce.

Things were going fine until the resident mime artist, with white clown's face and bowler hat and black suit, decided to choose me as his next victim. Amid jeers, catcalls and assorted good-natured piss-taking, I tried to feel my way round the walls of an imaginary room. Luckily, after a couple of vodka sorbet specials and some excellent white wine, I might well have looked a fool but I didn't feel any pain.

Each evening there is a brilliant moment when one of the waiters, clasping an enormous peppermill, runs like hell about thirty feet down the restaurant, takes a flying leap into the air and lands, legs akimbo, on two chairs placed in front of the diners. The rest of the staff line up behind him and they do the most hysterical mime to rock-'n'-roll from the jukebox. And this is the end of Day Eight in Sydney . . .

PS Their fish and chips were brilliant, the beer batter was good. But you can't beat a fillet of good old British cod, can you?

Creek Cottage, County Cork, Ireland, 30 September

I am back at my desk overlooking the estuary again and just shuffling through the Sydney section of this mighty tome. The heron still pops by from time to time and as autumn approaches and the leaves begin to turn, the wildlife on the estuary has changed dramatically. I must go into Kinsale and buy a book on seabirds and a pair of binoculars too. Hunched squinting over a hot typewriter all day wears out the old eyes, don't you know.

Anyway, it's one of those days. I thought I had finished the whole Sydney bit when I suddenly remembered that on my last day in the brilliant city, I had two splendidly contrasting snacks. According to my tape recorder:

▶PLAY Cabramatta, New South Wales, 11 May

• They say that Cabramatta is a suburb north of Sydney. In fact, it took the Floydmobile two or three hours to get to this strange, modern, 1960s township. It was like any other ghastly development: streets with wide pavements, shopping malls, supermarkets, banks and chain stores selling tacky clothing.

The only thing that was strange was that all the signs, all the notices, all the advertisements, were written in Vietnamese. For all I knew, we could have been in downtown Saigon. The smell of soups, prawns, lemon grass, ginger and chilli wafted down the crowded, straight streets.

● An Australian truck driver came up and said, 'What are you here for, spotting Aussies?' Australians are very insecure, threatened as they are by the Japanese, who come in and buy up the country in a major way. And the Vietnamese, who are so industrious and so clever and so hardworking, will surely become a major economic force in the country too, while the Australians stand there and 'Have another Fosters'.

▮▮ PAUSE

But Cabramatta deserves a fuller description, so here goes. Guided tour of markets, baskets piled high, with my chum Van Thu Phan, who spends much of her time helping her countrymen come to terms with the Australian way of life. Passed stalls piled high with mint, lemon grass, baskets of mung beans, bulbs and bulbs of ginger and garlic, sheaves of coriander leaves, piles of *bac ha* (a Vietnamese vegetable with green stalks used for stir-frying or in soups, a bit like celery really). There were pyramids of bean curd, cellophane-wrapped packets of noodles, baskets of rice, pyramids of tamarind, bottles of soy sauce, jars of green and red curry paste . . .

Into a Formica-tabled café with this beautifully elegant but serene Vietnamese woman who seems to speak about eighteen languages. Two big steaming bowls of meat, noodles and mint, chopsticks . . . luckily, the tape recorder was quite precise here, it actually explained how to prepare a bowl of typically Vietnamese food.

All you need is some really good clear beef or chicken stock. Into that you pop some thin noodles, and bring them to the boil. Then you add some very thin slices of cooked roast pork or beef, and a little chilli oil. By the way, if you haven't any cooked pork or beef you can just pop in some wafer-thin slivers of fillet steak. And if you wanted to be really smart, as you make the stock (beforehand of course), you could add a little chopped knuckle of veal or a bit of tripe into the stock to make it even richer.

Anyway, you get the picture, you end up with a big Chinese bowl filled with this clear liquid, jam-packed with noodles (they only take a couple of minutes to cook) and loads of slivers of beef, with a dash of chilli oil in it.

To make it really interesting, you also have to have some side dishes to tip into this kind of stew. And these are a delightful combination of fresh herbs and raw vegetables popped into the hot broth and noodles. So, what you need is a bowl of fresh basil leaves, a handful of fresh raw beansprouts, a handful of fresh mint leaves, some chopped spring onions. And you just sprinkle a few of all of those on top of your soup each time you take a mouthful out of the meat and noodles. You crunch it all up together – the fresh herbs, the hot spicy oil and the noodles. Fresh and invigorating. And if you like your coffee black, as they say, somewhere you can also sprinkle on a teaspoonful of finely-chopped fresh chillies, to give it a real 'oomph'.

The tape recording seems to have gone rather indistinct and I am having difficulty in transcribing it, but it was all something to do with standing in the rain in the dark, on a pavement by the docks, in front of what must be Sydney's premier gastronomic rendezvous – a caravan of some kind plastered with black and white photographs of film stars from the 1940s and 1950s, known as Harry's Café de Wheels, and patronised by the dinner-jacketed yuppies, leather-jacketed taxi drivers, drunken sailors and *le demimonde en gros*.

Where, after a long night of carousing, you buy one of those dreadfully brilliant meat pies with mushy peas, topped with tomato sauce.

And after a gastronomic tour that in Sydney alone has taken me through Thailand to Greece and Vietnam to France, which has filled my tummy and tickled my palate with the finest that this vibrant city can offer, there is nothing finer than pie and peas.

As the poet said: 'A surfeit of the sweetest things to the stomach a certain loathing brings.' Just thought I'd put that in to show the poets I can smoke and that I like Tom Paxton – work that out.

Of chain gangs, devils and tigers.

Creek Cottage, County Cork, Ireland, 20 July

The tide is in and the estuary outside my studio window is teeming with fish, some bass, some mullet and the occasional salmon. A soft, grey heron flapped casually by and landed on the stone jetty opposite. He would wait for the tide to turn before he started fishing. Across the estuary, or creek I suppose, the bank rises steeply with fat, foliaged trees. Some white birds were diving like Messerschmidts into the water, which has an opaque grey-green hue.

I am sitting at a desk that is polished and empty except for a battered, dark-green, Silver Reed, manual, portable typewriter, a box of typing paper sitting in its lid, a small tape recorder and a stack of mini-cassettes. I roll a fresh sheet of paper into the typewriter. It had been the trip of a lifetime and now I have to, somehow, commit the adventures, the food, the wine, the people, the journeys and all, to paper.

The tide has turned and is starting to ebb. The first mudbank appears as the water recedes. Slowly, silently, the heron begins to stalk. I am brimming with excitement but my fingers can't find the keys and my mind is emptying faster than the creek. I switched the tape recorder to playback and lit a cigarette.

▶**PLAY** • 'You're all rugged up for a cold winter's day,' means you've got lots of warm clothing on. Sign on the road to Eaglehawk Neck Bay, where we are going, 'Cow Dung For Sale'.

• Eaglehawk Neck Bay – and into the Tasman Sea. A wet and blustery day to go tuna fishing.

• All Australians live in cricket pavilions. Waves crashing on the sandy shore of Pirates Bay, a perfect semi-circle with trees running down the ribbon beach. Jetty by the Blow Hole – this is a hole in the rocks – a little Pirates Bay with the jetty going out a hundred feet, white tuna boats. Desolate and bleak, mists and clouds scudding over the wooded mountaintops. Little bungalow-type settlements round the shore.

• With Tony and Jack – Jack is the skipper on this lovely white boat – coming back into where Abel Tasman discovered Tasmania and a steely albatross flying behind us; bloody wide wingspans. Four, five tuna we've got, all roundabout sixty pounds; the biggest one this boat's caught was roundabout 270 pounds so that doesn't make us really brilliant . . .

• Sitting in the empty hotel's atrium overlooking Hobart Bay, with its steamboats, its fishing boats, its red roofs, the Georgian warehouses and former slave quarters, one of them now called the Drunken Admiral.

• A couple of Spanish guys fishing for squid off the end of a little jetty – where *Pauleta* was moored before we went tuna fishing.

• A few yachts coming in, slowly into harbour, as if coming home to tie up for the winter.

• That lazy dockside activity that's so beguiling on islands where much of the produce is brought in . . . and where boats play an important role in transport.

• A quick tour round the kitchen, with a glass of wine, tasting the Tasman salmon, smoked quails, strawberries and cream and all this before breakfast.

• Sunday night. Driving round Hobart. It was shut. No pub, no bar, nothing open.

• Local estate agent is L.J. Hooker!

• Tuna fish at Mures Restaurant: scallops of tuna fish brushed with olive oil and garlic, sautéed briefly, with a puréed tomato concasse underneath, served with rice, fennel and anchovy butter. A piece of piss. Very difficult to achieve.

• It is trite but true that all things that are good for you like sport are, the world over, sponsored by all things that are bad for you like booze.

• It's Wednesday morning and the helicopters come in at first light over the harbour. Still grey sea. Just a few lights twinkling, nothing moving in the harbour; the steamboat, the factories and a big container ship loading up. Low cloud over the hills in the bay.

● What kind of thing did we come in – what was it? A Squirrel – we arrived in a Squirrel and Graham decided to 'hot-fuel' it, which in the trade means fuel it while the engine's still running.

▶▶ FF

● *Lactarios deliciosus* and sometimes wild mushrooms are known as saffron-tops.

● Then down to a stream, rather like a bigger Exmoor/Dartmoor river, cook the dish and all that. Kookaburras ate the food. We had a big chopper. It was a highly, highly entertaining day. The forest ranger joined us and Graham, the chopper pilot, told me that flying down to the Antarctic was great.

● There's an expression in Hobart, 'If you don't like the weather, come back in five minutes.'

● Abalone, black beans . . . thin noodles, ginger, garlic, salt and pepper, oyster sauce; being filmed when the Fire Brigade burst in, in the Duck Palace.

▮▮ PAUSE

Jesus Christ, that isn't exactly what you would call comprehensive is it – I thought I had done more than that. Anyway, here goes.

If Abel Tasman sailed into Eaglehawk Neck Bay, Tasmania, today, nearly 350 years after his first sighting of the island, the only change he would see is a slender wooden jetty protruding into the grey swell, where three tuna boats, their observation platforms bristling with antennas, their sterns spiked with rods, ride against the rubber-tyred stanchions of the jetty. Under dove-grey clouds, tinged alternately with black linings or suddenly illuminated with a brief shaft of golden sunlight, the boats, blown northwards by a Force Six, tumbled, scudded and danced in harmony with the waves, which grew bigger as they headed out to the fishing grounds.

I leant against the gunwales, sucking on a damp cigarette, watching the tough coastline diminish as the *Pauleta* nosed steadily into wind and sea. Climbing high for a long minute, only to slide fast into a wall of spray on the other side. It was an exhilarating ride.

A hundred yards away an albatross held station astern. It was the first one I had seen. It is not a sinister bird – it is majestic and aloof. But then I was not struck calm in the doldrums or telling salty tales at wedding feasts.

Of Chain Gangs, Devils and Tigers

After an hour or so, the cliffs slid slowly from sight and the sea grew choppier and the sky darker. I sensed a vastness of ocean that you do not feel crossing the Channel. There is something awesome about the Tasman Sea, the South Atlantic, though a chopper pilot I'd met in a bar yesterday had said flying down to the Antarctic from Hobart was 'Okay'. Once you'd seen your first iceberg you'd seen them all.

The skipper and owner of the *Pauleta* is a mild-spoken man, approaching sixty, but looking forty, called Jack Collet. They say he's the best tuna man on the island. Do I mean island? That rather makes it sound like the Isle of Wight; in fact, Tassie is about the size of Ireland. Looks like Devon, could be Normandy or Scotland or, from some aspects, somewhere in Scandinavia. And to make matters more confusing, it has towns called Launceston, Swansea and Devonport, and the Derwent Estuary or the River Tamar, alongside the original names given by the Aborigines (who were, by the way, slaughtered or driven off the island).

The capital of Tasmania is Hobart, Australia's second oldest city, first settled in 1803. The island was much favoured as a penal colony and a naval base. These days it's a great place for a holiday, anything from sailing, wild mushroom hunting, to gambling, eating, walking, hiking, riding or just gazing at the spectacular scenery; it's got the lot. Especially trout fishing, although I, of course, arrived out of season. Tasmania grew prosperous on whaling and fishing. For a sombre day out, visit Port Arthur on the Isle of the Dead – where the convicts are buried.

Anyway, I digress. This is supposed to be a personal view of my brief sojourn, eating and drinking the delights of Tasmania. If you want the low-down on colonial Australia, read Robert Hughes's *The Fatal Shore*; it's grisly, dramatic and brilliant.

I tell Jack I have no fishing experience. It's the best way, then if I lose a fish as I usually do when I'm making Floyd programmes, he'll hopefully understand. We started out a noisy lot, babbling with excitement. Now the swell had got to most of the film crew, and you can clearly hear Jack asking other boats on the radio where the fish are. It's looking good. The *Barbara* has just hit a shoal two miles to the west. Jack says it's time to put on a harness, and stand by.

Tim, the sound man, is green and holding on to Bruce, who is wobbling. I'm lucky, I never get seasick, and I'm enjoying every minute. But, praying I will land a large one, or even a small one. Jack said the boat's record is a tuna of 270 pounds, kilos or tonnes, I don't remember, but it was one hell of a fish that took six hours to pull on to the deck. Jack wouldn't say exactly, but it sold for a fortune to a Japanese fish merchant who flew it by private plane to the sushi bars of Tokyo. Six sturdy rods are trailing brightly-coloured lures on hundred-pound lines way astern of the *Pauleta*, each rod with a huge multiplier reel. I'm strapped into a swivel seat, feet snug in Wellingtons, jammed against the stern as the boat rides up and crashes down on this rolling, thick, grey sea.

I can just hear the engine throb above the noise of the wind, and the albatross is still keeping aloof from the gulls that swarm around us. Then a rod dips fiercely and bends hard toward the water – the reel screams as a fish rips off the line. My heart leaps, I reach for the rod.

'Steady,' says Jack, 'hold on to the tip of the rod.'

Then, all of a sudden, another four rods dip and reels scream.

'It's a five-strike,' shouts Jack, but I'm too busy to notice the others grabbing the rods. I'm standing up, leaning back from this torpedo that is diving, diving, diving and then twisting and running straight at the boat. So I reel frantically in.

'Hold the rod up. Don't give him any slack. Lift the rod. Keep the line tight, dip the rod and wind like hell.' This is Jack, soft-spoken, and calmly instructing me. It's the heaviest fish I've ever hooked, I'm sure. My knees are wobbling. The director is demanding a piece to the camera, but the fish is more important than anything, so I ignore him. My arms are aching, but I'm making line. I can see the tuna now, just below the surface, he's trying to corkscrew down. I lose concentration for a second in the thrill of seeing the thing and he rips another thirty yards off me.

Jack is saying, 'Rod up, dip and wind like hell, dip and wind like hell.' The fish is tiring. Jack Collet's crew is on the marlin board with the gaff. Jack lunges once, and, one-handed, yanks on to the deck this black and blue silver missile that is a tuna. I exhale with relief, and stand grinning inanely, feebly trying to light a cigarette. I have landed my first tuna. It weighs seventy pounds, and I am thrilled.

Exhilarated and tired, we make the calm water of Eaglehawk Neck Bay with five tuna. We tie up to the jetty where a couple of Spanish men are catching squid. They admire the tuna and give me a couple of squid in exchange for an autograph. It's funny that Spanish immigrants to Australia always seem to watch Floyd programmes, but they do, and that makes us all feel good. It has been as they say: 'A top day'.

Later, I sat in the empty atrium of the Hobart Sheraton watching a tired yacht drift slowly into harbour. The fishing boats were tied up and the

Georgian warehouses reflected the last of the sun. The red corrugated roofs of the humbler buildings glowed in a friendly way as a container ship edged out to sea. I asked the waiter for another raspberry tart and a double ration of King Island cream.

There was snow on the top of Mount Wellington and the government buildings sat proud on the wide empty streets. Hobart has a Presbyterian air that is solid and reassuring, like Bergen or Kirkwall I felt. Last night, Sunday, David and I had gone in search of a lively pub. But on Sunday night Hobart is closed, though I ate a great Tasmania crayfish in the Drunken Admiral, a restaurant built in former convict quarters just across from the hotel. The bar is made of reclaimed timber from the steps to the prison, worn down by hundreds of pairs of shackled feet.

The crayfish was split in half, the flesh removed, then fried in a little butter and mixed in with a light cheese sauce with a hint of mustard, replaced in the shells and popped under a very hot grill till it was mainly golden-brown, but a little blackened too. It was an unpretentious version of a thermidor, but since the fish was spanking fresh and cooked to order it was very tasty.

The waitress told me that up to a short time ago, crayfish was considered poor food, suitable only for making fish cakes. Tourism had changed all that, she said. David had a popular local fish, a Trevally, rather like bream, cooked in the blackened way made famous by Paul Prudhomme in New Orleans (see page 151 for Paul's recipe).

In Western Australia, Trevally was considered suitable as bait for game fishing, I discovered later, but hardly eaten. As they say, one man's meat is another man's bait. Ugh. Of the five tuna, we'd given one to a local charity, three to Captain Jack – perk of the trade – and one to Mures Fish House, a modern Scandinavian-style restaurant on the opposite side of

the dock from the Drunken Admiral, which among other delights serves sushi, deftly prepared by a Japanese chef called Hero. So I toddled over for a sushi lesson.

You can use virtually any firm raw fish for sushi, but not only must it be fresh, if you choose tuna it must also be caught and killed carefully. Fish roughly gaffed in the side do not command the high price that those which have been quickly and neatly dispatched through the head do. This way the fish does not contort and tense up. If the fish has rigor mortis it has to be left for a day to relax. Most important, Hero said. So important that he rejected the fish I brought and used one of his own to show me how to prepare tuna for sushi.

He lifted the fish, with great care to avoid bruising, on to the worktop. Oh, by the way, the second the fish is landed it must be gutted and bled in much the same way that Muslims prepare their meat. First, he removed all the fins and then with a very sharp knife cut the fish in half lengthways to produce two boneless sides. Any slightly black flesh and thin bits were then trimmed off. Next, he cut the two sides lengthways again – see my brilliant little sketch.

Then cut into quarters - lengthways Trim off the skin

He trimmed the fillets into rectangular bars which were then cut into strips, ready to roll into those seaweed-covered rice tubes that look like the stuffed liquorice sweets in a bag of All-Sorts.

I don't suppose many readers will have to fillet their own tuna, but if you do decide to make sushi at home, apart from ordering a bit of fish cut as I have described from the fishmonger, you must also buy a few bits of roasted seaweed (*yaki sushi nori*) from your nearest Asian supermarket.

Also, you must cook some short-grained rice that has been well washed and allow it to cool. (Hero cooks three cups of rice to four and a quarter cups of water in a pan. Once it has come to the boil, he puts the lid on the pan, lets it simmer till the water has gone, then turns off the heat and allows the rice to cool naturally.) Then boil one cup of white wine vinegar with one cup of white sugar till you have a syrup. When this is cold, mix it into the cold rice. This makes 'sticky' rice, essential for sushi.

Spread some rice on to a sheet of roasted seaweed, lay a strip of tuna on the rice, roll up the sheet into a tube and, with a very sharp knife, cut into finger-sized portions. Serve with a dash of soy sauce, some Japanese mustard (from the same supermarket) and some grated white radish.

Hero prepared a plate of tuna sushi in a fraction of the time it took to write this, but then he'd served a four-year apprenticeship before he qualified and, like so many who are helping to make Australia the most exciting place, left the teeming streets of Tokyo for Tasmania, fame and, I hope, fortune.

I said goodbye and set out for the hotel. After the heat of the kitchen it was very cold, so I ran across the old cobbled dock and took the lift to my very extravagant, but absurdly luxurious, mezzanine-floored presidential suite. I rang room service for some baked beans on toast, which I ate in solitary splendour at a twelve-seater table in the dining room overlooking the Constitution Dock and Hobart Harbour.

The fishing boats bobbed softly, the lights from Mures Restaurant twinkled in the gentle swell and the big cranes that had loaded the container ship earlier cast shadows over the old government warehouses. Sometimes a car passed by. I finished my baked beans, sipped a glass of whisky in the bath, then stumbled upstairs to bed. I was too tired to read. It had been a top day.

I wake too late for breakfast – the chopper is due at 6.30 so I scramble into my clothes and dash across the road to the dock where the crew are waiting, stamping their feet against the cold and rubbing sleep from their eyes. There is still snow on Mount Wellington. The morning is grey, there is no sun yet and Hobart is asleep. I am going with Juan Nin into the hills to pick wild mushrooms and cook some quail.

Elsewhere in the world I'm sure you'd jump into a car and walk across a few fields. Here in Tassie you go by chopper – a neat white Squirrel with South Antarctic Division painted on the side – for Juan, the cameraman and me. The rest are going in a fixed-wing to Launceston and by road for the last bit. Juan is pointing to the spot on Graham, the pilot's, chart. Graham is tall, wears a Biggles flying jacket and achieves a laconic sense of humour by saying nothing. I suppose he was wondering what was so important about mushrooms that we needed a helicopter to take us there.

Graham grimaced when he saw the vast amount of equipment that we had to stow into his frail craft. Aluminium boxes of lenses, cameras, tripods, assorted packs of food, frying pans, billy cans, kettles, knives, and, of course, my magic stick. Now you don't know yet about my magic stick, but it was something I got from a forest just outside Sydney on the first day of my trip. It is a stick about three feet long with a small 'V' at the end that has been elegantly carved with a brand new knife I bought in town. With the aid of this stick, which is imbued with all sorts of magical powers, I can find rivers, I can find heiresses in wine bars. It is a sort of divining stick, an all-purpose divining stick; it is a talisman. Each time I travel from one part of Australia to another, I put a little airport tag on it, so it looks a bit like a Zulu warrior's ceremonial spear, though instead of being covered in feathers it is covered in airline tags. Consequently, airline staff look at me (a) as if I'm insane, or (b) as if I'm carrying an offensive weapon. However, Australian stewardesses are very helpful people and I have had no trouble yet in getting it on board.

Even though Graham thought it was rather odd, he didn't say anything – he just looked that way. Anyway, we strapped ourselves in and the chopper took off, circled around Hobart and set off north-easterly across the plains of Tasmania. Each time you go up in the air in Tasmania, you are reminded of yet another country. This journey over the Derwent Estuary, over the oyster beds and into the central region, was for all the world like leaving Fowey, Cornwall, only to find yourself flying over Exmoor.

We didn't seem to be flying too high and we sort of stopped and hovered in mid-air, moving neither forwards nor backwards, nor side-ways. I pressed the intercom button and said 'What are you waiting for, are you lost?'

'No, I'm not lost. I'm waiting for the fixed-wing to catch us up.'

And as he spoke, through the glass panel under my feet this white, twin-engine, fixed-wing aeroplane shot beneath us. It was terrifying. It seemed that the little craft was only ten or twelve feet above the ground. I grabbed my magic stick and cursed myself for forgetting the magic hip flask. What had been a dull dawn now gave way to beautiful clear blue skies, bright sunlight and Exmoor, or was it Tasmania, lay below us in all its autumnal beauty.

Soon Juan was leaning forward to shout landing instructions to Graham. We were hovering over the dense forest and, try as I might, I couldn't see any clearance where he could safely land the craft. However, with that insouciant way only the Australians have, he said, 'No worries, mate, hold on, here we go.'

And it was only as we came to treetop level that a small clearing revealed itself. There was probably only a patch of a hundred feet in diameter, but to the kind of guy who's used to landing on icebergs, he had no fear of the tree-lined clearing.

And as the rotor arms swished more and more slowly to a standstill and hung limp like the wings of a cormorant drying himself in the sun, I

But anyway, here we are in the middle of nowhere and Juan sniffing like a hunting dog saying, 'I think we will go this way.' Dragging our bits and pieces, cameras and other impedimenta of the filming crew through the thick forest we came upon a muddy clearing right in the centre of the forest. Here the forest rangers had thoughtfully created a crude wooden shelter made like a tepee and there was a tree trunk lying sideways shaved off like a massive chopping board. They had also been good enough to erect a rather striking barbecue. It was here we made our camp. Then, armed with the magic stick and a nice wicker basket, Juan and I trekked off into the woods. It was late autumn and though the trees were still full of leaves they were tinged from green to burnt

Juan and me down by the mushroom yard

amber, through orange, yellow and ochre. The earth was blackish with lots of white stones and the going was quite tough. Here and there we stumbled across a bush of wild raspberries, sometimes blackberries, sometimes nuts, which Juan did not know the names of and we had no reference books with us.

They were logging in the forest and, so as not to disturb the earth with the massive wheels of yellow tractors and orange JCBs, all the logs were hauled out by teams of buffalo, six to eight in harness. And it was not done for some quaint tourist attraction, but out of the very best principles of conservation.

As we ventured deeper into the forest, climbing higher all the time, so we started to see the odd moth- or beetle-eaten orange-coloured mushrooms.

'Don't bother to pick those,' Juan said; 'soon under the leaves and bushes you will find them in plenty, some perfectly-formed, saffron-coloured mushrooms.'

He was right, we did. Within half an hour our basket was full. It was time, we thought, to stop for a tinny. Although he was what they call a 'New Australian', Juan had adopted the custom that all Australians have, of not going anywhere without a few tubes of 'nectar'.

It was eleven-thirty on this autumnal Tasmanian morning. The sun was high. It streamed down through the immense trees, dancing on the leaves and cheering our spirits. Even posing to hold up a handful of these lovely saffron-coloured mushrooms for the camera was no problem on such a wonderful day. Neither was it a problem each time the director said, 'Walk back this way, swing the basket as you go, look cheerful and appear to be in an animated conversation.'

The usual repetitive rigours of filming did not intrude at all. After a happy refreshment we scrambled back to our base camp and on the big, big chopping board set out our feast. While Juan and I chopped, some of the crew kindly brushed our mushrooms clean. Juan said they were too delicious to wash and while John Chase, our producer, struggled yet again to assemble the portable stove, Juan and I took a little snack of King Island smoked salmon egg caviar with King Island cream, and a couple of very small nips of iced vodka, which he produced from a handsome, Spanish, chased-silver picnic set.

But the main dish was to cook some quails with wild rice and these scrumptious mushrooms and although I will tell you it was good, it was even better for having been cooked over a fire and after we had spent an energetic morning walking through the forest.

No exact quantities for this dish: all you need is one plump, free-range quail per person, three or four ounces of wild mushrooms per person, and some cooked wild basmati rice to accompany the dish.

First, marinate the quail in a mixture of teriyaki sauce (you can buy this), red wine vinegar, fennel seeds, a bit of star anise, and some grated fresh ginger for twenty-four hours.

Then sauté the quails in olive oil for about thirty minutes till they are cooked on all sides (it's easier if you flatten them first). Remove from the pan and keep warm. Add some more oil to the juices in the pan, add the

A Tassie Devil.

mushrooms and some chopped garlic, season with salt and pepper and fry them for ten minutes or so. Just before you serve the mushrooms toss in some chopped fresh coriander, and there you have it – sautéed quail with wild mushrooms and some rice. A splendid lunch. Wash it down with some Tasmanian wine, a light red from Moorilla Vinery is fine. It is a bit like a Côtes du Ventoux.

The scene was fabulous. In short, the bees were on the wing and the birds on the honeysuckle and God was in his heaven smiling down. It was then that disaster struck. It was this way, there was a lull in the filming and my bubbly blonde and New Zealand assistant Maggie was bringing over my cucumber sandwiches on the silver tray, when the kookaburra who had spent some time eyeing up my sizzling quails, swooped and to my horror snatched a sandwich from the tray.

I should explain that though I am surrounded by food on these merry jaunts, it is often impossible actually to eat anything, so to be certain that I had something simple and bland to keep me going Maggie produced cucumber sandwiches at midday, every day, in the bush, at sea or in the air. And now thanks to that damned kookaburra I would have to go hungry.

In this remote clearing with Graham's helicopter, we set up the picnic table laid out with fine linen and silver and I served the quail to Graham and a passing forest ranger. Anxious for approval (or not) I waited until they had finished eating. Their plates were clear, they had wiped them clean with bread and I stood expectantly by their table. They looked up at me and I said, 'Enjoy it?'

'Yeah, good tucker, mate.' I was beginning to get used to the Australians.

We were about to pack up and go when my director thought he saw a Tasmanian devil so we set off on a filmatic wild-goose chase, if you'll pardon the pun, looking for this beast, which everybody but David knew was now only found in wildlife parks. The upshot of this was that we were losing light fast and the chopper could not take us back to Hobart, but only as far as Launceston, where we made a rapid tarmac transfer into a fixed-wing Strike Commander that took us home.

We were coming into land when the pilot broke out of his landing approach and said, 'Sorry, mate, I forgot I've just got to scatter these ashes of this bloke who died the other day, over the oyster beds. It'll only take a second, no worries.' He banked the plane steeply, opened the window and shook out the cask.

Tasmania is rich in all manner of produce: cream, beef, salmon, oysters, shellfish, tuna, raspberries, wine, superb fish from King Island just off the mainland of Tasmania. But probably the most explosive and recherché are abalone. For a long time fishermen have dived for this curious mollusc. It is a dangerous task. You have to chip them off the side of rocks. And in former times when they used hard-hat diving techniques, that is to say they were connected to the ship by a tube with compressor, many lives were lost.

Yet it is not only the Australians who eat them, but the Japanese and there is a thriving abalone trade between Tasmania and Japan. Just to have a licence to fish them, never mind the cost of the boat itself, runs into thousands and thousands of dollars.

Unfortunately, we came a little too late in the season. The sea was too rough and the gales too strong for us to go fishing ourselves, but we did manage to procure one or two. The best thing would be to actually prepare them on the deck of one of the fishing boats. So off we set, down to the abalone fishing harbour with our portable stove, when lo and behold, the heavens opened and the most God Almighty squall hit us.

The conditions were quite unsuitable for filming outside, so we decided to prepare the abalone in the tranquil luxury of my presidential suite at the Hobart Sheraton. A local television crew had been shadowing us for a couple of days so we invited them back to my room. We set the cameras up and we set the ingredients up. I thought it would be appropriate if I put on my kimono and swept down the curving staircase from my bedroom to the dining room and started to cook. All the time ABC TV filming us, filming me.

I had just got to the stage where you flip the thin slices of abalone into the sizzling wok, when all hell broke loose. Alarms sounded, sirens screamed and a group of men dressed in green overalls, wearing white helmets and calling 'Fire' exploded into the room.

We had forgotten to switch off the smoke detectors and they were on the point of evacuating the hotel when, in between fits of giggles and sidesplitting attempts to try and be serious and sorry, we explained our situation. One thing I will say is no guest will ever be in danger of fire in that particular hotel. Their response to the emergency was very swift and efficient.

Anyway, abalone are a great thing to eat. The trouble is, in Britain in particular, you will only get them frozen or bottled and they just don't taste the same. The wonderful thing about Australia is that you can get anything you want and ingredients are no problem. But if you want to taste these things, all you need is a first-class airline ticket from Heathrow to Hobart, or possibly Tokyo!

You can cook them most ways but this is my favourite. I call it Abalone Stir-Fried The Sheraton Way. (Hope that's enough plugs for the Sheraton and hope they have forgiven me for trying to burn it down.)

You need 1 teaspoon chopped fresh root ginger and 1 teaspoon chopped garlic, a couple of tablespoons black bean sauce. Also, some soy sauce, a bottle of oyster sauce, some sesame oil, a packet of very thin noodles (you just pop them into boiling water for seconds, strain and serve them), a couple of leaves of *pak choy* per person, some thin slices of fresh abalone, salt and pepper. Oh, and two or so chopped spring onions.

Heat a wok till it's smoking, add a little sesame oil and quickly stir-fry the *pak choy* and the spring onions, toss on to a warm plate, then add a little more oil to the wok, plus the ginger and the garlic, and fry the abalone for a second or two on both sides. Add the black bean sauce, stir the lot together, reintroduce the *pak choy* and onion, mix with a little dash of oyster sauce, and serve on a bed of thin noodles. The whole operation should not take five minutes.

After all that excitement I decided to have a stroll around Hobart itself. If you are a student of architecture, or even if you just like architecture, you will love it. The little corrugated-roof houses along the coastline for all the world could be in Clovelly or St Ives or Bude except that they have verandahs, a colonial feature.

You can walk along Salamanca Place and enjoy the soft sandstone government buildings, the warehouses, the Courthouse, the Parliament building with its colonial splendour. The docks and the customs house are familiar, and yet somehow not in these outlandish locations. Anyone who has been to the West Indies, to Canada or wherever else the British Empire has spread itself, will feel at home, as it says in *Identifying Australian Architecture* (essential reading by the way), and I quote:

'Georgian architecture was the most visible piece of architectural baggage brought to Australia in the late eighteenth century by the first European settlers . . . As well as providing the aristocracy with an architecture that spoke of refinement and culture, the style had given a character of understated elegance to less exalted places of the urban vernacular.'

My sentiments entirely.

After the excitement of the day, I trotted down the several hundred floors to the atrium and consoled myself with a very refreshing whisky, ice and water. The hotel music system was playing that song again. Each time I sat in this vast glass-fronted mausoleum, they seemed to play the same song and I believe it is called 'Side by Side'. You know the one:

> *'Maybe we're ragged and funny,*
> *We don't have a lot of money,*
> *But we travel along, singing this song,*
> *Side by side.'*

After a couple of these reviving drinks I was beginning to see the bright side of life again, unlike the morning I arrived in Tasmania at ten past nine on a flight from Melbourne straight to a press reception of print, radio and TV journalists who, knowing full well I'd just got off the plane, asked me the leading question: What did I think of Tasmanian food? Difficult to answer, especially as at that stage I hadn't tasted any.

Sitting there, at leisure, I thought back over the last few days. There had been David's continuing obsession with Tassie devils. I bought him a little woollen one in a wooden cage in a gift shop of the hotel. It was hideous. Then there was our trip to the Cascade Brewery – a fabulous old place where they make a really good beer. Also, the label on the bottle was good, with two Tasmanian tigers standing side by side. There aren't any Tasmanian tigers any more. They got shot to death, hunted to extinction by the 1930s. There are two reasons for this: 1) they ate sheep and 2) their skins were in great demand. But there is still a band of hopefuls who believe the Tasmanian tiger is still around and the *National Geographic* magazine offers a fabulous prize for anybody who can find one.

Then there was the sunny morning sipping the wines of Julian Alcorso in his Moorilla winery just outside Hobart, where he cooked Tasmanian sea trout under a hot sun as the workers picked the grapes. It was extremely drinkable, and the sweet white was superb.

Australia's wine industry has had a chequered history. All went well in the late 1800s and early 1900s. Then disaster struck. The wine disease phylloxera devastated many vineyards. South Australia was comparatively fortunate and today still has the edge on, say, Victoria.

You'll find champagne-style sparkling wine at Seppelt's (developed by a pioneer who arrived in the 1970s and stayed); Barossa Valley wines (in the vanguard of the so-called 'cool climate' movement whereby vines are increasingly being planted in the cooler region of the country); Semillon sauternes emerging during the 1980s from the very hot regions of New South Wales. To name but a few.

Only since the 1960s has table wine been acknowledged here as the perfect accompaniment to food. Unless you are familiar with these amazingly intense and individual new cool-climate wines, it is difficult to choose food to complement them (and vice versa).

With new and replanted vineyards, plus a keen interest in local fare, perhaps Oz traditions of food and wine 'cuisine', in the European sense, may thrive. Add to this a migrant population, productive soil, climatic variations and the enthusiasm of the visionaries who, with purpose and dedication, strive for the highest reputation and promotion of their own particular area and produce – and you have a recipe for the success of the Aussie wine industry and a bright future indeed.

Then there was our cultural evening when I attended an exhibition of bizarre Tasmanian seascapes painted by Geoff Dyer, a voluble, gesticulating Alex Higgins of a man. A genteel event sponsored by Cascade Brewery that ended up in riotous hilarity around four in the morning.

All in all, Tasmania is one hell of a place and I shall look forward to returning one of these days.

Apropos of absolutely nothing, most people are quite convinced that the lot of the convicts on this fair island was a grisly one. They were flogged, hanged, starved, deprived and humiliated. No doubt when planning his work camps, Stalin took the British Government's correspondence course. I have already referred to Robert Hughes' book, *The Fatal Shore*. Now for another view of convict life you must read the twenty-third impression of *Shadow over Tasmania* by Coultman Smith, who seems to think that being a convict in Tasmania in the 1830s was an absolute doddle. I quote:

> '*Many women who came out free, or were freed, married convicts still under sentence and cases are on record where wives have had their spouses flogged by the authorities for misdemeanours. How does that sound to the modern woman demanding her rights?*'

He also points out that the most arduous work to which the male convict was applied was the chain gang.

> '*Chain gangs were kept in road-making and in fact the majority of the gangs kept on the roads did not wear chains although they were constantly under guard because of ample opportunities for making bush. Even then the severity of the work like all other hardships has been grossly exaggerated.*'

He goes on to say:

> '*In general terms, the life of a Tasmanian convict was much more agreeable than that of the average working man in England at the time.*'

Mr Coultman Smith is quite a liberal fellow, I am sure you will agree. Mr Coultman Smith also said that the convicts really ate terribly well. Be that as it may, I bet they never got to try the gastronomic delights of Bessie Baldwin, an ex-convict who was cook to Sir John and Lady Franklin at Government House, where a nice little snack would have been steamed kangaroo.

> '*Procure a young kangaroo, let it hang for a few days to dry well, then cut off tail, open the kangaroo and put all the bones to boil well for gravy (the tail is nice if boiled in stock to make soup). Cut trimmed flesh into square pieces, flour well and season with salt and pepper. Cut up some slices of bacon in small dice, make a seasoning as for veal and roll into small balls. Add a finely-cut onion if liked. Place in jar a layer of kangaroo pieces, then a layer of bacon and then a layer of seasoned balls [I don't know what she means by this]. Repeat this until you have placed the quantity you require to cook, then pour over this the gravy. Place the jar in water up to neck, tie down to keep it closed and steam it for three or four hours. Serve with redcurrant jelly. It is better to prepare this the day before cooking it so as to have the goodness from the juices for gravy. Kangaroo is also very nice finely cut and well seasoned and made into patties. Dip in well-beaten eggs, breadcrumbs seasoned all over and fried in plenty of hot dripping.*'

Presumably the first roo burger. The strange thing is, all the time we were in Tasmania I did not see a kangaroo – or a Tassie devil, or a Tasmanian tiger. One thing Bessie Baldwin and I do have in common is these rather loosely formulated recipes. Neither she nor I are too concerned about the precise quantities or precise times. Don't forget this is only one person's view of cooking, it is not a workshop manual.

Bessie's outrageous crime had been to demand a pay rise of one penny a week to bring her wages up to fivepence a week. Her pastry cook boss refused this modest request and Bessie, feeling a bit pissed off, 'Assaulted the said Thos. Edenwell by striking him with a rabbit pie and beating him about the head with the pie dish.' For this misdemeanour she got seven years' transportation to Tasmania. But Mr Coultman Smith would undoubtedly approve of the fact that after seven years as a convict she really improved herself, mended her ways and got the job as Head Cook at Government House.

Bessie Baldwin's great success story surely bears out Mr Coultman Smith's point: 'Britain's transportation of felons to the Australian territories was a far-sighted and on the whole successful colonisation system.'

PS It is true that the bath water goes down the drain in the opposite direction! END

Dear Henry,

Apparently, Britons are obsessed by a TV soap opera called Neighbours *(I haven't seen it, have you?), which is made here in Melbourne. So we spent yesterday filming a short cooking sketch with two of its stars, Harold and Madge. They run a restaurant or hotel in this imaginary yet typical Australian community. I don't know if those are their real or their characters' names but they were utterly charming people and a good time was had by all.*

It seems that a whole group of actors keep rushing in and out of each other's houses, drinking cups of tea, and chatting about the hopes and fears of everyday Melbourne folk. Some of the actors are teenagers and they rush in and out of each

other's houses as well, having just fallen in or out of love with somebody; and they either storm out of the house in anger and tears or curl up on a gaudy sofa and sulk.

By all accounts this gripping saga attracts a viewing audience in Britain slightly larger than the entire population of Australia.

I don't remember if you have been to Melbourne, but it's a rather elegant city with fine Victorian architecture and immensely wide streets. They were originally meant to be sixty-six feet wide but the seventeen-year-old prodigy who designed the place read the plans upside down and consequently they are ninety-nine feet wide! In my view it is a happy mistake and lends a very pleasing atmosphere to this elegant city.

People keep telling me that Melbourne has the largest population of Greek people outside Greece. I don't know if it is true, but it is certainly richly endowed with Greek restaurants. And if Melbourne is rich in one thing it is certainly restaurants. There are thousands of them, of all creeds and denominations, and the Melbournians are extremely proud of them. In fact, the Melbournians are very proud people because their city, unlike Sydney which was founded by convicts, was founded by free men who actually chose to be there of their own will.

Three-million Australians think that Australia's first city, Sydney, is a heap of absolute crap. Needless to say, these three-million all live in Melbourne – and the inter-city rivalry is intense. Melbourne regards itself as the cultural, financial and Establishment centre of the country and views Sydney as a brash, sleazy, hip town. Sydneysiders spend a lot of time gleefully reminding the people of Melbourne that they have the worst climate in Australia.

By the way, after filming last night I bumped into Pete Koren – you remember he was with Ogilvie & May in London a couple of years ago. Anyway, we went out for dinner and had a few drinks and he's asked me to send you his best wishes. He is pretty chuffed at the moment because he has just been appointed to the board of his company.

I must say the Sydney people are right about the weather down here. My suite is on the twentieth floor and I looked out of the window to discover that the whole of Melbourne is totally blanketed by fog below me. And apart from about two high-rise buildings and a couple of cranes, just the tops of which grew out of the mist, I could see nothing of the streets and buildings below.

Yet three hours later, after an erratic helicopter ride to the High Country north of Melbourne we spent a day spit-roasting a massive joint of beef and galloping round on horses pretending to be 'The Man from the Snowy River'. I don't know if it's been shown in England, but it is a film about this really tough horseman, a sort of Crocodile Dundee *I think, but without the crocodiles. It was fun. When we landed we were met by a powerfully-built red-faced man in old-fashioned blue dungarees, who spoke in the broadest Geordie accent, even though he explained that he had been living in Australia and hadn't been back to England for forty years.*

Actually, it was the same when I popped up to see Aunt Olive, my late father's sister, and Uncle Frank. They, who had been there since 1953 or something, still had the faint intonation of a West Midlands accent. I, on the other hand, get overtaken by accents in foreign countries: if I am in Ireland I start speaking in a lilting accent, and when I am here I slip into an Australian accent and say 'G'day' to everyone.

The object of the trip up to the High Country was to meet this chap who knew all about horses and lived this rugged life, but on the day he was a bit boring so it was rather a wasted journey and we shan't be using it in the programme, I think.

One of the nice features of Melbourne is the trams. It has wonderful trams that trundle up and down the streets and I spent an enchanting morning on one that had been converted into a restaurant, and had lots of canapés and a light lunch and some wine while it went round the sightseeing things of Melbourne. It was fun. What isn't is the Melbourne taxi, Henry. They are driven by non-English-speaking Europeans at breakneck speeds in the wrong direction and they overcharge you outrageously.

We are only here for a couple of days so the pace is pretty hectic. As you know, I'm a bit of a cultural philistine but I had a couple of hours unexpectedly spare so I took a stroll round the Victoria State Museum. It is stuffed with terrific Aboriginal art among other things and I have to say I thoroughly enjoyed it for an hour or so. I have been to Melbourne a couple of times before and have had a very good time. Whether it was the pressure of filming or the appalling weather, this visit was less joyous than previous times.

One splendid day's fun, though, was a game of cricket that the Lord's Taverners organised for me. The idea was that I would cook a meal for Frank Tyson, the great fast bowler, who now lives in Australia. It was an idyllic location, a lush green cricket pitch with a perfect replica of a 1920s cricket pavilion and the whole lot surrounded by vineyards. I spent more time padding up and putting on my Lord's Taverners cricket pullover than I did standing at the crease, because, of course, Frank bowled me clean on the first ball. Luckily, there is a rule in the Lord's Taverners that you are all allowed to score one run before you are out, so I had another go.

And that, me old mate, more or less sums up my couple of days in Melbourne. Tomorrow we are off to pastures new in South Australia and Adelaide.

Anyway, hope everything's all right with you, and if you can pop into the Maltsters Arms to see if they are all right I'd really appreciate it.

Floyd knocking Tyson for six with A.N. Other

Cheers, Old bean K.F.

PS *When making* On The Beach *Ava Gardner remarked that Melbourne was the perfect place to make a film about the end of the world. That says it all, really.*

Three

Pie floaters and red legs

I left Melbourne at 6 a.m. in freezing fog. Winter had really begun to set in and I was glad to leave. A couple of hours later the Australian Airlines plane flew out of the clouds, banked steeply over a rich blue sea fringed by a long white beach and landed in the neat, white-painted Adelaide International Airport – international I think because sometimes a plane arrives from New Zealand!

We drove the long, straight road into town through wide streets with fine government buildings, modern banks and many churches, on this warm Sunday morning. Adelaide was as light and airy as Melbourne had been dark and gloomy.

I told my driver the hotel and he sped through the empty streets and deposited me in front of a tatty hotel with big glass doors and windows that might have been okay when it was built in 1966. But I knew as I walked into reception that it was not for me.

The desk clerk was surprised that I had been booked in here. I had no intention of having anything but the best on this epic odyssey, so while I had a drink at the bar, the duty manager, with great good heart, set about checking me into what he thought would be the best room in town. (It is worth a note here that what we in Britain call the Catering Industry, Australians call the Hospitality Industry. And the standard of service, courteousness, consideration and warmth of welcome that I, at least, received in Australia is second to none. The Australians leave the much-vaunted American reputation for service standing.)

Within a few minutes a car collected me and whizzed me round to the Adelaide Hyatt, an imposing modern edifice next to the old railway station, now a casino. I was met with great pomp and ceremony by the duty manager, and whisked up to the most magnificent suite at the top of the hotel. It was a splendid room: it had a sauna, a dining room and kitchen, a sitting room, a grand piano, telescopes and lots and lots of telephones. No mini-bar here filled with 1/6-gill miniatures. The sideboard was packed with full-sized litre bottles of alcoholic excellence. Any President you know – Marcos, Salazar, Franco – would have approved heartily. I certainly did! It was terrific fun.

You could press buttons and butlers would spring out from behind concealed doors, housekeepers would materialise and return within minutes with freshly-pressed suits and replaced buttons. I did have a twinge of guilt when I discovered that the room rate was in excess of $2,000 a day, and that was, of course, before you started pressing those buttons! But what the hell! There would be occasion enough in the forthcoming weeks to pay penance by sleeping in a swag in the bush.

It was a fine Sunday. I sat in the Jacuzzi, Scotch in hand, and gazed at the Adelaide cricket oval with its neat terraces, archetypal pavilion and fine green grass. I am quite convinced that a flock of budgerigars, vivid little yellow and green things, swooped past my window. It was a rare Sunday off. We didn't start filming until tomorrow. So I pressed a bell and ordered cucumber sandwiches on white, with plenty of salt, please.

Monday morning, bright sun and high wispy clouds, and Maggie and I rolling along this lazily-curving, empty road through the low, soft, sparse hills. The 150-mile drive to location, almost unthinkable in England, is very much the norm here. Indeed in the bush, or so I am told, station hands would think nothing of driving 200 miles on dirt roads for a drink on Saturday night.

After a couple of hours, the soft slopes gave way to gentle hills, neatly planted in rows of vines, with yellow and ochre leaves dropping gently to reveal the bunches of grapes soon to be picked. We are passing through the Clare Valley. Where, among others, a gentleman by the name of Pike makes some jolly drinkable stuff. I like it more for the label than the wine, to be truthful – a wonderful pale-green pike drawn with a lot of love. However, this wasn't a wine trip.

I am on my way to see a sheep station, Bungaree, a vast estate settled in about 1840, I think. With its grand house made of Cotswold stone, the bunkhouses with Georgian windows and pleasing corrugated roofs, the shearing shed with its pillars and archways, for all the world it could be a slice of the Cotswolds. The only things that make it a bit different from Gloucestershire are the water towers and windmills. In the 'dry' they have a problem.

Bungaree is not so much a sheep station as a small self-contained town, founded by George C. Hawker and his brothers. It used to have council chambers, a manager's house, an office and a station store that sold food, nails, leather, laces, everything the workers would need. A men's kitchen, a swaggie's hut, a shearing shed, its own church. One hundred and forty years ago they used to have 100 shepherds and up to 50,000 sheep. But the bottom fell out of the market and they have two or three staff and 8,000 sheep. Anyway, today Sally Hawker and her husband Richard, who looks a bit like John Cleese and reminds me of my Scottish chum John Noble, supplement their income by taking in guests in this elegant home, like so many other homesteads founded by the odd naughty aristocrat sent by some red-jowled father to the Colonies for misdemeanours such as, perhaps, gambling debts or too much dalliance with the understairs staff.

I set up Clive in front of the bunkhouse and, with a certain amount of trepidation, began preparing a Kangaroo Tail Soup. Sally Hawker is bright and cheery, her husband is shyer. He occasionally appeared from behind some building on a huge horse and looked on incredulously as this mad little band made what must have been to him an unnecessary song and dance to film what for him must have been the last thing he would ever wish to eat, Kangaroo Soup. He squeezed the side of his horse and trotted away.

Anyway, Kangaroo Tail Soup (see page 139 for the delicious recipe). We were short of time so I cooked it in the pressure cooker. It took me about twenty minutes to learn how to put the lid on and take if off. However, we ate it and it isn't really dissimilar to oxtail except that it is sweeter. And to be truthful, I didn't really like it. And although there's a great move in South Australia to make *bresaola* from it and other classic dishes more usually associated with beef, I personally think that 160 miles is a long way to go for such a treat. But it is all in the cause of research. The best bits about it were the baby turnips, carrots, celeriac and celery hearts that Sally had grown in her own garden: they were quite delicious.

Going back to my brilliant feature film (you remember, the one with my port-swilling young blade as hero), to make sure of antipodean sales and screening we'll probably have to use some proper Australian phrases from time to time. You know, like even really important British films have to have an American actor in them so they can be sold to the States. Naturally enough, as one who has had a classical education, I am not familiar with the everyday parlance of the Australian hoi polloi, so I bought myself a brilliant book written by Crooked Mick of the Speewa and published by Child and Associates, so that I can slip in the odd phrase. And as a man of the people at heart, and to guarantee enormous sales, we will be able to have little phrases like 'bangs like a dunny door' – which of course means nothing to me but in fact, according to Crooked Mick, is 'used by males in reference to any female of the species who is said to be free with her sexual favours'. It invariably turns out to be a lie!

I will be dipping in and out of Crooked Mick's book so that if ever you go travelling in Australia, you too will be able to speak the lingo.

Many of you, as I write this, might think that I have got 'kangaroos in the top paddock', but without me you wouldn't know that it is one of many phrases indicating that someone is stark raving mad. Another well-known Australian phrase for such a person is, and I quote, 'one sandwich off the full picnic'.

Day 38, Kangaroo Island, South Australia, 15 March

The battered Toyota lurched crazily through the haunted and twisted stumps of burnt-out and rotting gum trees, ghost gums and eucalyptus trees of this brown muddy creek, blocked and choked by many fallen stumps. I am holding on to the grab-bar on the dash as my new chum Bill Addington tells me that the tiltover clock they thoughtfully placed on the dash of this four-wheeled drive is totally inaccurate and crooked. I am prepared to believe him, against my better judgement, because it is well beyond the thirty degrees recommended by the manufacturers.

We're off on a little yabbie fishing expedition. Every Australian boy goes yabbie fishing. It is his first experience of fishing. And by these small man-made puddles all over Australia you will find sitting side by side young men and girls in their hats dangling with corks. They hold a twig cut from the bush, with piece of string hanging from it, to which is attached a piece of lamb chop, and haul these succulent crustaceans out faster than rabbits are taking over New Zealand.

Another essential ingredient for yabbie fishing is a very large supply of tinnies – Victoria Bitter, Fosters or Cascade, it doesn't matter as long as you have at least a ute-full of them. Ute, by the way, is Australian for a pick-up truck. Most pick-up trucks, traversing as they do the red interior of this vast continent, tend to carry more refrigerated tinnies than they do emergency supplies of petrol.

However (this is instead of anyway!), you may be wondering what a yabbie is. In Louisiana they are called crawfish, in France they are known as *écrevisses*, and in the clear streams of good old Blighty (some hope), they are known as freshwater crayfish. But most of the ones you get in England come from Turkey.

Be that as it may, back to the fishing. I tied a piece of string on to my magic stick which, by the way, has now got a few more airline tags on it, and tied on a lamb chop at the other end. I squatted down beside Bill, who opened the first of a couple of tinnies, and I dropped the bait into the muddy water.

High in a tree above me a koala (they are not called bears, you know, they are just koalas) gazes scornfully down. Something tells me that Bill is having me over. We are not going to catch yabbies on the end of a piece of string, with a lamb chop, in a muddy pond.

'Straight up, sport,' he says, 'we will. Just have another tinny and wait. I promise you, trust me.'

We sat and we sat and we sat. The koala turned over and went to sleep. A kangaroo hopped by, a couple of parrots fluttered brilliantly by – and I was being bitten to death by some kind of mosquito-like insect. After an hour of this tomfoolery, Bill said, 'It's no good, mate, they aren't feeding today, it's lucky that I bought a pot of them from the farm.'

This, of course, completely changed the little piece to camera I had to give. I mean, I can't pretend that I have caught them myself. So I am busy rearranging my speechette, at the same time as chopping chillies and heating up the pan with olive oil. And in my excitement rubbed my eye with my hand, which is covered in bits of chilli. The eye begins to water, I am temporarily blinded, and thoroughly pissed off. It was fun to see the koala, though.

Having washed out my eye, recovered my composure – my beloved director, by the way, was the whole time practising knife-throwing into a gum tree, totally unaware of my discomfort as usual – I set about cooking them (see page 164 for my superb recipe).

David, who has never heard of the wise old proverb 'you can't get a quart into a pint pot', decided he'd like a few more sequences while we were on this wonderful Kangaroo Island. Which was, in fact, settled, I think, in 1819 by a chap known as Governor Wally. And he planted a

Above *Still a kid at heart.*
Yabbie fishing on Kangaroo
Island. **Right** *Bill cooking the*
books: attaching a bait to the
yabbie in case we don't catch one

fabulous mulberry tree, which to this day is still going strong and bearing fruit. (Actually, that might not be true, it might have been in around 1801 when one of the great British explorers, Matthew Flinders, in the good ship *Investigator*, discovered it.)

So we went off back to the part of the island where the famous mulberry tree grows. Rocky River is a terrific place for wildlife. Dark-faced kangaroos have learned to trust people and frequently pilfer from picnic hampers (so it says here on a beautiful map published by the Kangaroo Island Tourist Association Inc).

▶PLAY

● And did you know that Kangaroo Island is Australia's third largest isle (after Tasmania and Melville) and that it was isolated from the mainland about 10,000 years ago?

● Or that early settlers, bands of renegades and escaped convicts bartered salt and skins for whalers' provisions – rum, flour, tea and sugar

– and, according to one Captain Sutherland, 'they are complete savages . . . they smell like foxes'?

● That large volumes of medicinal cures such as 'Dreadnought – the best eucalyptus in the world' were once distilled here, but production has declined with demand?

● Or that another island industry thrived when yacca gum, 'jiggered' from the pithy trunk of the grass tree, played an important part in the manufacture of explosives, linoleum and varnish.

● And that you might find two common species of snake – the Black Tiger and Pigmy Copperhead – both venomous but which fortunately shy clear of humans!

FADE DOWN SOUND

That's enough ripping off stuff from the Tourist Guide, Ed.   ▮▮ PAUSE

It was getting dark, the sun was setting and a chill wind was beginning to blow when Bill, who was still a little peckish after my dish of yabbies, foolishly started talking about razor fish. Apparently, these are flat-shelled things that protrude from the sand, cut your feet to ribbons if you walk on them, are eaten raw and taste delicious.

'Ooh, yum, yum,' said Pritchard, 'let's have some of those' – ignoring my protestations that you can pick them only at low tide.

I had nearly talked him out of this foolhardy scheme, which would have involved me plunging into the chilly waters of the South Atlantic when Bill volunteered. Incredibly, he ripped off most of his clothes, waded 150 yards out to sea, and dived repeatedly. He stuffed these razor shells, which must have been about eight inches long, into his underpants, and waddled – he is a corpulent gentleman – back to the shore. I, naturallly, being of sound mind, supervised the operation from a distance. And the fact that the water temperature was marginally above freezing had nothing whatsoever to do with it.

We split them open and, once you have cleared away the mess that fills the shell, a small white disc about three times the size of a Trebor extra-strong mint reveals itself, which you cut from the shell and munch. The taste was exquisite. It was as if the moon had kissed the sea. But notwithstanding that, there is no way you'd get me to dive for the little bastards – for the little deliciousnesses I mean to say.

Bill was shivering and trembling. We dried him, we wrapped him up in blankets and repaired to the local pub where everyone ate mountains of chips and tomato ketchup and other unidentified frying objects. I had only had my cucumber sandwich all day. That's the trouble with these programmes, you are cooking delicious things like yabbies and such, but you never get to eat them.

But soon it was dark and time to go. So we drove the odd mile or so back to the dirt-strip airport and clambered into the twin-engined Short, made as you know in Belfast, and headed back for Adelaide – that brilliant, light and stylish city founded, in fact, by Colonel William Light. There are virtually no high-rises; it is actually very much a people-sized place where the tram and not the car is king.

Indeed, the delightful thing about South Australia in general is that it was settled, unlike so much of Australia, by free men and women who chose, rather than being transported here, to build their farms and their vineyards. In this rich and fertile garden of Australia, which reminds me so much of Provence, Germans have settled with their finance and their Lutheran wooden churches.

Greeks grow olives and harvest the fruit in a fashion that goes back to biblical times. They knock ripe olives from the trees with sticks and let them fall to the ground into baskets. The breeze takes away the leaves and the debris, leaving just the olives behind. One morning we stopped off to watch an olive harvest and shared a Greek breakfast feast of home-made bread spread with crushed garlic and freshly-ground black pepper and drenched in olive oil.

That moment of mists and mellow fruitfulness, standing in an olive grove sipping the best, the Barossa full and fruity, remains one of the most memorable of my Australian odyssey.

Anyway, picture yourself on a boat on the river or picture me in the elegance of my presidential suite, scrubbed, washed and shaved after a hard day's yabbie fishing on Kangaroo Island, contemplating dinner. I walked through the three or four rooms, pouring a drink here, gazing through the telescope there, or tinkling with the keys on my grand piano, waiting for gastronomic inspiration. Shall I have a Mongolian hotpot sent up from the Japanese restaurant or shall I perhaps order some caviar and a light sauté of kidneys? All day I have only eaten a cucumber sandwich, as I do every day, and I am hungry for something good.

I am determined to drink some Penfold's Grange Hermitage, probably the best red wine in Australia. I certainly want to drink some Noble

Botrytis. And there needs to be an excuse to commence the feast that I have agreed to choose, with some Lindeman's Chardonnay.

I press the button and Kelvin and Kevin, my round-the-clock butlers, manifest themselves, or so it seems to me, from behind the curtains. Pressing a button in the Hyatt in Adelaide is a bit like being in charge of the lamp. Every time you rub it, you can have a wish. In their starched white coats and carefully-creased black trousers, black bow ties and gold epaulettes, they stand, waiting for my order. I tell them the wine I want and they murmur approvingly, but when I order the food they blanch.

Because for my dinner party tonight for Pritchard, my personal assistant Maggie, and a young lady who shouldn't have been there in the first place, I ordered King Island cheddar cheese, severely grilled on toast. I ordered a massive bowl of strawberries and raspberries and King Island cream – but for the main course I wanted something very, very special indeed.

Outside the old railway station, which is now a casino, there is a retired tramcar. And in this tramcar, there are bubbling tubs of lurid green mushy peas, and there are glass-fronted hot cabinets stacked high with round, flat meat pies. On the Formica counters, there are bottles of Rosella tomato ketchup and white vinegar and salt and pepper shakers.

Under normal circumstances these pies, known as pie floaters, are eaten only at the intervals in football matches. Or when late at night while wheeling home, arm-in-arm, wide-eyed and legless in the company of carousing chums, you are hit by that overwhelming hunger that has no consideration for your digestive system.

So after a night at the theatre that led on to just a quick one at some grotesque nightclub, with your velvet cape over your shoulders, your black tie askew, the solid gold studs of your evening shirt undone – you stop at the Pie Cart and order a pie floater. And with half of it in your mouth, half of it over your pure silk evening shirt, the laces of one of your patent leather shoes undone, you stand under the sodium lamps munching, slurping, hiccupping, and giggling, hoping that a taxi will come and take you home.

What you don't do is tell your butlers that tonight at eight-thirty in the presidential suite you will have served, upon the best bone china, as a main course for a dinner party, four pie floaters – and make sure that the ketchup is Rosella's.

Kelvin and Keith (or were they called Wayne and Clive, I don't recall) were shocked. Their lower lips trembled, their eyes narrowed. You know

Pie-eyed and legless

that bit in the book where Jeeves refused to lay out Bertie's snazzy socks, and Bertie said, 'He gave me a look of withering disdain' – then you will get the drift of how Julian and Julian looked at me.

However, they are dedicated professionals and throughout dinner maintained station, moving only to dispense more wine or brew coffee. We were, of course, hysterical with the absurd juxtaposition of the gross Adelaide pie floaters served in such elegant, refined and distinguished surroundings. I hadn't enjoyed myself so much for ages.

And after my Jacuzzi that evening when I was relaxing with tingling skin in a cool, freshly-laundered towelling robe, I made a few pretty pertinent notes into my dictating machine, so that when I came to write this modest masterpiece, I would have all the material at my fingertips.

Herewith I reproduce some of the tape!

▶PLAY

● Cucumber sandwiches every day. Many Australian houses with little verandahs reminiscent of Hornby O-gauge tin country railway stations of youth! Low corrugated roofs, sort-of Cotswold stone bunkhouses, pieces of kitchen equipment, wooden draining board on the ceramic sink . . .

- Seafood consommé with seared abalone enhanced by lemon grass would be a smashing soup; and creamed curry soup with chicken *goujons* and ginger, Thai-based; grapefruit and Campari *nage*; then thickened with butter, and a carrot *mousseline* with lime and Cotton Bay scallops and some very thin slivers of grapefruit. There must be some fish stock, combined with grapefruit, reduced, the butter beaten into it; the carrot purée had a little sugar as well, with very, very fine lime zest in it.

- Of course, we didn't catch any yabbies but the beer bottles represented the passage of time.

- Casino in railway station. The bullpits where they crowd round, jeering soldiers, uniformed sailors, ladies in silk dresses, tossing up two coins into the pit.

- Dip in the Hyatt. Seared, grilled *darne* of salmon, champagne sauce, beansprouts, and salmon caviar.

- Geriatric train but very good fun. Little station with cabins, trees, kangaroos, camels, into a bar full of people who'd run away from home. No funny barmen!

That's enough garbled tape transcript, thank you, Ed.   **❚❚ PAUSE**

Garbled notes they may be, but, in fact, very useful ones because I had completely forgotten a super little dish that I had cooked at Maggie Beer's Pheasant Farm restaurant in the Barossa Valley. We had driven in the Floydmobile past the vineyards, the neat floral villages, past wineries and the odd corrugated-roof Lutheran church. Full of home-made Greek bread, soused in olive oil and garlic, and wine, I was in such good spirits, the weather was bright and sunny – but I didn't really want to do another cooking sketch.

In the original plan, David had said, we would merely observe Maggie Beer cooking one of her specialities, roast pheasant – and I'd write a commentary for it later. But when we got there, Maggie had invited a load of local wine-growers – Bob Maclean, Doug Lehmann and Robert O'Callaghan, to name but three of this jolly crowd.

So David, as usual, changed his mind and suggested I cooked a lunch for them, now! And all I really wanted to do was to sample the many different wines they had brought with them. Not least of all, Rockford's sparkling red, an amazing, fruity, and totally drinkable and unusual sparkling red wine – irreverently known as the legover of the 1950s! And, by the way, with typical candour, it was a woman who told me that. She said that more people had got married as a result of too much Rockford's than you could shake a stick at. You will obviously get my smutty implication here!

Anyway, lunch. Very simply, I roasted a couple of pheasants, breast down, in butter for about half an hour. Then I surrounded the pheasant with a load of peeled and parboiled baby beets – beetroots – and continued roasting them rather like potatoes, along with the pheasant. This was quite an inspirational dish, by the way, because as usual I had about ten minutes to raid Maggie Beer's fridges and devise a dish that was different from anything she had on her menu.

Just before the pheasants were beautifully roasted and the beetroots tender and sort of slightly crunchy on the outside, I strained the juices from the pan and returned the pheasants and beetroot to a low oven to keep warm. In a separate saucepan I browned finely-chopped onion in butter until it was almost caramelised, a little flour to make some roux, and cooked them until they started to go slightly golden. I added the juices previously taken from the pheasants, and a drop of red wine.

Then, as luck would have it, I found a bowl of jellied chicken stock (a luxurious optional extra) and added a couple of tablespoons of that. I bubbled up the sauce, and seasoned it with salt and pepper. It had a rich, gamey taste. And I strained it into a sauce jug ready to serve.

Another thing that Maggie happened to have were some large quince that she had peeled, cut into quarters, and stewed in caster sugar and lemon juice, which is a really simple thing to do. The resulting concoction resembles, a little bit, mango chutney.

My luck was holding. For the accompaniment, I didn't want to do potatoes and ordinary vegetables because I had the quince preserve and the roast beetroots and the rich wine sauce. Maggie had made some flat ribbon noodles. But if you haven't got a pasta machine, you can easily buy some.

So, I jointed the pheasant neatly on large white oval plates. I arranged the pheasant with the sauce under it, a little pile of the creamy yellow noodles with a garnish of purple roast beetroots and a dollop of the quince preserve.

And though I say it myself, it was quite delicious; I served it to the by now riotous assembly, and we began to talk and eat. Bottle after bottle was opened and the afternoon slipped downhill at one hell of a rate. As you can see from the following tape transcript, made on that day, after about three minutes I switched the tape off and decided to give in.

▶PLAY

- 30 May, Adelaide and we are visiting a pheasant farm in the Barossa Valley.
- Lunch started with Rockford's fizzy red . . . 1986 Henschke Rhine Riesling: aromatic with complex flavours and clean finish. Then 1986 Saltram . . . 1973 Rhine Riesling . . .
- 1976 Penfold's Grange Hermitage, made by Max Schubert, a Shiraz. Full and flat with a hint of mint and aftertaste of oak, at 1976 still a little young – even though it is now 1990. Also a hint of dark chocolate.
- Rhine Riesling won endless gold medals, slightly sweet, smoky after-taste – quite delicious and worked with tuna fish, an oily fish, very well. Reminded me of smoked apples.
- Brilliant sweet white wine is Peter Lehmann 1988, Botrytis . . . Semil-lon Sauternes . . . absolutely fantastic. 1981 Basedows Barossa Hermi-tage . . .
- The Wednesday Table, 3.30 – no rules except you enjoy the food and wine and probably make or sell it.

❚❚ PAUSE

Somebody told us later that we had had a really good time and I am quite prepared to believe them. But not only that, as you can see from the foregoing, I managed to make these brilliantly comprehensive wine-tasting notes.

It is fine, sipping iced melon juice, pink and sweet, on the Basque-rouge brick terrace of the Hyatt on this sunny Saturday Adelaide morning. Figures in stylish but unnecessary autumn coats crisscross the manicured garden piazza. Church spires shine in the soft sunlight. It is seventy-eight degrees Fahrenheit and the waitress, as she brings another tray, shivers, and places the glasses precariously on the wall. The tables, the chairs, the recliners and the parasols have long since been removed because it is winter.

It is not the same winter that I see today here in deepest, darkest Devon in December, a day of log fires, roasted chestnuts and heavy frosts. A day when, at low tide, we crunched through the frosty grass and rescued a flapping trout trapped by the falling tide in the icy waters of the Harbourne River that flows into Bow Creek. The creek that laps twinkling blue against the gnarled slimy roots of the woodland opposite my pub. A pair of kingfishers, a flash of papal blue and vermilion, are flying fast and low over the water.

It is 13 December and Adelaide is a long way away and it is hard to recapture my last Saturday in that fair city where, after drinking scented melon juice, I took the silent elevator up to the cool stainless steel kitchen to do a small cooking sketch with my chum Urs, another New Australian who has found not only the rainbow but the pot of gold that lies beneath it.

He is young, quiet, calm and very clean in white clogs and crisp overalls. And with the fingers of a concert pianist he chops, slices, stirs and shakes, sharp knives and gleaming pots, slivers of fish and whites of egg, until he has created an exquisite dish of garfish and sea urchins. A combination of tastes and flavours, it would be absurd in Hampstead, Devon, Wandsworth or Oxfordshire, but in Adelaide seems perfectly okay. Urs cooks with majesty. I don't care whether or not you can use the word 'majesty' in this sense. It's my book and I'll write it how I want.

I cooked a much simpler dish, quickly grilled *darne* of sea or salmon trout with a lemon butter sauce and beansprouts. It was hotter in the kitchen than it had been outside, because when you are filming 'they' don't like the extractor fans humming in the background. It makes too much noise for the sound recordist – though of course later they dub on all the ambient sounds of a kitchen, like the sizzling of a pan on gas and the hum of refrigerators and air-conditioning plants.

Happily, the sequences went well and by twenty to twelve the filming was over and David declared a wrap. Which meant that I could get on with the main event of the day, something much nearer to my heart than cooking – sport. In this case, an invitation to a lunch of the President's Men at Adelaide's premier Aussie Rules team, the Red Legs.

Trevor Armitage is President this year and every now and again he invites a few chums to the inner sanctuary of the club for a light lunch, some erudite conversation and a lot of booze before the match.

A light lunch consists of trays groaning with small handmade meat pies, loads of prawns, pieces of chicken, fried, and about four-million gallons of South Australian wine – notably fizzy red from my chum (see further back in the wine notes), the one affectionately known as the legover of the 1950s. The erudite conversation centred mainly on outrageous and untruthful boasts of sporting derring-do, of sexual prowess and tips on how to survive a twenty-four-hour drinking bout.

In case you haven't had the pleasure of watching a live Aussie Rules

*And every now
and again they go
off for a G & T
and have a rest*

game, very simply it is a question of thirty-six (eighteen-a-side) gladiators, assisted by four or five umpires, running round a large oval pitch knocking the living-be Jesus out of each other. If you are unfortunate enough as a player to receive the ball, you have two options: avoid it like the plague and endure the jeers of 'you yellow-livered poofy git' from the crowd, or get absolutely flattened by at least eight of the opposing team.

About every twenty minutes they stop and have a little rest, while scantily-clad cheer leaders parade the park. Every now and again a coach or a trainer will pop on to the field and offer some advice. And occasionally, if there has been a successful kick, a couple of chaps wearing white milking coats and straw hats, who stand behind the goalposts, make curiously military mechanical salutes with their arms.

At the end of about one and a half hours, you look up at the scoreboard to discover your team has won by 120 points to 87 and also by 13 to 8. I am sure you all now fully understand this elementary game! If the score is substantially in your favour, you then go back to the clubhouse for more meat pies, lots of drink and more deep and meaningful – even philo-sophical – conversation.

After a couple of hours you are in a perfect position to offer some advice to the actual players. After another hour you are ready to select next week's team. When you have done that, you can start retelling your tales of prodigious drinking, sexual prowess and sporting derring-do all over again.

It is with great relief that you see your chauffeur fighting his way through the crowded bar to take you back to the hotel, and sanity. As he opens the door in front of the hotel steps, you must straighten your tie, square your shoulders and try to mount them without slipping, tripping or in any way revealing to the ranks of doormen, porters, receptionists and duty managers that you are absolutely wide-eyed and legless!

A cold shower is all it takes and you are ready to don a dinner jacket, slide back into the limousine and, praying to God that if you do fall asleep during the second act of this damned musical, whose name I can't even remember but which was sponsored by the hotel whose guest you are – at least you won't snore.

The musical was noisy, enthusiastic, quite funny and had some very good songs. The set was superb. As I recall it was an ocean liner upon which a selection of lovers chased one another in and out of cabins and all lived happily ever after. I managed to avoid meeting the cast afterwards and swept out into the cool Adelaide evening air. And strode purposefully towards the Pie Cart, parked outside the casino.

Where, by arrangement, a South Australia politician presented me with a bow tie and made me Honorary Vice President of the Adelaide branch of the World Bow Tie Club. I thanked him, ordered a pie floater and with the gold studs of my shirt popped open, my velvet cape askew, made it manfully, once again, up the hotel steps and to bed.

Tomorrow the madness would end. We were taking *The Ghan* from Adelaide to Alice Springs – the Red Centre.

Day 365, The Ghan, 6 June

The Ghan is a big train of twenty coaches – sleeping cars, restaurants, bars, crew quarters and car transporters. It is a long, polished aluminium snake pulled by two diesel engines through 1,000 miles of scrub and bush and hard-baked earth from Adelaide to Alice Springs.

But on this day there was one extra coach. An elegant wood-panelled coach built for the Prince of Wales in 1920. And it had been hitched up so that I could make this epic journey in old-style comfort. It had a private dining room, double bedroom and kitchen with storeroom, as well as a cook, steward and butler.

And though the modern *Ghan* has every conceivable facility aboard from gaming room to cocktail bars, to sit in the splendour of this lovingly restored coach was much more to my liking. It was exciting too because our storeroom was stacked high with fresh provisions and at least

*Pitchard D.
breaking
the mile of a lifetime*

half-a-dozen bottles of each wine grown in South Australia. And I planned a sumptuous dinner party at the twelve-seater dining table for a load of hitherto unknown elegant Australian heiresses whom I felt sure would be travelling on the train.

There was only a handful of people on the platform to see the train off; the Station Master nodded to the driver and half a mile of metal snaked slowly into the fast approaching dusk. And twenty-two hours of clickety-clack, clickety-clack over 2,331,334 sleepers to the Red Centre of Australia.

Many years ago a telegraph link was established north from Adelaide, through Alice Springs, to Darwin and the rest of the world beyond. Men and machinery for this prodigious undertaking were transported by camel and their Afghan owners, whose memory is maintained in the name of the train. When the railway was planned these same camel drivers hauled the track and the sleepers for the railway. This, of course, was great for opening up the centre of Australia, but put the camel drivers out of business.

Anyway, I spent a self-indulgent hour unpacking or rather supervising the unpacking of my leather suitcases into the smoothly-sliding drawers of the panelled wardrobe in my bedroom. An exquisite place to sleep, with softly-turning fans on the arched ceiling and wonderful porcelain sinks with heavy chrome taps and polished brass wastepipes. A discreet tap at the door and a steward entered with a chased-silver tray bearing a decanter, ice, water and two glasses. And yes, cunning reader, you may have discovered I did not make the mistake of travelling alone.

The train rumbled and clattered through the evening at a dignified forty mph, making this creaking carriage feel like an elegant yacht gliding through a tranquil ocean on a light breeze. In deference to the regal surroundings I decided to dress for dinner in the white silk suit that was later to cause me so much grief at customs at Heathrow (I haven't worn it since, as on mature reflection I think it is a bit too flash and besides, I don't drive a BMW, or for that matter sell them).

Once dressed and the evening apéritif taken, I set off leading a crocodile of a film crew down the train, looking for someone, preferably female, blonde, vivacious, witty and intelligent, to have dinner with. And we staggered and swung along the zigzagging central corridor of the sleeping coaches, occasionally startling a perfectly innocent traveller trying to make his way in the opposite direction.

I must have looked like some modern-day witch doctor, lurching down the train in my white suit, holding before me and aloft my magic stick, which was still festooned with the gaily-coloured tags that airlines put on your baggage. Well, bless my soul, we went on and on down the coaches, through the first dining car, through the next bar, into the entertainment lounge, past the shop, into the next bar, and right down to the tail coaches where economy passengers made themselves comfortable in airline-type couchettes.

There was not a single heiress, blonde, brunette or redhead, on the whole goddam train. In fact, I don't think there was a female aboard under the age of about seventy-five. And whereas, of course, such ladies are great fun, it wasn't exactly what I had in mind, to have dinner with a blue-rinsed, real-life Edna Everage, Dame or just plain Mrs.

So I had no choice but to return to my stateroom and dine with the crew. What we had hoped to find, you see, was an attractive dinner companion whom we could use in the film to tell us about the lot of the Australian woman, their social position, relationships with the Australian man, sexuality – in short, we wanted to explore and expound the myth of modern-day sexual relationships and the meaning of life – the very Bruce and Sheila of it all. Alas, it was not to be, so we uncorked a few bottles of Hardy's wine and settled down to a simple but excellent dinner of steak, followed by pavlova, and some delicious King Island brie. We drank some Australian port, which I didn't like, and some *Noble Botrytis* (Australian sauterne), which I did. And went to bed.

Referring to my notes, I see that I was up at dawn, gazing out of my window on to a vast flat expanse of sterile, muddy-brown landscape sparsely dotted with stunted trees and bushes. But the air smelt fresh and good and the biggest sun I have ever seen rose majestically into the morning sky.

It was time for me to do a cooking sketch, something that went with *The Ghan*, so I decided to cook a modernised version of couscous, a recipe that my friend Tony Papas from Sydney had given me. Simple enough, of course, but there was one slight snag – we wanted the engine drivers to eat it and there was no communicating door to the engines. So we decided to

Food
Blood/on the tracks

stop the train. They don't normally make unscheduled stops, but they kindly made one for us. We set up a portable table and chairs in between the tracks, and in front of the engines fed two totally relaxed and unfazed engine drivers with couscous served on fine china plates upon a table decked with crisp linen and solid silver cutlery.

The train was on a slight curve and looking back along its immense length you could see hundreds of heads hanging out of windows, wondering what the hell was going on. So David, with his usual charm and tact, shouted at them: 'Would you all shut up please, we are trying to make a film.' The Australians are so laid back that this interruption to their journey caused them not a stir, and once one of the stewards had told them that it was just a bunch of Poms being silly, they retired to their couchettes or cabins, and breakfast.

Once again I was overawed by the silent vastness of the countryside and I wondered if anybody else had stood on this very spot in the middle of Australia. Except for perhaps the people who had laid the track, probably no one ever had. We packed up and the train trundled off, clickety-clacking through the nothingness. The earth was growing redder, a rich rust-red.

About a hundred miles before Alice we passed a group of some twenty Aboriginals sitting beside the track, sad and quiet in dirty shorts and sweatshirts, drinking beer from tins. They were there for no apparent reason, hundreds of miles from the nearest habitation. And Australians travelling on the train whom I asked just shrugged their shoulders and replied: 'Oh, they're just Abos, they like doing that sort of thing.' Nobody wanted to have a conversation about them, it seemed.

Towards noon, only an hour or so late, this long, silver train pulled into the desolate siding that is Alice Springs Station. The sky was overcast and it was very cold. I was glad I had my leather riding coat and gloves. The place was grey and flat. I felt depressed but the brightly-clothed pensioners gaily climbed aboard the waiting buses that would take them to their holiday hotels. From the station across the goods yards, past the wooden crates and the stacked oil drums, you could see no evidence of Alice itself.

I was told we were staying at a homestead some seventy miles east of Alice Springs and that this waiting Toyota would take me there. The crew would wait until the Floydmobile had been unloaded from the transporter at the end of the train. I was pleased that I didn't have to hang around for the two hours it would take to get the bus ready.

We set off with, to my mind, an overly cheerful, wisecracking young man, down a drab, empty metal road that was fringed with discarded rubbish. It was an untidy, unkempt road that took us through what I assumed to be the outskirts of Alice Springs. We drove over bridges that spanned dried-up watercourses. The driver said even the bridges were impassable in the 'wet'.

We passed some untidy bungalows set in gardens, or compounds really, which were filled with the rusting bric-a-brac of people who need to be self-sufficient to live here. Stacks of oil drums, piles of timber, several generations of pick-up trucks in varying stages of decomposition. Heaps of tyres, rusting cement mixers and small tractors. Most bungalows had paddocks with a horse or two mooching disconsolately round. We passed a wildlife park or zoo whose entrance gates and signs needed repainting.

My driver was chattering away thirteen-to-the-dozen about his sexual conquests, drinking bouts and his love of the outback. It struck me as a strange mixture of interests but I was feeling so low – perhaps it was those Abos huddled by the railway line, perhaps it was the sudden change of weather – that I wasn't paying attention to what he was saying anyway.

But truth to say, I reckon the real reason I was feeling a bit pissed off was because the journey on *The Ghan* had really been rather disappointing. The train itself is fabulous. The people who work on it were helpful and kind and everything you could wish for. But the food in the restaurant car (not I hasten to add in my own private quarters) was quite one of the worst meals I had ever had. It had been enough to choke a brown dog. My trusty dictionary informed me: 'Almost anything nasty will choke a brown dog. However, black or black and white dogs seem impervious to various types of culinary poisoning. The phrase normally goes, "Jeez [a euphemism for Jesus], that pie was as rough as guts, it would choke a brown dog, it would." Why brown dogs in Australia are more susceptible to ptomaine poisoning than those of a different colour remains a mystery.'

And where I had expected to find a train full of diverse characters – young backpackers, sophisticated advertising people, fascinating priests, villains and cardsharps, you know, the whole romantic bit that you associate with a long, long train journey – all it contained were several hundred pensioners trundling off on a journey that had no real reason, no real rationale. And, I am afraid to say, they were a jolly dull lot.

Anyway, every cloud has a silver lining and suddenly the clouds lifted above me. At the precise moment the metal-topped road ended and gave way to a long, straight dirt road cut between red rocks, the sun came out and illuminated gum and eucalyptus trees, and we passed a posse or a pack or whatever you call it of kangaroos – the first I had seen on my journey, except on postcards.

We were bowling along at sixty mph with a ball of red dust behind us that tailed back several hundred yards to a wisp. As the journey went on the road surface deteriorated. Tracks formed in the 'wet' had baked hard into ruts. And you hit potholes with a stomach-turning thump. I was holding on to the grab-bar on the dash but, of course, my driver steered with one hand and with the other pointed out outcrops of rocks, trees and black cockatoos with red tails.

We passed no other vehicle. A sign said 'Beware of Camels', but I didn't see any. After about an hour, thoroughly bounced and bruised, we came to the Ross River Homestead, which was a stone-built farmhouse, with a handful of barns and stockpens and a couple of dozen chalets dotted round a small swimming pool. There were some camels tethered to a fence and a little plump kangaroo lopped towards our truck.

The driver switched off the engine and the silence was deafening – until about eight-hundred pink and white galahs, which I had not seen sitting on the ground, screeched into the air like something out of a Hitchcock film. Galahs are the size of racing pigeons; I think they are beautiful, but Australians regard them as pests. We walked up to the main house and passed a lot of brightly-coloured birds, presumably parrots, in cages. My recently revived spirits – because the dirt road journey had been exhilarating – took a nosedive yet again. Why, oh why, in this spectacular landscape, with no people, hardly any vehicles, no telephones, no pollution and no worries (ha ha!) did all these exotic creatures have to be either in cages or tethered? Why do groups of Aboriginals sit beside railway lines all huddled together in the beds of dried-up rivers? And, another thing, if this was the Ross River Homestead, where was the Ross River?

Inside, the bar counter was made from the original wooden sleepers of *The Ghan* railroad, but there was nobody standing behind it to greet us. The menu was chalked on the blackboard: pie and chips, chicken Kiev and chips, chilli con carne, and two or three other totally uninspiring offerings, with the exception of a dish called barramundi – though where the fish actually came from I couldn't imagine. A glance at the map will demonstrate that you are thousands of miles from the nearest water. Anyway, not to worry about things like that.

We stood at the bar, waiting for some wizened, gnarled Australian bushman to serve us when, to my delight and surprise, a fresh-faced young lady bounced through the kitchen door and in a Yorkshire accent asked us how we were and what we would like to eat and drink.

As I took in my surroundings, I realised there were half-a-dozen blokes in the bar all dressed in moleys, high-heeled riding boots, kangaroo-leather belts and the kind of tough shirts that cowboys wear. As Australian as it is possible to be, they all appeared. But as the ice melted and conversation began to flow, it transpired that they were all from places like Milton Keynes.

But a love of horses and the brutality of the outback had lured them there, where they tended the stock and entertained the tourists and visitors by taking them on camel safaris and riding expeditions and camping trips. I soon realised that I had misinterpreted the natural reserve of true countrymen.

As the evening progressed, everyone relaxed and a good time was had by all. Except for the dinner. If the meal on *The Ghan* had been bad, then dinner here was absolutely atrocious. We discovered from the chef that they had some legs of lamb and we, who had been eating so much fine food, particularly in the big cities, were craving for a simple roast. So we explained most carefully, David and I, that if it wasn't too much trouble – there was virtually no one else staying there – we would adore a whole leg of lamb, placed on a baking tray in the oven, surrounded by a load of potatoes and served with some plain gravy. And if there was any chance of a dish of frozen peas, that would be a bonus. We also explained that we would eat it at the chef's convenience. It didn't matter if it took two or three hours to cook, whenever it was ready, we would eat it.

He told us about nine-thirty would be fine so we retired to our various cabins, unpacked, and with that wonderful image of roast leg of lamb and roast potatoes firmly in our minds, hearts and stomachs, we set off to do a bit of filming to fill the gap between now and dinner-time. I seem to remember it was a cooking sketch, alfresco, with the daughter of the owner, a precocious flaxen-haired little beauty of about seven years or maybe ten, who went to school on the radio, a system quite normal in the sparsely-populated areas of Australia. The system works very simply. The teacher works from a radio station in, say, Alice Springs, and each morning the kids, in a room in their own homes, turn on their radios and take their lessons over the air, something they take completely for granted. But it is, after all, the land of the Flying Doctor, which service in fact originated from Alice Springs, by a man called Flynn.

Anyway, back to the sketch. Very basic ingredients of breast of chicken, a bit of cheese, put in a frying pan on the Primus stove. I set about teaching young Heidi an easy dish in the spirit of the radio teacher. But under the observation of a stray, inquisitive young camel called Camilla, a blasted pet kangaroo and Heidi herself, chaos, confusion and darkness reigned and I was left a trembling wreck, roundly upstaged and out-acted by my young friend. That ignominy was compounded by the camel nicking the food from the frying pan and confused by the kangaroo hopping in and out of the shot. Still, it doesn't do any harm to have your ego totally annihilated from time to time, because television can deceive you into thinking that you are much more important and clever than you really are.

You don't have many bad days filming, by and large it is the most terrific fun, but this had been a bad day, plus I didn't really like the location very much. So I was glad when David Pritchard decided it was a wrap, and with the anticipation of a superb roast leg of lamb for supper, I squared my shoulders and accepted that I had made a mess of things and went happily to my cabin for a shower before dinner.

Once the sun had set, it became quite chilly, and the cabins with only small heaters were cold. So the roaring log fire that greeted us in the bar was a welcome sight, and we stood before it drinking great draughts of red wine, waiting with excited anticipation to be called into the little dining room to eat.

I was offered and declined Witchetty Grub Soup to start with, on the grounds that it was tinned and not fresh, but David had some and said it tasted like mushroom soup. It probably was. But the thought of eating anything to do with caterpillars made me feel sick. Nibbling a little bread so as not to spoil my appetite, I waited with some impatience for the others to finish their starters and finally, with much pomp and ceremony, a huge platter was set on the table before us.

'Thank you,' we cried, and then one by one we fell totally silent and stared at this extraordinary sight.

David put his fingers to his pursed lips, looked up in an amused way and called the waiter back: 'I'm sorry to trouble you,' he said very gently and politely, 'but I think you have given us the wrong order. We were expecting roast leg of lamb with roast potatoes and gravy.'

'No worries, mate,' the waiter replied, 'this is leg of lamb with roast potatoes and gravy.'

I said, 'It is not, at least I don't think it is.'

So the chef was called. 'It is roast leg of lamb,' he said.

'Well, why is it already in slices then?' we asked. 'And what are these peppers and onions and mushrooms and courgettes doing floating in it?'

It was a mishmash of the most appalling crap I have ever had in my life. The chef had chain-sawed a frozen leg of lamb into one-inch slices, roasted them in the oven, then boiled the aforesaid vegetables in neat red wine and poured the whole revolting hot vinegary mix over the crucified, sacrificed lamb. The disappointment was enormous, the food was terrible, the chef was mortified because he really had done, by his lights, his very best. It was just that when he said he understood what roast leg of lamb was English-style, he was telling porkies (so to speak).

I asked Maggie, my assistant, to make me three rounds of cucumber sandwiches. Rather unreasonable of me at eleven o'clock at night since she had to stumble outside with a torch and open up storage compartments of the Floydmobile and run round various 'eskies' (Australian for icebox) to find the wherewithal. I probably sound petulant and spoilt, I don't care if I do, it was the last straw. I hadn't really liked Alice Springs Station, I hadn't really liked the Ross River Station, and now I absolutely hated it. So I sulked and went to bed and left everyone else feeling totally pissed off.

I awoke early in my cold and slightly damp chalet and trudged over to the main house for breakfast, which we had ordered by arrangement the night before to be served at 6 a.m. Of course, the cook wasn't on duty, presumably still nursing his wounded ego from the night before. And the waiter, a strange Englishman who seemed right out of place, wasn't a very good cook. So a variety of undercooked and overcooked eggs, burnt or raw bacon, arrived at spasmodic intervals over the next hour and a half, and left the whole crew feeling completely disgruntled.

And it was an ill-tempered lot that piled into a load of four-wheel drives to follow 'No Worries' Chase to the location. We became even more disgruntled when he took us to the wrong place, because he can no more read a map than the idiot who had cooked us breakfast can cook.

Maggie, in a rare moment of forgetfulness, had omitted to buy us any fresh ingredients, so I was faced with baskets of stale vegetables and tins of strange Australian convenience food to conjure up a dazzling dish that would reflect the power and the eerie glory of this ancient, barren, majestic Red Centre of Australia. To make matters worse, when we did get to our location we found, would you believe it, another film crew there, doing fashion shots for the spring collection of some Melbourne store.

In fact, recalling these troubled times here has so depressed me, as I stand in the window, looking at the slate-grey mud outside my cottage in County Cork – although a puffin or some such bird has caught a shaft of sunlight – that I am going to have a small snooze before I write any more. (Jim came in and said it is not a puffin, there aren't any round here, it is a redshank. Jim, by the way, is a man who has been employed by my publishers to prevent me from hopping off into Kinsale for company and consolation when in fact I should be writing) . . .

. . . I have had a nice sleep now and I have woken up feeling very refreshed. It is the most sensible thing to have a little snooze when you are a bit grumpy or depressed. When we feel we lack inspiration David and I do what we call 'going for a walk in the garden'. In this case we were naturally despondent to find someone else using our chosen location, a dramatic spot of precipitous cliffs and soft red earth, with eagles swooping high in the brilliantly sparkling clear sky. So we went off for a stroll to think things out.

And David has a terrific knack of reversing a disadvantageous situation to our benefit. We had only walked half of our prescribed circle when he grabbed my magic stick from my hand and pointed it up to the eagle. He cried, 'I've got it, I really think I've got it.'

'You mean you want me to cook the eagle?' I said.

'No, no, dickbrain [an Australian term of endearment which he had become very fond of using], you can cook some food for the models. After all, you've been tramping halfway across Australia looking for attractive women and here are two for the taking – sorry, I'll rephrase that.'

So with spring in our step we returned to the trucks, made friends with Justin the photographer and Boris the designer (whom I thought would have shuddered at the very idea of watching any kind of horror movie), and asked them if we could borrow the girls for a little culinary, cultural filming sketch. Seeing a slightly miffed look on their faces, I kicked David in the shins and said it would be really good if Tarquin and Wayne (or whatever they were called, the photographers, that is) could join in too. Radiant smiles flowed on to their faces and they adjusted their silk safari suits and reknotted their flowing scarves.

I cooked a blinding little vegetable curry. The girls, shivering in their scanty costumes, put on brave faces and to the disappointment of the crew woofed the entire dish of curry and scraped the pot clean.

Then we all went back to the homestead, laughing and jolly, where I melted great slabs of cheese in front of the log fire while we waited for our excellent order of magnificently reheated industrial meat pies, served with mountains of chips and Rosella tomato sauce. And in an atmosphere of international conviviality we passed an outrageous evening telling each other, including the chef and the waiter, how wonderful we all were.

The next morning I had to sit on a rather uncomfortable horse for a long while, trotting up and down the dried riverbed underneath the sweet-smelling eucalyptus trees, pausing occasionally by ghost gum trees, chatting to Alec Ross, a half-caste Aboriginal, who was going to teach me how to cook the ubiquitous damper bread, beloved of stockmen and tourists the outback over. We were going to eat it with syrup, known as 'Cocky's Joy'. According to my little dictionary, syrup was the only cheap sweetening available to a cocky or farmer in the early days because jam cost too much. And the misery of the farmer's lot during the pioneering era is explained in the saying, 'The river flooded, me horse dropped dead, the damned wet dog got into me bedding and the ants got into me Cocky's Joy.'

As Alec and I sat by the camp fire waiting for the bread to cook in a heavy cast-iron pot Alec told me, without bitterness, of his childhood and being forcibly taken away from his mother because he was a half-caste, and 'brutally' educated in what the Australians of the time thought of as the enlightened approach to the 'Aboriginal problem'.

We sat there for a long time, munching on damper bread with butter and Cocky's Joy by the Ross River. Usually when I have finished a cooking sketch I can't wait to get back to the nearest bar for a quick Scottish one, but I felt content to stay in this place with this peaceful man.

It is tempting to be philosophical here. As a cook I can quite understand the old Aboriginal way of life as it was, or as it has been, for about forty-thousand years – gathering what you need for the day and when food gets low, moving on to another area for richer pickings; and as a Pom, it is arrogant for me to suggest that the Australians understand or care little for it. But central Australia is poised at a delicate moment in its life. Soon, very soon, no thanks to the sort of programmes that I make, tourists are going to come here not just in their hundreds but in their thousands and it would be outrageous if the rich culture and history of the Aboriginal people were overlooked in the process. They are in danger of becoming distant watchers, always on the outskirts and never a part of what really makes this region great.

Day 54, Alice Springs, 1 June

Everyone has heard of Alice Springs, and I had a preconceived idea of a place out of the Wild West, with Victorian façades, ornate balconies, saloons babbling with happy banter; a place with character, in fact. Alas, it isn't. It was as if some bright spark had transformed the town overnight, giving it all the elegance of a Home Counties new town.

Most of the Aboriginal people I saw preferred the outskirts, the riverbeds and the eucalyptus trees for company instead of the brash shopping malls.

Depressed yet again, I walked up the steep hill to the Anzac memorial, the highest point that overlooks the town and behind, across the plains to the ring of mountains that form a huge amphitheatre. By the memorial a simple white obelisk, erected in honour of Australian dead, not only from two World Wars, but from wars in Malaysia, Borneo, Korea and Vietnam. From the vantage point I could survey the whole of Alice, the modern shops, the pedestrian precincts, the rugby park – a lush green pitch completely at odds with the arid surroundings, with its neat white Fosters hospitality tent and smart four-wheel drives parked neatly by the excited supporters of the two teams.

From 300 or 400 feet up, I had an excellent view of a thrilling game, switching from one end of the field to the next, both sides scoring tries with skill and style. It looked so English, a cross between a real traditional church fête being held on the edges of a well-heeled village.

Eleven eagles were diving and swooping and gliding. I reluctantly abandoned the match and started to rejoin the crew, when some movement on the dried-up riverbed caught my eye. A group of presumably drunk Aboriginals were stoning a woman, who lay writhing on the earth. And I knew that as I stood high in the wind where eagles fly, I was watching the heart of Australia pumping with vitality and at the same moment broken and bleeding to death. Before the white man came, many thousands of years ago the Aboriginals roamed round this magical and beautiful place. They called it Dreamtime.

I didn't go to Ayers Rock. If you look at the map you think it is virtually at Alice Springs but, in fact, it is about 500 miles away. Anyway, the pilot on the plane – no names, no pack drill – did a quick detour and overflew it just so we could see it. But I didn't bother to look out of the window.

Four

Billionaires, bishops and the bush

I thought it would be a good idea to start this bit on my trip to Western Australia, home of billionaires, bishops and the bush, with some really useful factual information on its capital, Perth.

▶PLAY

● Did you know that Perth claims to be the sunniest state capital in Australia?

● Perth is usually referred to as Australia's youngest state capital since it was not founded until the late 1820s when Captain James Stirling was sent to explore suitable places for white settlements by the London Colonial Office, who feared otherwise the French would settle on the west coast.

● The colony grew slowly, however, even after convicts were taken there in 1850. But once gold was discovered in the 1890s, the population leapt to 30,000 and has been growing ever since. It is now hovering round the one-million mark and is nearly as big as Adelaide's. There has been a big influx of migrants from overseas and from the east coast to this modern, financial centre.

● Perth was definitely the city of millionaires in the 1980s, home to international wheeler-dealers like Alan Bond and the late Robert Holmes a Court. FADE DOWN SOUND

That's enough ripping off tourist guides, Ed.   ❚❚ PAUSE

Another Luxurious Hotel, Perth, Western Australia, 12 June

Woke up feeling very refreshed this morning, on the twenty-first floor of this amazingly plush hotel that is also a casino – which by the way I didn't bother to visit. I had an excellent breakfast in the atrium, a sort of subtropical grotto full of tinkling fountains and waterfalls and about eight-hundred serene Japanese businessmen. Many of the serving staff were Indian, the first I had encountered in my journey so far. Outside the weather was fine, warm and sunny, about seventeen degrees Centigrade, and if this is what Australians call winter, it suits me fine.

The leaves were turning golden and we had a pleasantly light day's filming ahead of us in the Swan Valley, another of Australia's noted wine areas. I do wish I had kept better notes on the wines because nearly all of them were highly drinkable. However, be that as it may.

And although we were not exactly singing like a rugby team in the Floydmobile as we drove along the banks of the Swan River, there was a decidedly happy atmosphere in the coach. I think everybody had been pretty pleased to escape from Alice Springs.

The mighty Floydmobile ground steadily up an ochre-yellow earth road through lush green fields, fruit trees and neat homesteads to our first location, which was a marron farm. Marrons are, I believe, unique to Western Australia. They are a type of freshwater crayfish except that they grow very, very much larger, nine inches long and possibly up to a pound in weight, the size of a small lobster. They are kept in a series of aerated freshwater dams, quite simply big ponds really.

It seems a very relaxing sort of business. Every now and again you wander past the almond trees, shooing off the parrots, which are so numerous they are almost considered pests, pick yourself a nice piece of fresh fruit – maybe an orange or a grapefruit – pause on a fence and have a small rest while you peel and finish off your orange or grapefruit, and lift out as many marrons as you have orders for, pack them gently into little polystyrene boxes and send them to market. On really hot days you can cool yourself by having a quick dip in one of the dams. It seems like the perfect life to me. That is, of course, if you are an Australian, used to such a way of life. To me it was exciting and fascinating, that in such a lovely climate with no threat of torrent or pestilence or monsoons or dangerous reptiles or horrible insects, you can wander out into your garden and pick any kind of fruit that you feel like. I felt a real thrill to be able to pick a basket of grapefruit and lemons and oranges and tanger- ines. And whereas I can take or leave a plateful of freshwater crayfish, which, quite frankly, unless they are cooked in the old Vaucluse way with a spicy tomato sauce, are a bit bland, a marron is somewhat different – it is heavier and feels plump and fat.

We did the film sequence with the owner, Tom Swannel, as quickly as we decently could because we wanted to have a few goes up and down the drive on his motorised Honda tricycle tractor, a sort of moon-buggy type of thing with great big tyres. It was terrific fun.

On the marron buggy

Then we ambled back down the hill to Kate Lamont's charming vineyard in the valley below. For all the world it reminded me of the Dordogne as cockerels and chickens pecked in and out of the neatly-ordered vines. The verandah of the house was infused, though, with the scent of citrus fruits, and all I had to do was drink a few glasses of Kate's wine, cook a marron, and the rest of the day was mine.

Kate was an utterly charming young woman, determined to make a success of both the vineyard and the restaurant, set among the vines. And like so many good Australian cooks, it has become clear to me, she was self-taught and unencumbered by tradition and misunderstood techniques. And with the undoubted advantage of having access to the most diverse and fresh produce.

And as all Australians here go out to eat a lot, there is no snobbery attached to it. There is no fuss. In fact, only the night before we had had an appallingly bad curry in a restaurant in Fremantle, where we had been assured all the visiting Indian cricket teams adored eating, and we had sat next to Robert Holmes a Court, who was undoubtedly one of Australia's most successful entrepreneurs, as well as a group of American matelots, a couple of tennis stars and a load of dock-workers – apart from the food, it had been great fun. And not only that, eating out is not outrageously expensive. Kate charges the equivalent of only about £6 for one of those wonderful freshwater lobster things.

Anyway, I popped a couple of marrons – as I dictate this I keep wanting to pronounce marrons without the 's' because it is the same as the French word for chestnut and it seems odd to me, sorry about that – into fiercely boiling water in a pan with a bit of salt, a bay leaf, some sliced onion, a sprig of parsley. And, as I hadn't come across them before, on Kate's advice I cooked them just for a few minutes until they turned a brilliant vermilion red.

Then I removed the flesh in one piece from the tail simply by twisting the tail off, and cracking it open. And with a flash of what I thought was inspiration, a squeeze each of lime, grapefruit, orange and lemon into the pan, which I then cooked over a fierce heat, stirring like fury, until I had the most delicious, slightly sweet and sour citrus sauce. The bitterness of that against the succulent sweetness of the marron flesh was a triumph. It was to me certainly a totally local dish. It was Swan Valley on a plate.

PS I hope they do a picture of this one.

*Me and Kate and
a dish called Marron*

Pritchard and I that evening amused ourselves by drinking cocktails in the hotel bar, watching some of the most stunningly beautiful women come and, sadly, go. Two months on the road and still not an heiress in sight.

Next day was another light one. Popped round to the riverside home of Australia's most loved and hated entrepreneur, Alan Bond. And after tripping over a couple of Bentleys and Jaguars, I cooked his wife Ellen a lightly-curried prawn dish beside her steaming pool. She was cheerful despite being incapacitated by a broken ankle.

Things were going well until I offered her a glass of what I thought to be good Australian wine. She almost spat it out. 'Jesus Christ, Floydie, where did you get that muck from?' – and promptly sent one of her servants (though Australians don't have servants) to raid the cellar for a drop of the good stuff, which turned out to be several bottles of Château Lafite.

Ellen Bond made a similar point to Kate: unencumbered by stuffy traditions, in Australia if you want to get up off your ass, you can do it.

As her ankle was playing up she held court resting on a chaise longue in a room stuffed with antiques, *objets d'art* and priceless pictures. She and her husband are, of course, very much victims of the Tall Poppy Syndrome. According to my brilliant little dictionary: 'Tall Poppy is any Australian who reads more than the sporting results and knows how to use snail tongs. Someone who aspires to intellectual excitement and cannot tell the difference between one make of car and another. The species is much hated in Australia and is always being cut down to size.'

When I told Ellen Bond that the next day we were flying north 2,000 miles to Broome she demanded a telephone, which was promptly brought to her side, dialled a number, asked for a man called Alan and said: 'Keith Floyd is flying to Broome tomorrow, you give him all the help he needs.' It wasn't an order, it wasn't a threat, it was just a statement of what would happen.

She is a good egg. It was only months later that I realised that on the very same day that she entertained us so generously, the Bonds were having to sell their house, worth many millions of dollars, to prop up their collapsing empire. I have no doubt that they will come bouncing back. I certainly hope so.

My three-day sojourn in the financial capital of Australia was terrific fun but as we boarded our Australian Airlines flight to Broome, John 'No Worries' Chase said: 'This is the last big plane you'll be on for some time now. From here on, matey, it's four-wheel drives, Cessnas, float planes and feet.'

It was absolutely fine by me. I was looking forward to a bit of real-life Australia – as long as it wasn't too rough! A few hours later we landed in thirty-three degrees Centigrade of burning heat at the tiny pearling township of Broome, which sits on the edge of the turquoise Indian Ocean. The terrain is flat and the colour of Kiwi ox-blood shoe polish. The heat was stifling. But at least we had travelled in luxury. Poor old John, the Floydmobile driver, had made the journey by road from Perth over 2,000 gruelling miles on his own, and was waiting at the airport to take us to the hotel.

And what a hotel it turned out to be. It is the most fabulous resort, an exciting complex of Indonesian-style chalets and bungalows, painted in powerful primary reds and greens that reflect the earth and the lush vegetation. It is a veritable oasis of greenery, bougainvilleas, rivers, streams, lakes and exotic trees. It is called The Cable Beach Club, Broome, and is the brainchild of Sir or Lord Alistair McAlpine.

To step on to the polished hardwood floor of the elegant and air-conditioned reception was like drinking a glass of chilled vintage Krug champagne. And my suite, with its balcony overlooking the white sands of a ninety-mile long beach, was furbished in the most exquisite taste. It too was cool and serene and smelt of all those lovely things that Shakespeare goes on about – woodbine, sandalwood and eucalyptus.

To make things even better, Pam Stockley elevated herself to the Dreamage in my eyes by announcing that because we had worked so hard we could all have a couple of days lazing by the pool before serious work started again. So I did. It was two heavenly days, with lovely satays, red prawn curry for lunch and cocktails by the pool, and in the evening more cocktails and *Nasi Goreng* for dinner. The place was stuffed with restaurants, fine or grill dining, barbecues, but I liked eating Indonesian-style food on the teak-decked verandah by the swimming pool. It was low-season in holiday terms so the place was agreeably unbusy.

The town of Broome is only a couple of miles away. It is a brilliant little place. It has the feel of a genuine frontier town. The architecture has a curiously oriental flavour, influenced by the Asian pearl divers, who used Broome as their base thirty years ago. It is what I had expected Alice Springs to be like, raised verandahs and cool dark shops that sold string and woks, hunting knives, fishing hooks, billy cans and swags. And even the shops that sold quite touristy things, cultivated pearls and shells and Aboriginal artefacts, displayed their wares in a pleasantly understated fashion.

One of the local hotels, set in the middle of town, had a couple of bunkhouses so that backpackers and others with little money could sleep and eat cheaply and cheerfully in communal comfort. Mind you, that is just a sentiment, I was glad I wasn't staying there.

At sunset I went on to the beach and walked slowly through the soft blue-milk waves and jumped back when the surf waves crashed deliciously on to the sand. The sky was cobalt-blue, with a million stars shining brightly like saucers of polished chrome.

For the first time on my trip I did some touristy shopping: I bought some carved boab nuts, a bit of polished red rock and some Aboriginal carvings. In the General Store, I bought a sheaf knife, and from Mr Wing's store a billy can, a wok, a torch and some basic foodstuffs – you know, like you expect to find in the middle of nowhere: Indonesian fish paste, red curry paste, oyster sauce, soy sauce, shrimp sauce, all manner of oriental canned comestible goodies.

For after our few days relaxing we were going on an expedition in four-wheel drives across the outback, to sleep in swags under the stars and

Dear Louise,

[who, as you know, is the editor of my book; she likes receiving postcards]

In the bay near Broome there is a landmark called Buccaneer Rock, dedicated to William Dampier and his ship, the Roebuck. *Dampier, an English pirate, visited the north-west coast of Australia (then known as New Holland) in the late seventeenth century – nearly a hundred years before Cook was to sail into Botany Bay. By the way, Dampier was the one who famously reported back that New Holland 'was a lousy place, inhabited by the miserablest people in the world.' Dampier had plenty of other derogatory remarks about the locals and certainly was not a founder member of pirates against racism!*

Broome did not really get going until the 1880s when the pearling industry was established. Apparently, the industry reached its peak in the early 1900s when the town's four-hundred pearling luggers, worked by over three-thousand men, supplied eighty per cent of the world's mother of pearl. The pearl divers and seamen were Japanese, Malays, Filipinos and others from all over the South Pacific and rivalry between them was intense. But when plastic buttons were introduced after the First World War the industry went into decline and today only a few lugger boats remain. There is, however, a Pearl Festival every August commemorating the pearling years.

I think these little bits of information will be really interesting in the book, don't you?

Love Keith
P.S. This is a command!
X X

cook camp stews and damper bread on wood fires. The morning of our departure we busied ourselves poring over maps, packing swags, pickaxes and shovels, loading jerry cans of petrol and water – there just aren't any filling stations in the bush.

And with an outrageous sense of gung-ho excitement because we were going off on our Boy's Own adventure we said goodbye to the women members of our crew and set off for the hundred-mile single-track drive to Derby. Despite the excitement, I was sad to leave Broome. I had visited the Japanese cemetery, the memorial to hundreds of pearl divers who perished in former times. I had visited the crocodile sanctuary, which for once wasn't just a tacky series of cages, but a carefully thought-out environment for these ancient monsters. I saw the footprints, fossilised in sandstone, of dinosaurs who trampled this land 130 million years ago. I spent a brilliant day fishing out in the ocean and landed, among others, a fifty-pound Spanish mackerel, the biggest the boat had taken for over three years.

I spent days in shorts soaking up the sun. I walked, slithered and scrambled up to my knees searching for cockles on the edge of the mangroves, chipped for rock oysters from the rocks, and caught an octopus trapped in a pool by the falling tide. I cooked Spanish mackerel for a crazy doctor and his wife, who had wandered innocently over the magnificent red cliffs. And all the while in this idyllic place Maggie kept making me cucumber sandwiches.

I cooked a chicken curry for a seventy-year-old Bishop, a former tank commander in the Second World War, whose diocese of Western Australia is bigger than Western Europe. He uses an aeroplane, which he pilots himself, to minister to his scattered flock.

We went to the local Races. Rough, tough, and dangerous. Rings of excited people holding fistfuls of dollars, betting on the outcome of two coins tossed into the air, was a popular sideshow. And the funniest and nicest thing about it all is that I was being paid for doing all of this. It was quite extraordinary. Once I nearly felt I was enjoying myself so much that I almost considered giving them their money back – but luckily a discreet tap on my bedroom door woke me and that awful dream was over, thank goodness.

But then I made the mistake of taking local advice and went to what they called 'the best Chinese restaurant in Broome'. Now if you consider Broome has probably only six- to seven-thousand inhabitants and about four Chinese restaurants, it was reasonable to suppose that I had been given the goods. But a bowl of chow mein without noodles is a terribly daunting prospect, and perhaps I am beginning to understand that the Australia outside of the cities has little to offer the travelling gastronaut.

At least in Broome, when I cooked the aforementioned curry for the Bishop of Western Australia, I could cut a coconut from a tree and pour its milk into the dish to make it succulent, light and delicious – whereas in Totnes, Devon, England, you are hard-pressed to find tinned coconut milk, not to mention the odd piece of fresh fish.

Anyway, that was Broome and it was great.

And now we are bombing along, slightly north-east, the metalled highway towards Derby – which after a while degenerates into a dust road that narrows and widens and looks as though oil has seeped through the ground. And occasionally you skid, swerve and slither as you move on to the soft shoulder to allow some oncoming vehicle to stay in the centre of the hard causeway.

DERBY
WESTERN
AUSTRALIA
16 JULY
OZ

Dear Mum,

We're now in Derby, which is about 130 miles north along the coast from Broome – not far by Australian standards. It is a tiny little place that is often used as a base for trips to the really spectacular gorges and rock formations of the Kimberley region.

You see masses of boab trees round here. Boab trees have cylindrical trunks a bit like very tall immersion heaters. And their branches, which spread from the very top of the trees, look like their roots.

Boabs can be centuries old and near Derby's airport is a huge one called the Prison Tree, with a hollow trunk about forty-five feet in diameter. It once served as a lock-up for the Aboriginal outlaw, Pigeon.

Lots of love Keith xx.
(how's the garden?)

You enter Derby from the bush with the windscreen caked in dust and a dry tickle in your throat. And suddenly you are in a neat, small hamlet of wooden bungalows with corrugated tin roofs, shaded lawns, a motel. *'Where the barmaid is yet again somebody who hitchhiked this far and finds it hard to leave when you just can't find the door.'*

In the supermarket or the general store, call it what you will, in Derby, I shopped for provisions that would take us on our journey further north and east. After piling several trolleys high with basic rations we reached the checkout point. The store manager was thrilled to bits to punch it through. He had never had a customer spend just under £1,000.

And we, of course, as a film crew have no means of paying it. So I did the decent thing and offered them one of my credit cards, which of course the machine rejects. It was not used to Coutts Gold Cards, naturally. And, of course, the producers whom I loved so much back in Broome for giving us two days off now became hated, exploitative horrors who weren't there to pick up the tab just when I needed it most. However, it all turned out all right. (Since I am in a terribly good humour this evening as I write this, it is fair to point out that the producers did reimburse me.)

After the shopping we went back to the Derby motel and had a very strange lunch of roast turkey and other cold cuts. So late in the afternoon we set off in a convoy in our Toyota four-wheel drives and headed east for the Windjana Gorge, which is an outstanding geological feature once used by an Aboriginal outlaw called Pigeon as a hideout. And he ran the police a dance for many years. The river has freshwater crocodiles, sea fish which were left behind by the melting ice of millions of years ago and have now adapted themselves to the freshwater. It is a museum of unlikely species.

Our vehicles bounced along the dirt roads several hundreds of yards apart to avoid being blinded by the plumes of red dust that trailed behind each one. I, of course, was all right, because I was in front. We drove on for about three hours in this monotonous but somehow spectacular terrain, until nightfall, when we reached our destination, Fairfield Cattle Station.

It was quite dark, there were no lights on in the house but there was the murmur of voices from half-a-dozen people sitting round the dying embers of a barbecue. We introduced ourselves to Ross, the station manager, whom I think had already had one or two. He didn't move from his chair but merely said: 'We expected you this afternoon and we've eaten all the bloody food.' A typically direct Australian greeting.

So we said: 'We don't care, we've got our own food, so we can cook our own.'

And under the headlights of our four-wheel drives, using an old barn door as a tabletop on top of a couple of oil drums, I set up my portable stove and in another oil drum, which had been cut in such a way to be formed into a wood-burning stove, I prepared a simple beef stew for the crew.

The bunkhouse where the station hands lived in some considerable squalor was raised on five-foot stilts, partly to keep them clear of the floods during the wet and partly as a precaution against snakes. Australia is full of highly dangerous snakes. Across the paddock I could see the faint silhouette of Spirit One, the station aircraft.

We were, of course, filming this little sketch when the activity attracted the attention of our truculent host, his Aboriginal wife June and half-a-dozen of the hands, who stood around sipping cans of beer and laughing at the various cock-ups I made. It naturally developed into a party, much swearing and cursing and drinking, an enormous amount of laughs, until it was time to lay our swags on the ground and go to sleep.

If you have never laid on your back in the bush at night under millions of galaxies, the Southern Cross bright and clear, you really haven't lived. The one thing it does for you is to make you realise how totally insignificant and meaningless you are. And with these deep and profound thoughts wafting through my head, I dozed happily into sleep.

Until David Pritchard started snoring. He woke the lot of us. Although it was cruel, a bit like something out of *Lord Of The Flies*, we made him take his swag four- or five-hundred yards away from our protective ring of swags that flickered red and gold and amber round the crackling fire. He was highly pissed off.

Morning came about four o'clock. A cowbell was ringing to call the hands to breakfast, which was served in a bleak canteen with a couple of Formica trestle tables, at the end of the bunkhouse. Walking through the bunkhouse, I glanced into the bedrooms of the hands. A mattress lay on each rusty bedstead, with a swag on it. Each room had just a rucksack or battered old suitcase with a few crumpled possessions tumbling from the hard-closed lids.

Breakfast was a massive stew of beef rib-bones cooked with potatoes, onions and courgettes. The gravy was rich and beefy and glistening with gold globules of fat. It was quite delicious. The people who work on the station have that breakfast every day of the year, before they mount their horses and ride out to repair fences until sunset. When they return to the station, they barbecue thick steaks and drink beer, every night of the year.

There was a time when the cattle station gave both shelter and provender to tribes of Aboriginals who, in exchange for at least some small sign of respect, would work the station. But when in a fit of enlightenment somebody suggested they should be paid as well, they were simply thrown off the estates. And today maybe as few as four or five people maintain a station of several thousand square kilometres.

After breakfast we reloaded our trucks, said our farewells and set off on

the next leg of our journey to the township at Fitzroy Crossing, bouncing through the bush past big boab trees. Forty-thousand years ago, the Aboriginals told me, the tree had displeased God, so it was ripped out and planted upside down as a punishment.

The Aboriginals don't know how old they are, they don't need to know, they don't want to. They want to be left in peace to wander across the bush as the hunter-gatherers they are. They don't farm, they don't store, when they are hungry they pick something to eat or track a goanna, a lizard-like creature.

They never had any cooking pots – they were too heavy to carry as they wandered round – so everything that had to be cooked was barbecued. It is they who created the Australian barbecue, not a load of flaxen-haired windsurfers in thongs and T-shirts.

Somewhere on the way to Fitzroy Crossing, 6 June

We had to borrow an axe so two old boys, Butcher and Mitch, took us to a cattle station where they thought we might borrow one. My notes of the day say: 'Butcher and Mitch stood shyly while two ladies in crisp white dresses and a man with a bush hat and highly-polished riding boots tended a horse lying on its side in the manicured garden.

'Neat green lawns, carefully-painted houses, green generator shed, pink, stone-built houses, set in luxuriant gardens.

'The bunkhouses outside the fence were stark breeze-block affairs. It

Butcher, Mitch and the Ugly

could have been a scene from *A Passage to India*. In fact, I even thought the ladies were wearing crinolines. Angry, they motioned us to be quiet until they had finished with the horse. It was perfectly obvious they knew Mitch and Butcher well since they had lived on their land, and they ordered them to be quiet so as not to disturb the horse and asked us in whispers what we wanted.'

Another line in my notes remarks on the sepia photographs in the bar of the motel at the station, celebrating the visit of some dignitary, half-a-dozen stockmen proudly holding on to the halters of prize cattle, rather like a regimental photograph or a school cricket team picture. Underneath was written in copperplate from left to right, 'Harry, Johnston, Hercules' etc. I looked long and hard before I realised they were the names of the cattle not the stockmen.

I spent hours with Mitch and Butcher tramping over the bush. To me a desolate landscape of thorny bushes and stunted trees, to them it is a well-stocked larder. The roots of this tree here has tubers that resemble potatoes on them, another tree severely slashed by an axe reveals a honeycomb oozing with sweet, sweet honey. The nuts, the berries, the tubers, the roots, the leaves, are for eating or for medicaments.

I felt a fraud in my straw hat and safari suit while these two old boys, who had no idea how old they were, marched tirelessly on in ancient jeans and sandals. They showed me a rock which, viewed from the right angle, reminded me of a statue of Queen Victoria. The rock was actually a holy lady. Millions of years ago, fleeing from some catastrophe and quite against the advice of the gods, she turned to look whence she had come and was promptly turned to stone.

Day 60, Fitzroy Crossing, 15 June

We rumbled into Fitzroy Crossing, thirsty, dusty, our faces caked with fine red mud, to find a motley collection of bungalows with corrugated roofs, the odd store, a motel and a pub. The pub was by the river and along the track which led to it from the dirt road you passed little knots of Aboriginals, squatting on carpets of squashed beer cans, drinking and chattering disconsolately.

The pub was frequented by Bush Rangers in neat uniforms, toothless, drunken half-castes and braggardly truck drivers, unshaven and wearing dirty white vests with their hats pushed to the back of their heads. It wasn't exactly Harry's Bar. But after the drive the iced beer tasted like liquid silver.

On the wall by the front door of the pub there is a noticeboard with the names of customers banned from the pub. I thought it quite humorous until it was explained to me that these bans were imposed by the local magistrates for petty crimes like being drunk and disorderly or whatever. But, of course, the only people who get banned are the Aboriginals. They have a low resistance to alcohol. They have no money. So the only punishment can be to ban them from the only pub for hundreds of miles.

In the motel not far from the pub, which was friendly and comfortable enough, we experienced yet another appallingly bad dinner that took three or four hours to arrive. And although it involved meat and bottled beans, I couldn't tell you exactly what it was. Later that night, we went to look for my two Aboriginal chums Mitch and Butcher and brought them back to the hotel for a drink, just to annoy the management.

'It isn't us who need educating,' they said, 'it's them. We would like to teach them everything we know. We are very happy to share our land with the white Australian.'

The next day was Sunday and the motel bar didn't open until six-thirty. They tried to make me pay fifteen dollars to go into the bar and you couldn't drink without eating. The fifteen dollars was a cover charge for a meal – which after last night's experience I had no intention of having. Maggie was making me some cucumber sandwiches.

Still, they refused to serve me a drink until I paid the fifteen dollars, even though I was a resident. So I climbed on to the highest of my high horses and wore them down with logical, well-balanced, reasonable and diplomatic arguments like: 'You are going to look really good in a series that goes out to twenty-two countries when I explain that you and your pub are a heap of absolute rubbish.'

I know I was being a bully but when a man is thirsty, a man's gotta do what a man's gotta do. Actually, I thought I might make a film about this bloke who rides into town looking for a drink . . .

WESTERN AUSTRALIA

I'm sorry that I sound a
bit sour but I was cross about
the Aussie attitude to my
chums – but when I think back
I didn't have such a bad time
there. Anyway, onto the next
place.

Five

Banquets in the bush,
A load of bull dust!!

Fitzroy Crossing, Kimberley District, North-Western Australia, ? June 8 a.m.

Hanging about the dirt strip while two cheerful young pilots tried, finally successfully, to load us and our equipment on to a six-seater, twin-engine Cessna and a four-seater, single-engine fixed-wing, I worried like hell about the overloading. Paul Shire, the stills photographer, said the pilots knew what they were doing – 'Don't worry'.

I really like these dirt airstrips with the aviation fuel stacked in brightly-coloured drums, owner-pilots tinkering with the engines and other craft, the informal coming and going of it all, the crackling of the two-way radio in the background, light breezes, big sky, high sun.

We are going to Katherine, famous for its spectacular gorge, about 500 miles away in what John 'No Worries' Chase calls the 'Top End'.

In the event, most of the equipment and Bruce the cameraman went in the single-engined plane, the rest of us squeezed into the Cessna. Chase had done some deal with the charter company, Air North, to take some air-to-air shots as we flew, perilously close to my mind, wing-tip to wing-tip.

After a while, we climbed higher and left the smaller plane following us, way behind. David and Pies (the grip) locked into one of their interminable chess games. Paul was suffering silently with another of his head-splitting migraines, Tim (the sound recordist) was up front with the pilot, interrogating him with enthusiastic questions about the instruments and controls. The producers, Maggie, Barbara and the rest, were making a tedious journey to Katherine overland in the Greyhound Floydmobile. I was wishing I was back in the aluminium boat fishing for mangrove jacks on the Drysdale River . . .

Sometime between Broome and Fairfield Station, we had taken a couple of days off to go barramundi fishing. We set off from a man-made lake at Kununurra, in a red Beaver float plane, powered by a 450-horsepower, nine-cylinder, supercharged radial Pratt and Whitney engine; the plane must have been at least thirty years old.

We clambered aboard over a jetty made up of boards lashed to oil drums and squeezed in. Craig, the pilot, fired the engine, his mate slipped the moorings and we nosed out into the centre of the lake and back up it to give ourselves sufficient length of water to make our take-off. I recall I felt that this plane was severely overladen. I had been in one before and reckoned it should lift off at about eighty mph and I also calculated that Craig's actual take-off point would be directly opposite his oil-drum jetty and the little shack with its air sock that served as his office. The poor old plane was shuddering, grinding and screaming; once or twice the floats got an inch or so out of the water. Craig was operating every damned control on board and goodness knows what else. And we were still only doing sixty mph when we went past his shack. I could feel that he was willing this lovely old plane to free itself from the water and finally, some 500 metres past the jetty, the choppy waters of the lake reluctantly released their grip on the floats and, slowly, the plane eased up into the sky.

We flew north-west for about three hours over featureless terrain which, as we neared the coast, gave way to featureless grey salt and mud flats. To remind myself of this trip, I have been today flipping through the glossy brochure published by the Kimberley Tourist Association. Underneath a spectacular picture of a jabiru (a beautifully-coloured heron-like bird), there is a headline 'Drysdale River' and underneath that, in smaller letters 'No Facilities or Access'. And by golly, it was true, in this desolate spot you could only reach by float plane or very long sea voyage.

Despite the noise, the shuddering and the cold, I had dozed off, but the change in engine noise woke me and through the window I could see we were going in to land (do float planes land?) on a thin strip of river that flowed between walls of rock, which looked as though they had been made of vast cubes of red Turkish Delight. At this point it seemed that the wingspan was wider than the river.

Craig banked the little plane steeply, turned 180 degrees and at thirty mph we bounced on to the water. He back-throttled the engine and switched off. The prop flopped slowly to a standstill and there was the sound of water lapping against the aluminium floats. Everything else was as quiet and still as an empty cave. Craig drifted the boat over to the mooring buoy. We transferred ourselves and our equipment into two shallow-bottomed aluminium boats with massive outboard engines.

'We must hurry, it'll be dark in twenty minutes – and by the way, be careful where you put your feet, this river is infested with sallies.' Which you and I both know are the dangerous, very dangerous, man-eating crocodiles. Incidentally, Craig's little charter firm was charmingly called 'Alligator Airways'.

Crocodiles are not for cooking – just for looking at

We made the boat secure, unloaded the gear and clambered up a ramp to a small amphitheatre that some god had carved out of the rock and where Craig had, some years previously, set up the Boy's Own camp of camps to end all camps. Rough frames from tree branches draped in netting formed a kitchen; there was an open-air dining area protected by a corrugated roof, with a crude table and tressels.

The first job was to start the generator. As it spluttered into life a load of naked light bulbs hanging from branches illuminated this enchanting scene. Rough wooden shelves were stacked with every kind of provision, banks of fishing rods hung from the rough walls like so many rifles in a Wild West cavalry fort.

The two-way radio crackled into life. Pies and David settled down to play chess and Tim and Bruce checked equipment. Craig called back to base to say we had arrived, and as I busied myself preparing an enormous pot of minced beef with onions, mashed potatoes and frozen peas, the daily life of Australians in this remote area chattered away out of the radio. An anxious husband called up the Flying Doctor because his wife was going to give birth; a farmer ordered fifty drums of diesel; a girl told a man and the whole world that she loved him. And all this sometimes interrupted by the rapid two-way exchanges of Taiwanese fishing boats that were pillaging the Timor Sea.

There was a washhouse, again made from tree trunks hung with hessian, and a Heath Robinson arrangement of pipes and tubes that sprinkled agreeably soft warm water. There was a workbench with neatly-arranged tools, boxes of spark plugs, spare batteries, First Aid kits, splints and stretchers. It was a great camp. It was called Alligator Camp.

And the fishing was fine too. We caught bream, barracuda and shark. We caught cod, threadfin salmon, queenfish, and everything you could think of except what we were looking for, which was barramundi . . .

But back to our journey to Katherine. We had been in the air about one and a half hours since leaving Fitzroy Crossing. And the pilot said he'd put down for some fuel. I suppose the mark of a good writer is that he can convincingly describe the plateaus and the plains, the faults and folds of this ancient land – but it is beyond me. It was brown, it was rust, it was black, it was purple, and it was desolate. No houses, no roads. From time to time we would fly over a huge lake set on a mountaintop and you could see so well that there was no stream leading into it or river flowing out of it.

As the hills gave way to a plain I saw the huddled buildings of a cattle station. The pilot headed the plain towards the station and landed on a grass strip. A couple of dogs barked but no one came from the house to see who we were. Presumably they knew. We taxied the plane right up to a couple of oil drums and, while we stretched our legs on the field, the pilot refuelled the plane with a handpump. Twenty minutes later we were airborne again and just over an hour to run to Katherine. ·

Paul was still suffering from his migraine, David and Pies had started another game of chess. I was intrigued by the casual way you could land an aircraft in a farmer's field and refuel it, without anyone being the least bit curious about the passengers. That's Australia, I suppose.

And as we climbed back to 12,000 feet I could see the little single-engined plane carrying Bruce and the equipment coming down to make its refuelling stop. Then, at 3,000 feet, there was Katherine below us. Tiny town, brightly-coloured buildings, laid out in a neat grid system like an architect's model, set in the centre of a vast sheet of hessian that is the Northern Territory.

Within twenty minutes of landing we were eating cold chicken and salad beside the swimming pool of a friendly motel. David wants to play chess, but Pies is having more fun with Tim, doing backward flips into the pool with the express intention of impressing a young lady reclining in her deckchair.

After an invigorating swim, almost two lengths of the pool, I retire for a siesta. Only to be rudely awakened by an urgent phone call from England. It was my accountant, phoning to say that I must approve and sign last year's company accounts within twenty-four hours, otherwise I would face serious penalties. Naturally, I exploded. How the hell could I organise that when I was many thousands of miles away and had been for the last three months, as they well knew. They were 'terribly sorry, old boy', but they'd been a bit busy. This bombshell gave me a sleepless night but by dint of frantic faxing I managed to appoint a temporary director to look over the accounts, approve them, sign them and get them back. I confidently expected that I would be given a massive reduction in their fees for a) their having been totally inefficient b) having caused me a near heart attack and c) putting me to an awful amount of needless inconvenience. No doubt at about the time you read this book, you will also be reading the court case of a firm of accountants, sueing me for failure to pay their bill.

Anyway, to calm my troubled self, I jumped into a car and drove twenty miles to have a look at the Katherine Gorge, which everyone said was highly impressive. I got there as the sun was setting, too late to explore. It was a tranquil place and very good for the soul. Big dried autumn leaves like well-cooked poppadoms drifted down from the blackness above. I collected a dozen as some kind of memento and drove back to Katherine.

Katherine has a fabulous climate and very fertile land which produces good fruit and vegetables, but the main industry is beef, and in a day or two we are going into the bush to round a few up. Not on horseback, of course, but with the aid of some jeeps.

For some time now you will have noticed the absence of lyrical descriptions of food and meals. Since we left Broome some weeks ago we have been living on pretty basic rations – beef stew, mince and mash, steak and chips. In this sparsely-populated part of the continent (incidentally the world's largest island and the fifth largest continent), Le Manoir aux Quat' Saisons would go bust in forty-three minutes flat. People don't travel up here to eat, they come for the mountains, the lakes, the spectacular sunsets, the stars, to look for fossils and minerals, to study birds and crocodiles, and to rejoice in the sense of freedom that this magnificent country offers.

Anyway, as long as I had the lovely Maggie to keep administering cucumber sandwiches, I was happy as a lark. For the three months' duration of my trip she never failed once to produce the goods. Occasionally she might have been a little too liberal with the salt and at odd times she left the crusts on, but apart from these relatively minor faults – or should I say lapses of concentration – she never let me down.

Katherine, Monday Morning, 18 June

Heading north on the dirt road. Maggie, who is supposed to be driving, is asleep beside me. The dirt road is straight and smooth; it looks wet and shines as if it has been sprayed with oil. As far as the eye can see, there are galaxies of anthills, some ten or twelve feet high; it is a surreal scene. It is as if the anthills had invaded from some other planet, landed and been petrified. There is a bright sun, the road undulates in long, slow, sickening crests and troughs. The top of each crest shimmers eerily. You must maintain a steady speed and a constant but gentle pressure on the throttle. The road is treacherous and by accelerating too rapidly three times, I have almost ditched us.

The verges are like quicksand. The shimmering in the distance is hurting my eyes and causing me to lose concentration. In this strange light it looks as though the road stops about a mile and a half ahead and there is no land beyond it. I realise I am seeing mirages. Two or three times I have braked sharply because I am convinced we have run out of road.

I wake Maggie and thankfully she agrees, they are mirages and it is very disturbing. We have left the anthills behind, there is just scrub now. In three hours of driving we haven't passed a house, a vehicle, or a human being. Sometimes a flock of carrion squawk angrily up from the half-devoured rotting carcass of a dead steer.

I check the petrol gauge. It is very low. They said it was only 125 miles. We have already done 300. The mirages are getting me down, making me

Dear Patrick,

Everybody goes on about Ned Kelly in this country so I looked him up in the Dinkum Aussie Dictionary. *It says:*

'A misguided socialist of vague Irish descent who was stupid enough (thanks to his Irish ancestry) to make a mere half suit of armour, thus allowing the forces of law and order to shoot and capture him. He was then hanged for his stupidity. Before dying he did not utter the words, "Such, such is life"; a reporter from the Melbourne Age *did. Because of this misguided dottiness Ned Kelly has become Australia's folk hero, giving rise to the phrase, "as game as Ned Kelly".'*

Fascinating, ain't it? The weather is fine, wish you were here.

Ho! Ho!

love Dad x

jumpy, and despite my better judgement I keep slamming on the brakes in panic; this time I spun 180 degrees before making it back on the main track (mental note, cancel my entry for the Paris–Dakar rally, if I get back).

Maggie says she can see a wind-driven water pump on the horizon. A little later we can make out some buildings. A badly-faded sign says 'Top Springs', a godforsaken rendezvous for travellers, a motley collection of sheds, workshops, a café and a bar, set on the edge of the road with a vast dustyard for parking to the side of it.

A gnarled old tree leans over, dying, into the dried, cracked, artificial, concrete ornamental pond that some enthusiast happily cherished years ago. There is a tacky General Store and an unpainted motel behind the bar. Outside the generators and refrigeration plants chatter behind wire-netting cages. There is an enormous radio mast and there are satellite dishes and solar panels on the rooftops.

A beaten-up ute with a dozen Aboriginals clinging to the uncanvassed frame careers up to the petrol pump. They fill up two fifty-gallon drums and depart. A couple of scrawny cows, undernourished flesh hanging off their bones, wander round the place.

The Greyhound Floydmobile is parked close to the bar, which inside is cool, untidy and filthy – as are the customers, half-a-dozen farmers or station hands drinking beer from bottles cased in polystyrene sleeves to keep them cool. Two Bush Rangers in neat shorts, bush shirts and knee-length socks are eating doorstep steak sandwiches, traditionally garnished with fried eggs and pickled beetroot. It is a desolate spot. It makes Katherine look like Monte Carlo.

Anyway, I'm out here to meet a breed of truck driver – the Australian road train driver. Road trains are those huge engines with three trailers behind hauling cattle and milk and oil and newspapers. The very lifeline of communications around here because, of course, there are no railways. And do you also know that these guys, despite their butch, outgoing masculine ways, are sensitive little souls? They press flowers, they do crochet, they like to eat low-cholesterol food, delicate fresh fruit salads and things like that – so I've invited a couple to lunch here.

The ingredients, locally produced from Katherine. A little bit of chicken, some lovely big tomatoes stuffed with garlic butter, parsley and anchovies, some chillies and garlic, some beautiful courgettes and red and green peppers, aubergines and onions and some very light, freshly-made pasta to go underneath it all. So without further ado let's whack it into the pot and get things going.

By the way, this is the first time I've ever cooked on the Floydmobile, my wonderful Greyhound bus. It's quite splendid. These are my quarters down here, my dining room. This is the galley. Behind are the seats for my personal attendants, the hairdresser, my manicurist and people like that, and of course, the director.

Right, straight into the pot with our chicken, seasoned with a little pepper and salt, first of all. Get that sizzling away. Shake it round. Brown it on all sides. Stay there, Bruce, I'll get some more ingredients to pop into that. My garlic and chillies go into that now, sizzle, sizzle. Now the chicken is sealed we're going to roast it in the oven for about fifteen minutes or so and I'll get the rest of the stuff happening here.

It makes a change from the bush. I've got a sink, electric lights, fans, everything – it's absolutely splendid. Right, lightly stir-fried vegetables, which remind me of Provence and this is a kind of dish that is a mixture of Provence in the South of France and the Asian influence of cooking you get so much of in Australia. It's a kind of stir-fried ratatouille, really. A little smattering of oregano into that. A bit of salt and a bit of pepper.

And then the final bit. I'll just finish off stuffing these tomatoes. I've taken out the pips because you know what lorry drivers are like, they don't want rough pips when they're chewing delicate little morsels. A tiny bit of

O
U
T
B
A
C
K

Bobby thumbed a diesel down
just before it rained

anchovy fillet in there, garlic and parsley butter inside like that and then all three tomatoes topped off with breadcrumbs and popped under the grill. The luxury of this equipment you cannot believe. In the pot with the stir-fried ratatouille and chicken and there it is.

Anyway, I am sitting back and waiting for my guests; some hope. The Floydmobile is too hot; you can't run the air-conditioning without running the engine. So I pace up and down outside fighting off the flies and choking in the thick dust – bull dust they call it – which a gust of wind stirs from time to time. This fine red sand is so thick that even as I walk, slowly and carefully, little puffs explode from under my feet.

The table laid in preparation for my guests gets dirtier by the minute. I go back into the Floydmobile to turn the oven down. If they don't come soon, my feast will be ruined. Some of the crew are playing cards in the café, Pies and David are as usual playing chess.

An awesome flapping of wings, squawking, clucking and crowing startles me. The sky is thick and overcast with thousands of galahs that have suddenly taken off. My chum, Crooked Mick's, book tells me, by the way, that galahs is a term of abuse applied to anyone who is a prat in general, but to politicians in particular.

It is now four o'clock in the afternoon and my biorhythms are troughing. I hope they come soon because when we filmed the cooking sketch three hours ago I was bright and the eating sequence and subsequent conversation that go with it where I deftly probe the psyche and lifestyle of the Australian road train driver must be in the same mood.

Somebody shouts out 'They are coming' and half a mile or so away you can see the telltale cloud of dust in the distance. It could be Monty and the Desert Rats. Fifteen minutes later two mighty trucks, three trailers long, grind into the parking yard. The dust they create blocks everything from view.

They swing round through a massive 360-degree circle and park within inches of each other, side by side. They kill the engines, which shudder to silence, and as the dust begins to settle, two men climb from their cabs and head straight for the bar. David is impatient to film and sends Pies to get them straight away. I tell him to wait, after all they have probably come 1,000 miles.

The trailers are packed with cattle that must be crazed and dazed with the jolting road. But they are packed so tight they can barely get a swing with their feet, and half-heartedly kick out at the wooden sides of the trailers.

'Strawberry' and 'The Padre' gaze down the necks of their beer bottles in embarrassed silence. Strawberry is about thirty. He wears denims, cowboy boots, a heavy-duty waisted shirt and a leather belt with a big buckle. He is six feet tall. The Padre is short, fat, fifty-plus, and tough. He wears a dark-brown trilby hat that is fossilised papier-mâché, hardened by years of sweat and dust. They are road train drivers and don't like being filmed. Strawb tips back his head and drains the bottle. The gust of red dust catches his long blond hair.

It is noon, hot and windy and the fine red dust from the yard swirls round us and the two Mack road trains, each hitched to three cattle

Strawb and The Padre taking Communion

107

transporting trailers – sixty tons unladen and over 150 feet long. I count the wheels. They have sixty-two apiece. The prime movers have been coach painted like gypsy caravans. The radiators are burnished stainless steel. So are the fuel tanks, compressed air cylinders, and the exhausts that protrude from the cab roof. In the absence of a rail network these road trains are the lifeline, hauling everything and anything that won't fit on a plane, from Western Australia to Queensland, thousands of miles on single dirt-track roads. Across the desert, trailing quarter of a mile of dust skirts behind them, they are an awesome sight as they thunder at sixty or seventy mph. When you've seen these you realise that there is no vehicle on the British or Continental roads that can truly be called a juggernaut.

Strawberry and The Padre are real buggers. They have eaten all the food, are steadily emptying the eskie of Victoria bitter and they won't talk when the camera is turning over. The Padre leaves the table and climbs up on to the trailers and with an electric wand electrocutes the cattle just to check that they are still alive.

The truth is these men are shy in the bar of some remote truck stop. They will swap joke for joke and drink for drink with their confrères at the rodeo and they'll swagger round; they'll gamble at the races with cool bravado; they'll talk the Levis off a long-legged, blonde Danish back-packer, or a short fat one in a denim mini skirt for that matter. They can cook a meal, change a wheel, rope a steer or punch you in the face if you do it wrong. They'll drive right through you if you don't pull over when they're smoking down the track, and they'll drive without rest to make a dollar and deliver the load on time. If 'Banjo' Paterson had been alive at the time – you know, the man who wrote 'Waltzing Matilda' – he'd have immortalised them in song: 'Once a jolly truck man, drunk by a billabong'.

Anyway, that is what I was told they thought of themselves. I thought they were brilliant but I know for a fact they would have preferred a thirty-two-ounce steak any day. And to be perfectly honest, all I wanted was a cucumber sandwich.

It is nearly dark and joy, oh joy, John 'No Worries' Chase has arranged for me to be flown back from Top Springs to Katherine by helicopter, which is just as well because I forgot to tell you that as we turned into the place this morning, and rolled to a stop outside the bar, the hire car blew up. So John, he of 'No Worries', had the spare parts flown up from Katherine so it could be fixed. And I could return in the chopper – hip, hip, hooray – because by Floydmobile it would take at least four hours and 'I'll be in the bar afore ye'.

Fifty miles outside of Katherine in the opposite direction from yesterday, Tuesday 9 a.m.

In Devon, when you need to round up your beef cattle to take to market, you wander into a well-hedged lush green field with a dog and boy and shoo them gently up the ramp to a cattle truck that is parked in the gateway, have a few words with the driver and amble back to the farmhouse for a spot of lunch.

Rounding up cattle for market in Northern Australia – mustering they call it – is a bit different. Instead of a boy, a dog and a stick you need a six-wheel drive, converted Second World War personnel carrier, loaded with a half a mile of hessian, a hundred metal poles six or seven feet high; a modular corral and fencing kit, some spare wheels, engines, axles and gearboxes for the two stripped-down, four-wheel drive jeeps that are also obligatory, a huge dog called Alf, a couple of the ubiquitous fifty-gallon oil drums, a two-way radio, picks, shovels, axes, basic rations and the wherewithal to cook them, and last but not least, a couple of enormous eskies packed tightly with tinnies. You also need a helicopter, complete with pilot of course. It is very important that you start the day well before sun up so that you can be where the bulls are bright and early.

The two jeeps are stripped to the barest essentials, the windscreens have been removed. Lights, windows, everything of glass has been taken away. Sheets of steel are welded down the sides and the bullbar across the radiator is padded with old tyres. It is best to wear goggles or sunglasses and a bandanna across your mouth because the dust is frightful.

You start off on a track that eventually fizzles out and now you bounce and jolt across the bush, which is criss-crossed with dried-up gulleys, ditches and miniature gorges, none of which you can see because they are obscured by the tall, spiky, prickly grass and thorny little bushes. You spend a lot of time reversing out of them. At the appointed spot, you unload the modular fencing and in the shelter of some trees – short, stunted things – you erect a corral, about twenty-five yards square, maybe a bit more. From a gate in the corral, using the steel posts and the hessian, you create a funnel which at its widest part, three- or four-hundred yards away from the corral, is probably fifty to a hundred yards wide.

This exhausting operation takes about two hours to set up. While this is happening and you are trapping the ends of your fingers in the bits of fencing, the helicopter pilot is out looking for the bulls. The idea is that he flies down low on them, only feet above the ground and inches above their horns, and stampedes them to the gaping mouth of the funnel. They are so angry and confused by the time they hit the mouth – they are probably going at fifty mph or something – they think the hessian walls are solid and charge obediently into the corral. At least, that is the theory of it.

To make sure that they go down the mouth of the funnel, the two jeeps hide on either side of the funnel mouth and, as the main wave come charging and snorting towards the gap, you smack the jeeps into gear, gun the engines and chase them like hell into the corral. As the walls narrow towards the corral, you just drive into their backsides to force them right in. If you think it sounds easy, try doing it with a camera strapped to the crash-bar over your head, delivering a piece to camera as you do it. If you combine the San Fermin festival in Pamplona with the 'chicken run' scene from *Rebel Without A Cause*, you will have some idea of what it's really like.

But some of the bulls are mavericks. They have been out in the bush for years and have survived many musters. Not all of them are easily fooled or frightened and there are always half a dozen who recognise the trap and career off across the bush. This is where the fun really starts.

The men who round up the cattle this way are 'Journeymen' and are paid by the number of head of beef they catch. By the time you have pulled out of the corral the maverick beasts, unconcerned about the pits, the trees, and the gulleys, have a start on you.

You whack the jeep into gear and drive fast after the escaping bull. It is a hell of a chase. It zigzags, it swerves, it about-turns. There is no off-road eventing, no fairground with a Dodgem-car circuit, no motor-bike trial that can come near this extremely dangerous caper.

You must get the bull no matter what the terrain. The idea of the steel plates on the side of the vehicles is that they enable you to broadside on to a tree and do a 180-degree turn against it. If you were lucky – and you weren't that often – the bull would break off open ground and at fifty mph you would aim to hit it in the side with the rubber tyres at the front of the jeep, knock it on to its back, rope its legs together, and leave it there stunned and hogtied to be picked up later, while you went charging off for the next one.

It is only when you stop, some hours later, that you realise that you are bruised, your bones ache and you can't walk. It is the most exciting, exhilarating experience. When I have the time to become a real writer I would like to turn these small cameos, of which this book is comprised, into really brilliant short stories.

But on this occasion my real purpose for being here is to film a little cooking sketch. And since yesterday, cooking for the road train drivers, we had exhausted Katherine's supply of interesting ingredients, we had to pad this one out a bit.

By the way, my chum, the incredible Alf spent most of this time during the chase on the goddam bonnet, would you believe. True, he fell off a few times, but he always came bouncing back and scrambled on again. My

What's it all about, Alfie?

Dinkum Aussie dictionary says that he is known as a black bastard: 'A term of endearment used to describe Australia's only home-bred dog strain, other than the disputed Kelpie, officially known as the blue heeler, Queensland blue or Queensland cattle dog. All blues are regarded by their owners as being as "thick as two bricks" but "as game as Ned Kelly". They are also renowned for their biting ability.'

Anyway, the cooking sketch. I wanted to prove the point that you could cook a steak, the sort of thing that cowboys would eat in the Wild West of America in the olden days, when they used to put a bit of beef under their saddle as they rode out after the cattle so it would be tender when they wanted to cook it.

Well, I wanted to link up with some sort of modern-day equipment so I decided, with the aid of bits of wire, cut-down beer tinnies, tin foil and the manifold of one of the jeeps, you could cook your lunch at the same time as you were working.

Take a pound of sirloin or rump steak, season it with salt and pepper, garlic and herbs if you like, wrap tightly in tin foil, place it on the manifold of your jeep, wrap that around with a cut-down beer can, wire it on to the manifold and charge off after another maverick bull. Experience has taught me, in a stripped-down 1962 Toyota four-wheel drive jeep, a one-pound steak will cook perfectly in the time that it takes you to knock over one bull. Experience has also taught me that if you don't take off your steak by the time you have run over four bulls, it is cooked to buggery and it only has two possible uses – one is to let it cool and use it to resole your shoes, or toss it to the ever-obliging Alf, who will devour it in about one-second flat.

And so with the bulls corralled awaiting collection by the road train, with our faces caked in red dust, our hands chapped and gnarled, bruised and bleeding, we sat round the brightly burning camp fire drinking beer and watching the sun set. Another day in paradise was over. Tomorrow we fly east again in the two little planes, to Normanton.

Do you ever get your mind obsessed by a stupid tune? Flying in the twin-engined Cessna from Katherine to Normanton, I found myself repeatedly singing, 'Wind whistle blowing all along the track, all bound for Normanton and never coming back.' I suppose it was too long spent in the desert and the sun had got to what was left of my brain.

Anyway, apart from my irritating the crew with this tuneless repetition, the flight to Normanton was uneventful. The usual scenario – Paul gripped with a punishing migraine, Pies and David playing chess, and me dozing and dreaming.

Normanton was uneventful too. But this remote township, little more than a crossroads, fringed by a few buildings and 500 miles from anywhere (everywhere seems to be 500 miles from anywhere in this place), quite touched my heart. The small generating station, again the satellite dishes, the tall radio masts, the clapboard buildings with their ornate verandahs and raised sidewalks, the watered-down colonial architecture carved in wood and corrugated iron instead of granite, marble and slate, sort of Bush Gothic.

I bought a brilliant pair of R.M. Williams riding boots in the General Store on Sunday while waiting for the pub to open. The pub is called the Purple Pub. Quite simply, because this outstanding monument of Bush Gothic, instead of being painted in sombre greens, cool creams and finished with polished hardwood, is painted from top to bottom in a vomit-inducing purple.

There is a two-coach diesel train that takes tourists to the disused gold mines. Old steam engines lie rusting on their sides in a gulch behind the brightly-painted, flower-decked station. On this warm Sunday morning the community is divided into three. One lot are rehearsing for the rodeo on the outskirts of town, another are playing golf in the bush (the greens, by the way, are sandpits soaked in oil and patted flat). Despite the hot weather the players wear thick gloves, a precaution against snake bites when they retrieve a ball from the undergrowth. In the neat clubhouse, wives are excitedly preparing a barbie. The other third of the community are black and they are sitting on the steps of the Purple Pub waiting for it to open. I sit high on a wind-blasted fence while the men break in horses.

Normanton was founded in the late 1800s and in former times prospered on gold. It is hard to see how people live these days, neat and thriving though the town appears to be – they probably take in each other's washing. We spent the night at the town's only motel, which has so much been the case on this trip. It is friendly, helpful and kind, and here they talk about Aboriginals and are pleased about what they see as progressive integration. In the centre of town there is a tidy street of little bungalows where they live.

A dull grey river flows from Normanton to the sea, 280 miles away. The river is infested with saltwater crocodiles. 'No Swimming' signs are no joke. The main street is wide and tree-lined. The town hall and the county library, in common with the other old buildings in the place, with the totally excusable exception of the Purple Pub, have been painstakingly restored and are beautifully maintained.

It is still Sunday. The golfers will golf until sunset, the rodeo club will ride until they are sore, and the Aboriginals will drink until the pub shuts. Oil drums are painted and used as refuse bins. They are used to make barbecues from, they are stacked behind the bungalows. Normanton is a frontier town. To me it is the essence of this country, the eau de vie of the frontier spirit.

After walking through the graveyard, filled with the bones of past pioneers, swagmen and jackeroos and the postman who, after living in town for twenty years, went to Sydney for an operation and came back as a woman and continued his business without causing a stir, I wonder if this is *A Town Like Alice*.

We flew to Cairns in a Sunshine Airways twenty-seater plane piloted by two terribly attractive young ladies. After weeks in the bush and the outback it was wonderful coming in to land at the international airport of a big city.

Cairns is bordered to the east by the ocean and the landward side is fertile and green. Behind are the mountains, covered in tropical rain-

Dear Poppy,

The wildlife here is really extraordinary and I have been reading up about it.

Did you know, for instance, that Joseph Banks collected a wallaby in New South Wales and took the skin back to England where it was stuffed and then painted by George Stubbs? Banks also reported that kangaroo tasted like tough venison and I must say that I haven't taken much to the taste either.

I also discovered that Australia's most venomous spider is the funnel-web, which is mainly found in New South Wales. A sting from it can be fatal, though an anti-venom has recently been developed. My guidebook helpfully says: 'extreme care should be taken with any funnel-web species. If bitten, seek help immediately.'

In fact, there are loads of dangerous things here, like stonefish, which cleverly disguise themselves on the Great Barrier Reef, and then inject you with poison if you tread on one. Blue-ring octopus sound jolly too; they lurk round in rock pools and can sting you to death.

Lots of love, Daddy xx

forests. And inland from the spectacular beaches were miles and miles of bright green sugar cane plantations. Cairns is a bustling modern city with high-rise hotels, stylish shops, nightclubs and marinas.

And Cairns was the end of our journey. From here, after a couple of days' filming, I would fly back to England. I checked in at the Radisson Plaza Hotel and was given a room with a spectacular view of both the rainforests and the South Pacific Ocean. It was uncompromisingly luxurious. I was back in the land of telephones, television, fax machines and room service. Back in the land of neatly-pressed shirts and lightweight shoes, instead of moleskins and heavy riding boots and bush jackets. Back in the land of long drinks tinkling with ice. It was great.

Now that we were so close to leaving Australia, for the first time I felt a little homesick for Devon. Being in Cairns was a bit like arriving at the railway station five hours too early for the train.

Another curious thing occurred to me while I was sitting in my Jacuzzi, my first proper bath for some weeks. And it was that Pritchard and I, in almost three months of very close contact, hadn't exchanged a single cross word – in marked contrast to our last trip together, when we were filming 'American Pie', and when we fell out so often that we communicated either by letter or through an intermediary. It says something for

Australia I think; it is such a grand place to visit. And though it had been a very hard trip in terms of schedules and travelling, it had been a very easy and comfortable one, a very happy one, thanks to the relaxed attitude of the Australian people, I suppose.

Anyway, enough of all of that, I mustn't get too soft and sentimental. Let me tell you what we did for these last few days. First, we took a trip to Kuranda, a little town high up in the rainforest, where I was going to cook some mud crabs for a troupe of Aboriginal dancers.

It was a Mud Bug Boogie

And although the journey from Cairns only took an hour, it is the most incredible journey. This old train snakes up the precipitous sides of mountains, crosses vast waterfalls, bends almost double on itself as it climbs higher and higher. Every now and again through the lush vegetation you catch a glimpse of the South Pacific, hundreds and hundreds of feet below. You can pick, though you mustn't, exotic blooms from the window of your carriage, so closely and thickly does the foliage – do the bushes and the trees and the shrubs – come to the railway track.

It was a great feat of engineering. Thousands of men with little more than shovels and pickaxes and in some cases bare hands, forged this spectacular link, excavating and blasting and tunnelling made more hazardous by frequent torrential rainstorms. These days the carriages are pulled by a chirpy little diesel engine. I think the carriages, with their tiny observation platforms, are the original ones.

I am not noted for attending arts festivals or sitting in open-air theatres watching ethnic dance troupes, and know absolutely nothing about the symbolism of Aboriginal dancing except that it goes back to the Stone Age, but I was extremely moved by the performance of a dance celebrating animals and birds and a way of life that existed before the tall ships, which brought an alien culture and the brutal process of civilisation, arrived.

The Tjakpuik dance troupe performed this dance for us on the edge of a lake in the middle of the jungle. They were painted in the traditional ochre (for camouflage) made from crushed clay and decorated with the symbolic colours of the sun, the earth, blood and air – yellow, brown, red and white – as they stalked round the clearing to the haunting strains of the didgeridoo that had nothing to do with 'Tie me kangaroo down, sport'.

After a while I thought I was back in the Stone Age, but as soon as we stepped back into the town, which was thronged with tourists, the illusion quickly evaporated. When I was in Alice Springs I had nearly bought a didgeridoo and I went into a shop that sold Aboriginal artefacts, drawn as I was by the haunting music that it makes. But the man playing it was a Dutch hippy, so I didn't.

This was the first time on our trip that we had really behaved like tourists and it was the most terrific fun. For next we went to see another set of dancers, this time at the Kewarra, a fabulously beautiful hotel set in lush tropical vegetation with banana groves and coconut trees – to watch the Torres Strait islanders, descendants from inhabitants of the South Pacific islands, do some dancing too.

What normally happens is you get a ticket in the hotel and they bus sixty or seventy up to the hotel where the Torres islanders, in full tribal costume, perform some great dances. And then you have a feast of pork and chicken and fish, which is cooked on hot stones in holes in the ground. Since it is a commercial operation, they have rationalised the process and built permanent brick-lined ovens. They put the food, wrapped in tin foil, on to the hot stones, cover it with hessian, and leave it until it is cooked.

And that's exactly what I did, on this pure white deserted beach, the South Pacific lapping gently on the sand. I dug my own hole, got my own stones, did the whole thing properly. The only thing I didn't do was weave the palm leaves into baskets to put the food in.

I cooked a boned-out chicken stuffed with rice and crayfish; a wonder-

ful spicy vegetable dish of sweet potatoes, pumpkins and plantains, seasoned with ginger, turmeric and local cane sugar; and a whole barramundi stuffed with chillies, ginger and lemon grass. And to my surprise and delight three hours later when I lifted it out of the sand and out of the palm leaves, they were all perfectly cooked. It was delicious. And a damned sight better than the stuff they had done in their concrete pits, wrapped up in tin foil.

But the real way to do it, the way the islanders would have originally done it, would be to dig a hole (about four feet deep) in the beach or earth, fill it with wood, then put smooth round stones from the riverbed on top and light the fire. Meanwhile, you carefully wrap all the food, a whole pig or a huge fish or chicken, in banana leaves, not tin foil. When the fire is burnt out and the stones are amazingly hot, across the stones you lay some chopped-up banana palm trunks because they will create steam, you place your baskets of food on top of the hot stones, cover them with the broad-leaved coconut palms and fill in the hole with sand.

You then go away and do a dance or have a few drinks, come back a few hours later and eat until you are fit to burst. Actually, I must confess, when I said I did it on my own, I sort of did it on my own – with a little help from the entire staff and management of the Kewarra Beach resort. And they said it would be a delight to go back to the old-fashioned way of doing it if they could possibly see any commercial return in about fifteen people spending two and a half days to produce a load of food for a one-minute, twenty-second segment of a television programme.

But joking apart, it is something you ought to try at home one day. Dig a hole in the garden, light a blazing fire in the hole, cover it with stones, get a nice piece of pork or a chicken, wrap it up in tin foil, pop it on top of the stones, cover the food with a load of soaking wet hessian sacks, make yourself lots of exotic cocktails containing coconut and rum and things like that, and have a party.

It was a schizophrenic few days: daytimes were spent stepping back in time and night-times after work, back to the future with a bang, cruising round the bars and nightclubs of this fun city.

My last day in Australia started with a waterfront service conducted by the Bishop of Queensland from the flying bridge of a sleek game fishing boat moored on Pier 5 in front of the Radisson Hotel. It was the annual blessing of the Cairns game fishing charter fleet. Some thirty or forty boats were crowded with anglers raring to start a new season. A couple of hundred spectators crowded on to the narrow pier, among them a vociferous group of Animal Rights activists who heckled the Bishop.

The service over, amid a cacophony of klaxons, hooters, horns and bells, the little flotilla put out to sea, among cheers and singing and shouted abuse at the luckless protesters. The crowd on the pier dispersed and Sunday normality settled once again on the wooden piers. Honey-mooners strolled hand in hand, joggers in flamboyant tracksuits padded up and down and day-trippers filed on to the glass-bottomed ferries that would take them to look at the Great Barrier Reef, which is only a few miles off the coast from Cairns.

Once again, thanks to our privileged treatment, we were spared the raucous tinny-swigging crowds, because we had our own fifty-foot launch, complete with Japanese chef, to take us to do the same thing. I was kitted out immaculately in bleached-blue canvas trousers, deck shoes, dark-blue Aertex shirt, a dark-blue Guernsey knotted loosely over my shoulders, my craggy, handsome, suntanned face peering intently out to sea from behind Zeiss (naturally) sunglasses. David Pritchard was as usual wearing his Doc Martens and Ray Bans – but then he has worked for the BBC for over twenty years.

After we cleared the shelter of the harbour we ran into a stiff breeze on the nose. David was lying on the forward deck, sunbathing, when the breeze freshened considerably and our boat was pitching and rolling like one of the horses I had seen them try to break in at Normanton a few days previously. It grew overcast and chilly. The movement of the boat was such that David couldn't get back from the deck and was periodically drenched by the stinging South Pacific Ocean waves.

Happily, the bad weather was short-lived and as we approached the reef the clouds disappeared. A big sun warmed us and the sea settled to a gentle roll. I was surprised to discover – I must admit my ignorance – that the reef is under the water. For some reason I thought it protruded like some sort of coral Hadrian's Wall. The first you see of it is merely the darkening of the water and as you get closer you can see that it is, in some cases, only inches below the surface. It must be a navigator's nightmare, to make sure he doesn't rip the bottom of his boat out.

Once we reached the reef one of the deckhands jumped over the side of the boat and with the utmost delicacy, so as not to damage the fragility of the reef, attached the anchor to it in a hole he had discovered previously, while diving. The beautiful green ocean rolled and rushed over the top of the reef and was sucked back by the current, occasionally revealing glimpses of the reef itself.

I, as usual, had to do a cooking sketch and on our way to the reef we had stopped at a little island where it was intended we should collect some clams that I could use to this end. But unfortunately they weren't the small variety that you can quickly toss in a hot pan with butter, oil, garlic and parsley and feast upon. They were huge, gnarled, cultured clams and were being bred for export to Japan to be sliced in the sushi bars.

So, as is so often the case on this trip, I had to resort to stir-frying my faithful stand-by, some large beautiful fresh prawns – and this I did. In the five or six years that I have been lucky enough to go on these little adventures, I think that cooking prawns on the bridge of a fishing boat tethered to the Great Barrier Reef must be the high point, the most exotic location of all that I have visited. The vastness of the ocean, the incomprehensible beauty of the reef that picture postcards and glossy magazines can't do justice to, is an experience I shall never forget.

The water was very warm, apparently, and before a light lunch most of the crew dived over the side and had a swim. David pulled his pink wet suit over his corpulent frame and floated on his back, occasionally flapping a flippered foot. I remembered thinking that he was fortunate that there were no marine biologists in the area, they'd have got overexcited and netted him and taken him back to the laboratory for further study.

I only put in this cruel jibe because, as you remember, I said earlier that in almost three months – contrary to our normal performance – we hadn't had a cross word. Well, it had to happen didn't it, on this our last working day.

'Listen,' he said, 'what I want you to do is to put on a wet suit, goggles and snorkel. You do a backward somersault into the water à la James Bond. I'll have the underwater cameraman ready and you just swim up to the reef, point out the turtle grass, the brown fire coral, the stinging hydroids and the gorgoneion [which is white fan coral, by the way]. Tap a few parrotfish on the head and generally do a sort of three- or four-minute Hans and Lotte Hass number.'

Now it may come as a surprise to you that if my director asks me to do something, like a good soldier I obey without hesitation, notwithstanding that my better sense tells me different. Whether it is travelling over the Vosges Mountains in Alsace in a hot air balloon, galloping down the mountainside in the Snowy Mountains in Victoria on an untamed horse, or whether it is risking life and limb hurtling across the bush chasing bulls in an unsafe four-wheel drive jeep – no matter what, I do it. I might complain like a stuck pig afterwards, but I do it. So I donned the wet suit, rinsed out my face mask, somersaulted into the ocean and struck out determinedly for the reef.

I couldn't breathe, my mouth was full of water, I couldn't see, the waves were crashing me on to the reef, the current was sucking me away from it. I reached out to touch bits of coral and weed and stuff and found that they were yards in front of me. The distance between the reef and me was increasing and I started to panic. I couldn't see the underwater cameraman. I didn't know in which direction to swim. I was lost and in genuine danger of drowning.

Somehow I struggled to the surface and managed to turn myself in the direction of the boat, frantically waving. I was exhausted from swimming. I could see David on the stern with a glass of wine in his hand. He waved back and went down into the cabin. I was really desperate now. I don't know how long I was in the water, but I was virtually unconscious when two of the crew on the boat dragged me up over the stern.

Maggie, who had been watching, told me she had asked David on several occasions to tell the divers to go and bring me back but he said, 'No, he's fine.'

I was frightened and badly shaken. When my voice came back I said: 'You bastard, you nearly drowned me.'

And David said: 'Oh sorry, I was just finishing up the prawns, they are delicious.'

The day that started with a religious service almost ended with one too.

Then you'd know
what a drag it
    is
    to
    see
    you

Food thoughts from Oz

Like all countries, Australia has its fair share of mediocre food: international hotels with cuisine for the culinary unadventurous and some fanciful and enthusiastic bistros for the gullible. At its best there are fantastic fish, succulent steaks, terrific wines, wonderful fruits and incredible ethnic dishes. At its worst there are canned three-bean salads, 'seafood' cocktails with bottled sauce, packet tomato soups and unrecognisable *coq au vins*. Not only that, but over the years some adaptations bear little resemblance to the original, leaving you to wonder where the translation was at fault.

And another thing, as elsewhere, you really can't tell just by the look of the place, how good or bad the food will be. Once you've sampled it, of course, it's too late. There are danger signs to watch out for – but that's another story. Recommendations are a better guide, though even these aren't infallible. But good food can be found in unexpected places. Fast food, innocuous enough and sometimes quite acceptable, is everywhere, fuelling you until something better can be found.

In January 1788 Captain Arthur Phillip arrived on the east coast of Australia with the First Fleet, and it's recorded that in Sydney Cove there was a rum-drinking celebration followed by a cold collation – for the officers, naturally.

The seeds that Phillip and his crew brought over were a disaster. The climate, the type of soil and salt winds killed off the cabbages and wheat as well as the vine cuttings. Not many cattle survived the journey either. So for many years the white man was dependent on the stores ships from England, the Cape and India. So started, and still survives in country areas today, the practice of living off 'rations' – mainly boiled potatoes and salt beef.

By the mid-nineteenth century boiled mutton and the occasional treat of pickled kangaroo haunch were the main fare in country areas. What you ate reflected what you were. In the coastal cities, with farming now established close by, things were beginning to change. Takeaways arrived. Those higher up the social scale added local snapper to their menus, supplementing game pies and turtles and the still popular traditional dried salt cod.

The settlers found little food and they didn't care for fish. Nobody bothered to listen to the Aboriginals, who could have taught them so much – still could, for that matter. About cooking in wet clay small birds and animals – complete with fur, feather and scales which tear off easily when the food is cooked. About baking food wrapped in leaves or seaweed. About making breads from wild grasses. About the medicinal uses of plants.

Foodwise, not much happened for the fifty years between the beginning of this century with the federation of the Australian states until well after the Second World War. Influences from Ireland (soda bread and stew) and Scotland (smoked fish) were there, but by and large immigrants – the Greeks, the Italians, the Chinese and so on – kept their cuisines to themselves.

As livestock needed the water in inland areas for much of the year, country women turned to baking. Hence the Victoria sponge and the Lamington (a small square sponge cake covered with melted chocolate and coconut and said to be named after Baron Lamington, who was Governor of Queensland in the late nineteenth century). Aussie cake shops still flourish here and there. Try some.

Salads of tomato, cucumber, onion and lettuce immersed in malt vinegar with sugar became popular, though some brawny men scorned these as something Sheilas ate – I had a steak sandwich stuffed with this bizarre mixture, and actually enjoyed it! A strange mayonnaise made from sweetened condensed milk and vinegar, mustard powder and sugar was 'invented'. And the still-popular mixed bean salad.

By the 1940s Australia had started to adopt American food fashions – the soda fountain, the milk bar, chewing gum and Spam. But it was the 'populate or perish' policy of the postwar Labour government, and the attitude of the 1945 returners, who had escaped the 'motherland' influence, that really changed things.

And while the backbone of food culture still remained the same, people discovered that foreign foods were really rather palatable. That spiced sausages were vastly preferable to the local offerings of Camp Pie.

Even so, a standard night out in the 1950s was still to go to a Chinese or Greek restaurant. Punters at Chinese places would eat Anglo-Saxon versions totally unlike real Chinese food. The Greeks served up steak with egg and burgers. Bistros followed – blackboards and chalk, phoney French accents. Then, of course, just like the rest of the world Australia was attacked by *nouvelle cuisine*, but luckily the Ozzies didn't really fall for that one.

And today in the 1990s food in Australia is really very exciting and the multi-cultural make-up of this population enables you to eat your way across the world without leaving Sydney or Melbourne.

But for me by far the most delightful aspect of the whole thing was the Asian influence, so many of the recipes I have decided to include in this book reflect this. Ingredients are now not too difficult to find, and the dishes are great fun to cook. There are some common denominators to Asian food – rice, noodles, spices, herbs, curries, thin soups, and snack stalls (their version of fast foods). By the way, did you know that chop suey has never been heard of in China – it was invented in San Francisco.

Australia, no less than Britain, has a truly indigenous national cuisine. One of its great traditions is the barbecue. Every Australian home has one as does every national park and beach throughout the country. They are very simple affairs, usually brick-built with a solid steel plate with a shelf underneath where the fire is lit, to heat up the metal sheet. And when that is searing hot, Australians throw on big steaks or dozens of fresh prawns and cook them with the minimum of fuss. And serve them with mountains of salad and fresh bread, washed down by copious quantities of Australian wine or lager.

Above all, my experience of Australian food was that it was served by cheerful, helpful people, it was fun, not outrageously expensive, and in most cases really good. Don't be put off by the snobby Australian you so often meet in London, who spends his whole time slagging off the food, the wine and the culture of his own country. Because he is wrong.

Home-made stocks – chicken, beef, veal, vegetable, fish – impart a marvellous flavour to soups, stews and sauces alike – and they're simple and satisfying to make. But don't forget to skim them well.

You can also now buy good stocks in tubs from some supermarkets and delicatessens – they're called Fonds de Cuisine and are well worth a try.

Chicken Stock
. . . .

MAKES ABOUT 900 ML (1½ pints)

*1 chicken carcass and bones from a
  carved chicken*
1 onion, roughly chopped
1 turnip, roughly chopped

1 small carrot, chopped
few sprigs of fresh herbs
1 bay leaf
1 litre (1¾ pints) cold water

Put the chicken carcass into a large pan with the vegetables and herbs. Cover with the water and bring to the boil, then reduce the heat, cover and simmer gently for at least 2 hours. Cool slightly, then strain through a very fine sieve. Cool completely, refrigerate and use within 2 days, or freeze and keep for up to 3 months.

Beef Stock
. . . .

MAKES ABOUT 1.5 LITRES (2½ pints)

450 g (1 lb) marrow bones
450 g (1 lb) shin of beef, cut into chunks
2 litres (3½ pints) cold water
1 carrot, sliced

1 onion, chopped
2 sticks of celery, sliced
½ teaspoon salt
bouquet garni

Brown the bones and the shin of beef in a roasting tin in a preheated oven, 200°C/400°F (gas mark 6), for about 30 minutes. Transfer to a large pan and cover with the water. Add the vegetables to the roasting pan and roast them for about 10 minutes, until browned. Tip them into the pan with the bones, add the salt and bouquet garni, then bring to the boil. Reduce the heat, cover and simmer for about 3–4 hours, skimming off any fat or scum from the surface from time to time.

Cool slightly, then strain through a fine sieve. Cool completely and refrigerate. Use within 2 days or freeze and use within 3 months.

Veal Stock

· ·

MAKES ABOUT 2 LITRES (3 ½ pints)

2 kg (4½ lb) veal bones
1 onion, chopped
2 large carrots, chopped
2 sticks of celery, chopped

2 cloves of garlic, finely chopped
300 ml (10 fl oz) dry white wine
4 litres (7 pints) cold water
bouquet garni

Put the veal bones into a roasting tin and brown them in a preheated oven, 200°C/400°F (gas mark 6), for about 30 minutes, turning once. Transfer to a large pan. Cook the onion, carrots, celery and garlic in the same roasting pan for a few minutes, but without browning. Then over a direct heat stir in the wine and allow to bubble until reduced by half. Tip the vegetables and reduced liquid into the pan with the bones. Cover with the water, bring to the boil, then reduce the heat and simmer, skimming off any fat or scum from the surface.

Add the bouquet garni and allow to simmer very gently for 2–3 hours. Cool slightly, then strain through a very fine sieve. Cool, refrigerate and use within 2 days, or freeze and keep for up to 3 months.

Fish Stock

· ·

MAKES ABOUT 900 ML (1 ½ pints)

450 g (1 lb) fish trimmings – head, tails,
*   leftover bones, etc*
1 onion, chopped
1 carrot, chopped
1 leek, chopped

few white peppercorns
bouquet garni
150 ml (5 fl oz) dry white wine
1 litre (1¾ pints) water

Put all the ingredients into a large pan, bring to the boil, then reduce the heat. Cover and simmer very gently for 30 minutes. Cool slightly, then strain through a fine sieve. Cool completely, refrigerate and use within 1 day, or freeze and keep for up to 1 month.

Vegetable Stock

. . . .

MAKES ABOUT 1.2 LITRES (2 pints)

1 large onion, stuck with whole cloves
2 carrots, sliced
2 leeks, chopped
bouquet garni
wedge of lemon

750 ml (1¼ pints) cold water
750 ml (1¼ pints) dry white wine or dry
   cider
1 tablespoon white wine vinegar

Put all the ingredients into a large pan. Bring to the boil, then reduce the
heat, cover and simmer for about 30 minutes. Cool slightly, then strain
through a very fine sieve. Cool completely, refrigerate and use within 2
days, or freeze and keep for up to 3 months.

Thai Soup Stock

. . . .

A terrifically versatile, basic stock. Freeze in ice-cube trays or little pots for
emergency or impromptu use – or for sheer convenience.

MAKES 1.5–2 LITRES (2½–3½ pints)

2.25 litres (4 pints) cold water
700 g (1½ lb) chicken, beef, pork or fish
   bones, depending on the flavour of the
   stock you need
2 sticks of celery, chopped
2 onions, chopped

2 coriander roots, chopped, see page 235
4 lime leaves, see page 236
2.5 cm (1 inch) piece of fresh root ginger,
   chopped
salt
freshly ground black pepper

Put all the ingredients into a very large pan. Bring to the boil, then reduce
the heat and simmer, covered, for about 1 hour, skimming the fat from
the surface from time to time.

   Strain through a fine sieve and discard all but the stock, then strain
again, lining the sieve with muslin to achieve a clear liquid. Cool and
refrigerate, then skim off any fat from the surface. Use within 2 days, or
freeze and keep for up to 3 months. Use in Thai soup recipes.

Fresh Tomato Sauce

. . . .

MAKES 300 ML (½ pint)

2 tablespoons olive oil
2 large onions, chopped
2 cloves of garlic, crushed
450 g (1 lb) tomatoes, skinned and
   chopped

1 teaspoon caster sugar
few sprigs fresh rosemary and thyme,
   chopped

Heat the oil in a large pan and fry the onions and garlic for about 3–4 minutes, until softened and golden. Tip in the tomatoes, sugar and herbs. Cover and simmer gently for at least half an hour, until you have a rich, red sauce. Whizz in a food processor or blender or rub through a sieve. Serve with Tuna Steaks, see page 162.

Spit Roast Sauce

. . . .

The essence of being a good cook is all about having patience and being prepared for situations. If you suddenly want to make a sauce, it is utterly boring if you have to simmer ingredients for a while first. So, if you are practical, every now and again you could make some of this sauce in advance and freeze it in little old yoghurt tubs or ice-cube trays. Then when a whim hits you, as it did me in the Snowy Mountains, you already have some ready.

SERVE WITH CHOPS, STEAKS, BARBECUED CHICKEN – ENOUGH FOR 4

50 g (2 oz) butter
6 shallots, finely chopped
225 g (8 oz) wild mushrooms, chopped –
   or use field mushrooms if you can't get
   any

1 wineglass red wine
150 ml (5 fl oz) beef stock, see page 125
2 tablespoons tomato purée
salt
freshly ground black pepper

Melt the butter in a medium pan and fry the shallots for about 3–4 minutes, until softened. Add the mushrooms and cook for 2 more minutes. Pour in the red wine and stock, then stir in the tomato purée. Bring to the boil and simmer for 5 minutes. Season to taste with salt and pepper, then serve the sauce as it is or whizz until smooth in a food processor or blender.

Green or Red Curry Paste

. . . .

Of course, when I made this curry paste for Thai Chicken Curry, see page 190, I sat up in my hotel room the night before, grinding it with a mortar and pestle, while the rest of the crew were out on the town. But what you could do is whack the whole lot through a spice grinder or coffee mill.

MAKES ENOUGH FOR 5–8 CURRIES

1 teaspoon cumin seeds or 1 teaspoon
 ground cumin
1 tablespoon coriander seeds or 1
 tablespoon ground coriander
1 whole nutmeg or 2 teaspoons ground
 nutmeg
12 black peppercorns or 1½ teaspoons
 ground black pepper
2.5 cm (1 inch) piece of dried galingale,
 chopped, or 1 tablespoon dried
 galingale powder, see page 235
1 blade of lemon grass, finely chopped,
 see page 236

10 whole green chilli peppers, stemmed
 and finely chopped, or for red curry
 paste 12 medium dried red chilli
 peppers, seeded and chopped
grated zest of 1 lime
5 cloves of garlic, chopped
4 shallots, finely chopped
1 teaspoon shrimp paste, see page 237,
 or anchovy essence
2 tablespoons coriander roots, finely
 chopped, see page 235
1 teaspoon salt
4 tablespoons vegetable oil

If using whole spices, put the cumin and coriander seeds, nutmeg, peppercorns, dried galingale and lemon grass into an electric spice mill or coffee grinder and grind to a powder. Alternatively, grind them using a mortar and pestle. Put the ground spices into a processor or blender and add all the remaining ingredients. Whizz until a smooth paste is formed.

Keep the paste in a screw-topped jar and store in the refrigerator for up to 1 month. Use in Thai recipes.

Garam Masala

. . . .

The base for much Indian cooking, there are many recipes for *garam masala*. In this one, use either bleached or green cardamons. *Garam masala* should keep for up to six months in an airtight jar.

MAKES ENOUGH FOR 10 FABULOUS CURRIES

1½ tablespoons whole cardamon pods
5 tablespoons whole coriander seeds
1 tablespoon whole cumin seeds

1½ tablespoons whole cloves
6 tablespoons black peppercorns

Remove the seeds from the cardamons, then put them on a baking tray with the remaining spices. Bake in a preheated oven, 240°C/475°F (gas mark 9), for 10 minutes, then allow to cool.

Grind to a fine powder using a pestle and mortar, or whizz in an electric coffee or spice grinder. Store in a jar with a tight-fitting lid for 3–6 months.

Crispy Omelette in a Basket

This is the perfect brunch dish, ideal on a Sunday morning with some chilled champagne and freshly-squeezed orange juice. Don't panic about making the potato baskets – you just need two wire or metal strainers, one slightly smaller than the other. The potato mixture is sandwiched between the baskets and deep-fried in hot oil. I would suggest, though, that you make these up in advance – better still, ask your spouse to do it.

SERVES 4 – 6

2 tablespoons vegetable oil
1 onion, finely shredded
2 sticks of celery, finely chopped
1/2 red pepper, finely chopped
5 large cap mushrooms, thickly sliced
150 g (5 oz) beansprouts

salt
freshly ground black pepper
6 eggs, beaten
1 large potato basket, see page 132
3 spring onions, trimmed and finely chopped
1 tablespoon chopped cashew nuts

Heat the oil in a frying pan or wok that has a lid and stir-fry the onion, celery and pepper for 2 minutes. Pop in the mushrooms and beansprouts, season to taste with salt and pepper, and stir-fry for 1 more minute. Pour in the eggs and allow to set – about 1 minute. Flip the omelette on to the lid of the pan to turn it and slide it back in – cook the other side for about 1 minute. It is important to cook the omelette until it is quite set so that no egg seeps out when it is shredded.

Lift out the omelette and cut into strips. Arrange in the potato basket, sprinkle with the spring onions and cashews and serve immediately.

Crispy Omelette in a Basket

Potato Baskets

. . . .

See also the notes on page 130 about preparing these.

MAKES 1 LARGE BASKET

450 g (1 lb) grated potato
2 tablespoons cornflour
salt

freshly ground black pepper
vegetable oil, for deep-frying

Mix together the potato and cornflour and season to taste with salt and pepper. Heat enough oil in a large pan or deep-fryer so that the sieves or strainers will be completely immersed. Test how hot the oil is by popping in a cube of bread to see if it sizzles. Dip wire sieves or strainers into the hot oil and remove. Put the potato mixture into the larger basket and arrange so that the surface is covered completely.

Put the smaller basket on top, sandwiching the potato in between. Holding the handles of both baskets together, dip into the hot oil to cover.

After about 3 minutes, when the potato has set, remove the smaller basket. Continue cooking for 10 minutes more, until the potato basket is crisp and golden. With a metal spatula, loosen the potato gently from the strainer. Drain on kitchen paper. Arrange the shredded omelette in the basket and continue as on page 130.

Son-In-Law Eggs

. . . .

Fascinating name, isn't it? Maybe it is what many mothers would like to do to their sons-in-law! In Thailand the dish is famous for its name as well as a classic recipe. You could serve these as a snack, starter, or in a salad.

SERVES 4 SURPRISED PEOPLE, WHO THOUGHT THEY
HAD TRIED EVERY WAY OF EATING EGGS

3 tablespoons vegetable oil
4 shallots or 1 small onion, finely
  chopped
4 hard-boiled eggs, shelled and halved
2 tablespoons fish sauce, see page 235

1 tablespoon cold water
1 tablespoon soft brown sugar
fresh coriander leaves or parsley, to
  garnish

Heat the oil in a frying pan or wok and fry the shallots or onion for about 5 minutes, until brown. Lift out with a slotted spoon and put to one side.

Add the eggs to the pan and fry them until they look crisp and 'blistered' on the outside. Remove and set aside.

Add the fish sauce, water and sugar to the pan and stir well to dissolve the sugar. Reduce the heat and simmer for 5 minutes, until the sauce is thick, brown and blended. Return the eggs to the pan and reheat for 2 minutes, stirring carefully. Serve immediately with the fried shallots or onion, garnished with sprigs of coriander or parsley.

Crunchy Pork and Prawn Snacks

. . . .

These make the perfect drinks party or Sunday brunch snacks.

SERVES ABOUT 8

225 g (8 oz) lean pork, cubed
225 g (8 oz) peeled prawns
1 bunch of spring onions, trimmed and
* roughly chopped*
1 clove of garlic
1 egg
1 tablespoon fish sauce, see page 235

freshly ground black pepper
10–12 slices of white or brown bread,
* crusts cut off*
vegetable oil, for frying
fresh coriander leaves or parsley, to
* garnish*

Put the pork, prawns, spring onions, garlic, egg, fish sauce and black pepper into a food processor or blender and whizz together for a few seconds until chopped and well mixed, but not too smooth. Spread thickly on to the bread, right up to the edges, then cut the slices into neat little triangles.

Pour some vegetable oil into a large frying pan to a depth of 1 cm (½ inch). Heat it – test by popping in a cube of bread to see if it sizzles – and shallow-fry the triangles, topping-side down, for 1–2 minutes. Turn over and fry the other side until golden. Lift out with a slotted spoon and drain on kitchen paper. Garnish with coriander leaves or parsley and serve hot.

Sushimi

. . . .

If you fancy your skills as a Japanese sushi chef, you may like to try your hand at preparing sushimi – thinly-sliced raw fish, which is usually served as a first course.

SERVES 4

450 g (1 lb) selection of very fresh fish
   fillet (use sea bass, sea bream, halibut,
   salmon or tuna), skinned and boned

TO SERVE:

1 carrot ⎫ *peeled, pared into thin strips*
1 white radish (daikon) ⎬ *and soaked in iced water until needed*
few tablespoons Japanese soy sauce
wasabi paste (Japanese green horseradish paste)
few spring onions, trimmed and finely chopped

Wash the fish in plenty of icy cold water. Pat dry with kitchen paper or a cloth. Slice some of the fish into pieces about 1 cm (¼ inch) thick and 2.5 cm (1 inch) wide, and the rest into paper-thin slices. Arrange simply and attractively on individual serving plates, garnished with the pared carrot and radish. Serve the soy sauce, wasabi and spring onions in separate bowls to accompany the sushimi.

Damper Bread

. . . .

If you happen to be a stockman on one of those vast Australian cattle ranches when you work out in the bush for days and days on end, you have to be a pretty self-reliant type. As long as you have a billy can to make tea, a pot to cook the stew in, a bit of beef and the wherewithal to make some kind of bread, you can survive – I wouldn't exactly say happily, but at least you won't starve.

Damper bread is very, very simple to make, but you need what they call a camp stove. A camp stove is a cast-iron pot with a lid, probably about 30.5–36 cm (12–14 inches) in diameter, with sides about 10–12.5 cm (4–5 inches) high, like a big Le Creuset stewpot, preferably the enamelled kind.

And, by the way, this is not a far-fetched recipe, it is the sort of thing that if you are on a camping holiday or pretending to be self-sufficient in the wastes of rural Surrey, you could easily make.

3 handfuls of self-raising flour   *1 handful of powdered milk*

And into those you pour between 1 and 2 cans of lager. You knead it all into a wet dough and plop it into your pot, and put on the lid. Then set the pot on to the embers of the wood fire that you have previously lit. Drag the embers up the sides of the pot and sit back to watch the sunset.

It takes between 30 and 40 minutes to cook, depending on the amount of dough you have in the pot and how hot the coals are. Traditionally, in the bush, the bread is then sliced hot and smeared with syrup.

Sweetcorn and Red Pepper Fritters

A brilliant alternative to fried bread at leisurely weekend breakfasts – and quite a bit more interesting. The recipe comes from Tony Papas at Sydney's Bayswater Brasserie.

SERVES 4 – 6

225 g (8 oz) canned sweetcorn, well-
    drained
75 ml (3 fl oz) milk
75 g (3 oz) butter
75 g (3 oz) plain flour
2 eggs, beaten

2 red peppers, chopped
few drops of Tabasco sauce
salt
freshly ground black pepper
200 ml (8 fl oz) vegetable oil

Purée half the sweetcorn in a food processor or blender, then mix with the rest of the sweetcorn.

Heat together the milk and butter in a pan until just beginning to boil. Shoot in the flour all at once from a funnel made from greaseproof paper. Cook the mixture, stirring constantly, for 3–4 minutes, or until it comes away from the sides of the pan. Remove from the heat, mix in the corn, then add the eggs gradually, thoroughly mixing after each addition. Stir through the peppers and Tabasco, then season with plenty of salt and pepper.

Heat the oil in a frying pan or wok and fry tablespoonfuls of the mixture, turning once, for about 5–6 minutes, until golden-brown on both sides. Drain on kitchen paper and serve immediately.

Red Pepper Purée with Salt Cod and Poached Egg

. . . .

This is an excellent summer lunch dish, cleverly created by Tony Papas of the Bayswater Brasserie in Sydney.

It is an example of how the new wave of Australian cooks are drawing on their European heritage to delight our tummies.

SERVES 8

FOR THE SALT COD AND POTATOES:
*400 g (14 oz) dried salt cod – this is
    1 side of cod
4 large potatoes
4–5 tablespoons olive oil*

FOR THE RED PEPPER PURÉE:
*3 tablespoons olive oil
2 onions, roughly chopped
1 leek, roughly chopped
1 kg (2 lb 3 oz) red peppers, roughly
    chopped
750 ml (1¼ pints) fish stock, see page
    126
freshly ground black pepper
8 eggs
chopped fresh basil and parsley*

Soak the salt cod in plenty of cold water overnight, changing the water a few times if you can. Drain and rinse well. Put the fish in a pan, cover with cold water and poach for 15–20 minutes, until just tender. When it is cool enough to handle, skin the fish and flake the flesh from the bones. Measure out the cooking liquid and make it up to 750 ml (1¼ pints) with cold water.

Wash the potatoes and boil them, without peeling, until almost cooked, then peel and slice or roughly chop them.

Next, make the red pepper purée. Heat the oil in a large pan and sauté the onions, leek and peppers for 5 minutes or so, until soft. Cover with the fish stock and the reserved cooking liquid from the salt cod. Bubble away for about 30–40 minutes, or until all the vegetables are cooked through, then whizz to a purée in a food processor or blender and return to a clean pan. Season to taste with black pepper.

Heat the olive oil in a pan and sauté the cooked potatoes for about 10 minutes, until golden-brown, then add, with the salt cod, to the purée and simmer gently for 15 minutes more. Meanwhile, poach the eggs. Serve the fish, potatoes and purée in individual dishes, topped with poached eggs and garnished with some basil and parsley.

Pumpkin and Coconut Soup

. . . .

Those of you who used to make artichoke and watercress soup and things like that in the 1960s for your dinner parties will have no difficulty in creating this sophisticated, tangy little number.

SERVES 4

450 g (1 lb) pumpkin, peeled and cut into
*   2.5 cm (1 inch) cubes*
juice of 1/2 lemon
100 g (4 oz) uncooked prawns, peeled
*   with back vein removed – see page 175*
*   for how to do this*
1 large onion, roughly chopped
1/2 teaspoon shrimp paste, see page 237 –
*   or use anchovy paste*
2 red chilli peppers, seeded (optional)

1 blade of lemon grass, bruised and
*   roughly chopped*
750 ml (1 1/4 pints) coconut milk, see page
*   234*
300 ml (10 fl oz) cold water
1 tablespoon fish sauce, see page 235
1 teaspoon caster sugar
freshly ground black pepper
salt
handful of fresh basil leaves, chopped

Sprinkle the pumpkin with the lemon juice and let it stand for 15–20 minutes. Put the prawns, onion, shrimp or anchovy paste, chillies, lemon grass and a couple of tablespoons of cold water into a food processor or blender and switch on for 15–20 seconds to make a smooth paste.

Skim off the thick coconut cream from the top of the coconut milk and save for later. Put the coconut milk and water into a large pan and stir in the blended paste, fish sauce, sugar and black pepper. Bring to the boil, stirring, then reduce the heat and add the pumpkin. Cover and simmer gently for about 20 minutes, or until the pumpkin is tender. Check the seasoning, adding a touch more black pepper, salt or fish sauce if necessary. Stir in the basil leaves and reserved coconut cream and ladle into serving bowls.

Pork Noodle Soup

Photograph on pages 142–3

. . . .

Another nourishing soup, practically a main course in its own right. And, as long as you already have some Roast Red Pork, see page 217, cooked, it is something you can knock up in literally minutes. All you need are soup spoons and chopsticks and a bottle of rice wine, and you can't go wrong.

SERVES 4

2 litres (3½ pints) chicken Thai soup
  stock, see page 127
225 g (8 oz) Roast Red Pork, see page
  217, or any cooked lean pork, cut into
  thin slices
1 tablespoon caster sugar
2 tablespoons fish sauce, see page 235
150 g (6 oz) very thin, Chinese dried egg
  noodles
4 cloves of garlic, finely chopped and
  fried until crisp

50 g (2 oz) beansprouts
3 crunchy lettuce leaves, shredded

TO GARNISH:

2 tablespoons fresh coriander leaves,
  chopped
2 tablespoons roasted peanuts, finely
  chopped

Bring the chicken stock to the boil in a large pan, then add the pork. Stir in the sugar and fish sauce. Reduce the heat and tip in the egg noodles. Simmer gently for 5 minutes, until tender, then add the garlic, beansprouts and shredded lettuce. Pour into serving bowls and sprinkle with chopped coriander. Serve the chopped peanuts in a separate dish so that people can help themselves.

Crab and Sweetcorn Soup

. . . .

This really tantalises the tastebuds, but if you don't have any crab you could always use chicken (and chicken stock) instead.

SERVES 6–8

1 tablespoon vegetable oil
½ teaspoon chopped fresh root ginger
225 g (8 oz) crabmeat, flaked (fresh or
  canned)
1.5 litres (2½ pints) fish stock, seasoned,
  see page 126
1 tablespoon dry sherry

100 g (4 oz) sweetcorn
1 tablespoon cornflour mixed with 2
  tablespoons fish stock or water
2 egg whites, lightly beaten
trimmed and chopped spring onions, to
  garnish

Heat the oil in a large pan or wok and stir-fry the ginger and crabmeat for 2 minutes. Tip in the stock, sherry and sweetcorn. Bring to the boil, then stir in the cornflour mixture to thicken. Remove the pan from the heat and pour in the egg whites in a thin stream. Garnish with the spring onions and serve immediately.

Kangaroo Tail Soup

. . . .

This is the recipe I cooked at Bungaree, the sheep station owned by Richard and Sally Hawker, in South Australia. Make it with oxtail.

SERVES 4

1 kg (2–2¼ lb) kangaroo tail pieces (or use oxtail)
50 g (2 oz) butter or 2 tablespoons vegetable oil
2 onions, sliced
1.2 litres (2 pints) veal or beef stock, see page 126 or 125
225 g (8 oz) baby carrots, trimmed
225 g (8 oz) baby turnips, trimmed

175 g (6 oz) celeriac, chopped into large chunks
4 celery hearts, or use 175 g (6 oz) celery, sliced
2 bay leaves
few sprigs of fresh thyme
salt
freshly ground black pepper
chopped parsley, to garnish

Remove any skin and sinews from the kangaroo tail pieces and discard, then chop into 5 cm (2 inch) pieces. If using oxtail, trim off any fat. Heat the butter or oil in a large pan or flameproof casserole and fry the onions for 3–4 minutes, until transparent. Add the tail pieces or oxtail and fry for 6–8 minutes, until well-browned on all sides. Pour in the stock, bring to the boil, then reduce the heat, cover and simmer gently for about 2 hours, while you go walkabout, until the meat is tender. Alternatively, cook for 20 minutes in a pressure cooker at 15 lb pressure.

When the meat is cooked, skim off any fat, add all the fresh vegetables and herbs and simmer for 10 more minutes or so, until just tender. Taste and adjust the seasoning before serving, and sprinkle with the parsley.

F
I
S
H
.
S
H
E
L
L
F
I
S
H

Lemon Sole with White Wine and Grapes

. . . .

To Celebrate Julian Alcorso's vineyard – Moorilla's

If you are ever in Tasmania you must visit Julian Alcorso's vineyard and try some of his excellent wine. I spent a happy day there during the vintage, and I include this recipe to celebrate the fine fish, fruit, wine and cream of Tasmania.

SERVES 4

100 g (4 oz) seedless white grapes, halved if large
1 tablespoon brandy or Calvados
8 × 100–125g (4–5 oz) lemon sole fillets, skinned
50 g (2 oz) butter
6 shallots or 1 large Spanish onion, finely chopped
300 ml (10 fl oz) fish stock, see page 126, or water
1 bay leaf
1 bouquet garni
4 tablespoons Australian dry white wine
1 tablespoon cornflour mixed with a little water
4 tablespoons double cream
salt
ground white pepper

Put the grapes into a bowl with the brandy or Calvados, stir through and leave to soak for 20 minutes or so.

Rinse the sole fillets and pat dry with kitchen paper, then roll them up from the tail end and secure with cocktail sticks. Pop them into a buttered ovenproof dish.

Melt the butter in a small, heavy-based pan and fry the shallots or onion for about 3–4 minutes, until transparent. Reserve 2 tablespoons onion and set to one side, then add the fish stock or water, bay leaf and bouquet garni to the pan. Bring to the boil, then carefully pour over the rolled fish fillets. Cover and bake in a preheated oven, 180°C/350°F (gas mark 4), until tender.

When the fish is cooked, strain off the liquid and pour 150 ml (5 fl oz) into the small pan, adding the reserved onion. Discard any remaining liquid. Add the wine to the pan and heat gently until simmering. Thicken the liquid with the blended cornflour and cook for 1 minute more. Remove from the heat, then stir in the grapes and cream. Reheat very gently, but do not allow to boil. Taste and adjust the seasoning, then pour the sauce over the fish. Delicious served with creamed potatoes and lightly cooked broccoli.

PS Avoid the possibility of death by cocktail stick – remove before serving!

Whole Baked Snapper with Pine Nut Stuffing

Photograph on page 179

. . . .

As you know, Australians are obsessed with barbecuing and this recipe can be as happily prepared wrapped in foil on the barbecue or baked in the oven. You could use red mullet or gurnard or any firm-fleshed fish.

SERVES 4

2 red snapper, weighing about 450 g
(1 lb) each, cleaned and scaled – smile
at your fishmonger
olive oil
½ red onion, sliced into rings

FOR THE STUFFING:

6 tablespoons long-grain rice, cooked
a few oysters, fresh preferably, but
bottled will do
3 tablespoons pine nuts
1 tablespoon raisins or sultanas
grated zest of ½ lemon or 1 lime
1 teaspoon fresh marjoram, chopped
salt
freshly ground black pepper

Wash the fish well and pat dry. With a sharp knife, make diagonal slashes across the back of each fish. Brush a large baking dish with olive oil, pop in the fish and olive-oil them liberally.

Mix together all the ingredients for the stuffing and whack this mixture into the cavity of each fish, securing with cocktail sticks. Arrange a few red onion rings on top of each fish. Cover the dish with a lid or sheet of foil and bake in a preheated oven, 180°C/350°F (gas mark 4), for about 20 minutes, until the fish are cooked and tender. (The flesh should be firm yet moist, and it should flake easily.) Serve with buttered new potatoes and fresh vegetables.

Next page, ▷
clockwise from top:
Warm Minced
Chicken Salad
with Fresh Herbs
(page 183);
Pork Noodle Soup
(page 138);
Roast Red Pork
(page 217)

Grilled Snapper

. . . .

This is a good, spicy dish, ideal for summer lunches or even dinner parties. It is inspired by a dish I had at the brilliant Last Aussie Fish Caf in Sydney.

If you can't find or don't like snapper, you could use whole little bream or red mullet or, in fact, virtually any fish that you liked.

SERVES 2

1 red snapper, weighing 350–400 g
(12–14 oz)
seasoned flour
25 g (1 oz) ghee, see page 236
½ lemon
3 tablespoons sesame oil
6 tablespoons peanut oil

2 leeks
1 red pepper, seeded
50 g (2 oz) fresh root ginger
1 bunch of spring onions, trimmed
2 small green chilli peppers, seeded
(optional)
light soy sauce
sesame seeds, toasted

} *cut into julienne strips*

Scale, clean and gut the fish thoroughly. Remove the fins, but keep on the head and tail. With a sharp knife slash the fish diagonally about three times on each side, then roll in the seasoned flour. Heat the ghee in a large frying pan and cook the fish for 2–3 minutes on each side, depending on its size, or until brown. Now squeeze the lemon over the top of the fish and pop under a preheated hot grill for 2–3 minutes. While the fish is sizzling away, heat the sesame and peanut oils in a small pan until starting to smoke.

Put the cooked fish on a warmed serving plate and arrange the julienne on top lengthways. Sprinkle with a few drops of light soy sauce and spoon the hot oil over the top so as to create a crackling sensation. Scatter over some sesame seeds.

Queensland Barramundi

. . . .

Barramundi is highly esteemed, particularly in Queensland and the Northern Territory, as a fine fighting fish for sport anglers as well as a delicately-flavoured fish for the table. The nearest UK equivalent would be bass.

Serve this dish with lightly seasoned, buttered and steamed vegetables such as mangetout, asparagus, baby corn or broccoli.

SERVES 4

4 barramundi fillets – or other white fish, for example, sea bass or red mullet	*½ red or Spanish onion, finely chopped*
	4 saffron strands
4 tablespoons good quality dry white wine	*225–275 g (8–10 oz) unsalted butter, slightly softened*
8 tablespoons freshly-squeezed lime juice	*chopped fresh chives*
4 tablespoons double cream	*salt*

Wash the fillets and pat dry with kitchen paper. Flash-fry the fillets for about 30 seconds on each side to seal them, then put into a buttered ovenproof dish. Bake in a preheated oven, 180°C/350°F (gas mark 4), for 10–15 minutes, until the fish is cooked.

While the fish is cooking, make the sauce. Put the wine, lime juice, cream, onion and saffron strands in a small pan and bubble away until the sauce is reduced by about one-third. Remove from the heat and strain through a fine sieve, discarding the onions. While the sauce is still warm, gradually beat in the butter. Add the chives and salt to taste. Serve the fish with the sauce poured round, scattered with more chopped chives and accompanied by plenty of steamed vegetables.

I travelled about 18,000 miles in Australia but I did not catch this delicious, elusive fish!!

King Prawn and Barramundi Luxor

. . . .

This dish, a cross between a soup and a salad, served in a generous bowl, sums up the fun of Vietnamese cooking. And the delightful mixture of fresh fish, a spicy sauce and herbs is outstanding. It is a sort of Asian *bouillabaisse*, but lighter and, in fact, even more tasty.

SERVES 6 – 8

225 g (8 oz) barramundi fillets (failing that, use any firm white fish such as sea bream or sea bass)
100 g (4 oz) uncooked (green) prawns
1.5 litres (2½ pints) fish Thai soup stock, see page 127
3 tablespoons fish sauce, see page 235
2 green chilli peppers, stemmed and finely chopped
4 shallots, finely chopped
1 blade of lemon grass, finely chopped
150 ml (5 fl oz) evaporated milk
100 g (4 oz) creamed coconut, chopped

1 tablespoon red curry paste, see page 237
50 g (2 oz) thread noodles or vermicelli
1 lettuce heart, finely shredded
2 tablespoons vegetable oil
2 shallots, finely sliced
2 cloves of garlic, finely sliced
salt
freshly ground black pepper
1 handful of beansprouts
fresh coriander and mint leaves
coriander vinegar (optional)

Rinse the barramundi, bream or bass and pat it dry with kitchen paper. Now slice it into thin slivers. Shell the prawns, keeping their tails intact, then remove the vein that runs along the back.

Heat the fish stock with the fish sauce, chilli peppers, the first lot of shallots and lemon grass. When it is simmering, add the evaporated milk, creamed coconut and curry paste. Heat gently until simmering again, then throw in the slivers of fish and cook for a couple of minutes. Add the prawns and noodles and cook for 2–3 more minutes. Avoid overcooking or the fish will fall apart.

Meanwhile, put the shredded lettuce into serving bowls. Then heat the vegetable oil in a small frying pan and fry the second lot of shallots and garlic until crisp and golden – about 3–4 minutes. Check the seasoning of the soup, adding salt and pepper to taste, then ladle it into the bowls. Now chuck a few beansprouts on each and top with the fried shallots and garlic, adding a few coriander and mint leaves for good measure. If you like, add a dash of spicy coriander vinegar to each bowl.

Whole Fried Fish with Ginger and Spring Onions

· · · · · · · · · · · · · · · · · · · ·

Score the whole fish first to prevent it from bursting and to enable the flesh to absorb easily the flavours of the seasoning and sauce.

SERVES 4

750 g (1½ lb) fish (for example, bream, sea trout, red snapper), cleaned and scaled
1 teaspoon salt
2 tablespoons plain flour
3 tablespoons vegetable oil
3–4 spring onions, trimmed and cut into 2.5 cm (1 inch) lengths
2.5 cm (1 inch) piece of fresh root ginger, shredded
fresh coriander leaves or parsley, to garnish

FOR THE SAUCE:

2 tablespoons soy sauce
2 tablespoons dry sherry or white wine
150 ml (¼ pint) chicken stock, see page 125, or cold water
1 teaspoon cornflour
freshly ground black pepper

With a sharp knife, slash the fish diagonally 2 or 3 times on each side, sprinkle with salt and roll in the flour to coat. Heat the oil in a large frying pan or wok until almost smoking, then add the fish. Reduce the heat a little and fry the fish for about 2–3 minutes on each side, until it is crisp and golden on the outside and the flesh is deliciously moist but firm. Carefully lift out the fish from the pan.

Quickly mix together the sauce ingredients. Add the spring onions and ginger to the oil remaining in the pan and stir-fry for about 30 seconds. Stir in the sauce and return the fish to the pan. Bubble away for a couple of minutes, then lift the fish on to a warmed serving plate. Pour over the sauce and garnish with coriander or parsley. Serve with rice or noodles.

Another Recipe for Whole Fish with Ginger

. . . .

Serve this with plain, steamed rice – the ginger sauce is exotic enough on its own. The Thais and Vietnamese, unless making a specific rice dish, always eat plain, steamed rice as it has to accompany several dishes at once.

I'm often asked how long it takes to cook the fish. Apart from the obvious like it depends how large your fish is and how hot your fire is, a general rule when barbecuing or grilling is that the fish is cooked when the skin starts to blister.

SERVES 4

750 g (1½ lb) whole fish, for example,
    red snapper or bream, cleaned and
    scaled
1 tablespoon vegetable oil
1 clove of garlic, finely chopped
4 spring onions, trimmed and cut into
    2.5 cm (1 inch) pieces
2.5 cm (1 inch) piece of fresh root ginger,
    finely chopped
1½ tablespoons caster sugar
1 tablespoon ground turmeric
250 ml (9 fl oz) chicken stock, see page
    125, or cold water

1 tablespoon tamarind water, see page
    237
½ teaspoon white pepper
1 tablespoon fish sauce, see page 235
1 tablespoon cornflour mixed to a thin
    paste with cold water
25 g (1 oz) red or green pepper, cut into
    fine strips
50 g (2 oz) onion, finely sliced
few sprigs of fresh coriander, to garnish

Wash the fish and pat dry, then with a sharp knife slash the flesh diagonally a couple of times on each side. Cook it by barbecuing, grilling, frying or steaming, until the flesh is moist and tender, about 8–10 minutes.

Heat the oil in a frying pan or wok and fry the garlic, spring onions, ginger and sugar over a medium heat for 3–4 minutes. Stir in the turmeric, stock or water, tamarind water, pepper and fish sauce, then remove from the heat and add the cornflour paste. Return to the heat and stir until the sauce is smooth and thickened. Add the red or green pepper and onion and cook for a couple more minutes. Put the fish on to a warmed serving plate, pour over the sauce and garnish with coriander. Serve immediately.

Bream Sweet and Sour

. . . .

The bream is a popular fish in Oz — but this recipe can be applied to virtually any fish you choose.

SERVES 4

1 kg (2 lb) bream, cleaned and scaled (or
   use other firm-fleshed fish such as red
   snapper or sea trout)
1/4 teaspoon salt
3 tablespoons vegetable oil
1 large carrot, cut into matchsticks
1 red pepper, cut into matchsticks
1 onion, finely sliced
1 small leek, finely sliced
2.5 cm (1 inch) piece of fresh root ginger,
   coarsely grated
3 shallots or spring onions, finely sliced

3 tomatoes, skinned and chopped
2 cloves of garlic, crushed
1 tablespoon brown sugar
2 tablespoons soy sauce
1 tablespoon oyster sauce
2 tablespoons rice wine vinegar (or use
   cider vinegar)
1 tablespoon rice flour (or cornflour)
   mixed with a little water
salt
freshly ground black pepper

With a sharp knife slash the fish diagonally across one side and rub in the salt. Brush the fish all over with a little of the oil and barbecue or grill for 8–10 minutes, turning once, until the flesh is firm but moist.

Heat the remaining oil in a large frying pan or wok and stir-fry the carrot, pepper, onion and leek for 30 seconds. Add the ginger, shallots or spring onions, tomatoes and garlic and stir-fry for 30 seconds more. Tip in the sugar, soy and oyster sauces and vinegar and stir until the sugar has dissolved. Add the blended rice flour or cornflour, bring to the boil and bubble until the sauce has thickened. Season with a little salt and black pepper. Serve the cooked fish on a warmed serving plate with the sauce poured over, with lots of Coconut Rice, see page 222.

Thai Fish Cakes from Oscar's, Port Douglas in Queensland

· · · · · · · · · · · · · · · · · · · ·

This was one of the most stunningly fresh-flavoured, exciting dishes that I had on my whole trip.

SERVES 4

450 g (1 lb) white fish fillets, skinned, boned and cut into chunks – or try mackerel instead
1 blade of lemon grass, bruised and roughly chopped
1 clove of garlic, roughly chopped
1 cm (½ inch) piece of fresh root ginger, roughly chopped
1 red chilli pepper, seeded and chopped
1 tablespoon fresh coriander leaves, chopped
1 teaspoon red curry paste, see page 237

2 tablespoons thick coconut milk, see page 234
1 tablespoon fish sauce, see page 235
2 lime leaves, see page 236, roughly chopped – if possible
freshly ground black pepper
1 red pepper, seeded and finely chopped
vegetable oil, for shallow-frying
white wine vinegar
100 g (4 oz) dwarf green beans, chopped
chopped fresh coriander leaves, to garnish

Whack everything, apart from the red pepper, vinegar and green beans into a food processor or blender and switch on for about 15 seconds or so, to make sure that you have a well-blended, spicy fish mush. Tip it out into a large bowl and mix in the red pepper. Form into fish cakes (you may have to flour your hands to do this).

Heat up some vegetable oil in a frying pan to a depth of about ½ cm (¼ inch) and fry the fish cakes lightly for about 3 minutes on each side, until they are golden-brown, cooked and delicious. Lift out and keep warm. Then into the oil in which you have fried the fish should go a dash of white wine vinegar and the green beans. Fry that up very quickly, pour back over the fish cakes and strew with lots of chopped coriander.

In the States they serve this with →
"DIRTY RICE" – in fact, it's not dirty it's just rice with the husk still on. (Available from good food shops.)

Paul Prudhomme's Blackened Redfish

. . . .

Although this recipe appeared in *Floyd's American Pie*, it is so brilliant that I am including it here too. When we were in Hobart, my director, David Pritchard, was served a local fish, called a Trevally, which is rather like bream, cooked in this deliciously blackened way.

SERVES 6

350 g (12 oz) unsalted butter, melted
6 × 225–275 g (8–10 oz) fish fillets,
  preferably snapper or bream, cut
  about 1 cm (½ inch) thick

FOR THE SEASONING MIX:

1 tablespoon paprika
2½ tablespoons salt
1 teaspoon onion powder
1 teaspoon garlic powder
1 teaspoon cayenne pepper
¾ teaspoon white pepper
¾ teaspoon freshly ground black pepper
½ teaspoon dried thyme
½ teaspoon dried oregano

Heat a large, heavy, cast-iron frying pan over a very high heat for at least 10 minutes, or until it is beyond the smoking stage and you can see white ash in the bottom – the pan cannot be too hot for this dish.

While the pan is heating, pour 2 tablespoons of the melted butter into each of 6 small ramekins. Put to one side and keep warm. Put all the ingredients for the seasoning mix into a small bowl and mix together well.

Dip each fish fillet into the remaining melted butter, coating both sides well. Sprinkle the seasoning mix generously over both sides of the fillets, patting it in with your hands.

Cram as many fillets into the heated frying pan as will fit comfortably in one layer and pour 1 teaspoon melted butter on top of each one – but be careful when you do this as the butter may flame up. Cook, uncovered, over a high heat for 2 minutes or so, or until the underside of the fish looks charred. The time will, of course, vary depending on the fillets' thickness and the heat of the pan. Turn over the fish and again pour 1 teaspoon melted butter on top. Cook for about 2 minutes more, or until the fish is done. Repeat with the remaining fillets.

Serve each fillet while piping hot. Put one fillet and a ramekin of butter on to warmed plates. Accompany with some boiled rice.

Spanish Mackerel Oriental

Photograph on pages 154–5

I went deep-sea fishing in a motor boat in the Indian Ocean off Broome in Western Australia and caught a huge fish weighing fifty pounds that was called Spanish mackerel. So I decided to cook it. It is, in fact, a very, very big mackerel and the flesh tastes like the mighty tuna.

So you could indeed use for this dish some firm mackerel or tuna fillets or even monkfish.

SERVES 4

4 × 225 g (8 oz) mackerel or tuna fillets, or use 4 medium fish, cleaned and scaled
4 tablespoons sesame oil
225 g (8 oz) Chinese dried egg noodles, soaked in warm water for 5 minutes, then drained
75 g (3 oz) oyster mushrooms
50 g (2 oz) canned straw mushrooms, see page 236, drained
25 g (1 oz) dried black Chinese mushrooms, soaked for 20 minutes, stalks discarded, then chopped

50 g (2 oz) pak choy (Chinese cabbage) or Chinese leaves, shredded
100 g (4 oz) fresh beancurd, cut into cubes
1 cm (1/2 inch) piece of fresh root ginger, grated
1 clove of garlic, crushed
salt
freshly ground black pepper
2 tablespoons black bean sauce, see page 234
drop of beer – 2 or 3 tablespoons

Rinse the fish well and pat dry with kitchen paper. If using whole fish, slash them diagonally on each side. Brush the fish with a little sesame oil and grill for 2–3 minutes on each side, until cooked.

Heat 2 tablespoons of the oil in a large frying pan or wok and gently fry the well-drained noodles. In a separate frying pan, heat the remaining oil and fry the three types of mushroom for a few seconds, then stir in the *pak choy* or Chinese leaves and stir-fry for 1 minute. Add the beancurd, half the ginger and half the garlic to the noodles and stir gently to avoid breaking up the beancurd. Season with salt and black pepper and turn out on to warmed serving plates. Top with the stir-fried mushrooms and cabbage, then place the cooked fish on top.

Sprinkle the remaining ginger and garlic over the fish, then spoon over the black bean sauce and the beer. Serve immediately.

PS Beancurd or tofu is made from cooking and curdling soya milk; though beancurd has little taste when uncooked, it soaks up other flavours wonderfully. Buy it from oriental stores or health food shops.

Mackerel with a Mustard Sauce

. . . .

People are a bit snobby about mackerel these days but, quite honestly, a freshly-caught one, swiftly cleaned and cooked, takes a lot of beating. This one is served with a mustard sauce.

SERVES 4

4 mackerel, cleaned and scaled
2 cloves of garlic, crushed
1 tablespoon olive oil
salt

freshly ground black pepper
100 ml (4 fl oz) double cream
50 g (2 oz) butter, cut into small pieces
2 tablespoons wholegrain mustard

With a sharp knife, slash the mackerel on each side, then rub the garlic into the fish. Brush with oil, season with salt and pepper, and wrap each one in foil. Barbecue or grill for about 20 minutes, turning them every 5 minutes or so.

While the fish are cooking, heat the cream in a small pan and add the butter bit by bit, whisking as you do so, which will thicken the cream. Pop in the mustard and season to taste with salt and pepper. Continue cooking and whisking over a low heat for 2–3 minutes more, and serve the fish accompanied by the sauce.

Mixed Grilled Fish

Photograph on page 122

. . . .

SERVES 4

1.4 kg (3 lb) equal-sized fish, for example,
*   red mullet, parrotfish, small soles,*
*   large sardines*
100 ml (4 fl oz) olive oil
juice of 1 lemon

salt
freshly ground black pepper
1 teaspoon mixed dried herbs
lime wedges, to serve

Scale, clean and gut the fish thoroughly – or ask your fishmonger to do this for you. Wash the fish and pat dry. Mix together the oil, lemon juice, salt, pepper and herbs in a bowl (not aluminium). Add the fish and leave to marinate for at least 1 hour, turning them from time to time.

Lift out the fish, reserving the marinade, and pop them under the grill. Cook for about 10–15 minutes, depending on their size, basting them with the remaining marinade and turning them occasionally. Serve with lime wedges – they also look good served on a bed of spring onions.

Next page, ▷
clockwise from top:
Spanish Mackerel
Oriental (page
152); Butter-crust
Trout Tartlets
(page 157);
Floyd's Tasmania
on a Plate (page
159)

F
I
S
H
·
S
H
E
L
L
F
I
S
H

Sea Trout with Champagne Sauce

. . . .

My friend Urs cooked me this exquisite dish when I was staying at the Hyatt in Adelaide, which was the place – you will remember if you have read the first half of this book – where I also had the waiters completely confused by having pie floaters and tomato sauce served up in my presidential suite.

SERVES 4

FOR THE CHAMPAGNE SAUCE:

4 tablespoons fish stock, see page 126
4 tablespoons dry white wine
225 g (8 oz) cold butter, cut into pieces
2 tablespoons double cream
4 tablespoons champagne or sparkling
  wine (Australian, of course)

1 kg (2 lb) salmon trout (sea trout) fillet,
  cut diagonally into 1 cm (½ inch)
  thick escalopes, or use 4 × 175–200 g
  (6–7 oz) fillets
1 tablespoon sunflower oil
225 g (8 oz) beansprouts
grated zest of 1 lime
50 g (2 oz) salmon caviar (optional)

First, make the sauce. Put the fish stock and wine in a pan and simmer together until reduced to 2 tablespoons. Remove from the heat and whisk in the cold butter, a little at a time. Stir in the cream and reheat very gently, preferably over a pan of simmering water. Add the champagne or sparkling wine just before serving.

To cook the fish, heat the oil in a large frying pan. Add the trout escalopes and cook quickly on both sides – about 2 minutes in total. If cooking fillets, allow 5–8 minutes, depending on their thickness. Transfer to a warmed serving dish. Briskly stir-fry the beansprouts for a few seconds and serve with the fish. Pour the sauce round and garnish with lime zest and salmon caviar, if using.

Did you know that some famous French champagne growers own vast tracts of Australian vineyards?

Butter-crust Trout Tartlets

Photograph on pages 154–5

. . . .

If you go to Tasmania you can't escape the similar feel to England's West Country because of its lovely cream, cheese, raspberries and the famous sea trout farming industry. And it is a West Country type of place. So here is an appropriate recipe for you to try out.

MAKES ABOUT 20

10 pieces of thin-cut white sliced bread
75 g (3 oz) butter, melted
350 g (12 oz) smoked trout or mackerel,
  skinned and boned
3 spring onions, trimmed and finely
  chopped
2 tablespoons bought or home-made
  mayonnaise
1 tablespoon natural yoghurt

1 teaspoon bought or home-made
  horseradish sauce
1 teaspoon wholegrain mustard
1 tablespoon fresh parsley, finely
  chopped
freshly ground black pepper
lemon wedges or cucumber, to garnish
  (optional)

Cut the bread into squares, trim off the crusts and go and feed the birds. When you're back, flatten the slices of bread with a rolling pin, then brush the bread squares with melted butter and lightly press into deep tartlet tins. Do not trim. Bake in a preheated oven, 190°C/375°F (gas mark 5), for about 10 minutes, until crisp and golden. Allow to cool.

Put all the remaining ingredients into a food processor or blender and switch on until smooth and well-blended. Tip the mixture out into a bowl, then cover and chill until you are about to fill the cooled bread tartlets. (Don't do this too far in advance of serving, otherwise you'll get soggy bottoms!) Lift out the toasted bread from the tins very carefully and garnish with lemon or cucumber slices, if you like.

Grilled Trout

. . . .

SERVES 4

4 trout
juice of 1 lemon
salt
4 tablespoons mixed chopped fresh fennel
  leaves, parsley, thyme and chervil

1–2 cloves of garlic, finely chopped
100 ml (4 fl oz) olive oil
4 lemon wedges

Scale, clean and gut the fish thoroughly. Remove the fins but keep on the heads and tails. With a sharp knife slash the fish on each side and sprinkle inside and out with some of the lemon juice and salt. Stuff the herbs and some of the garlic into the fish.

Mix together the remaining garlic, lemon juice and oil. Grill or barbecue the fish for at least 5 minutes on each side until tender, basting with the garlic, lemon and oil mixture. Serve with a wedge of lemon.

Monkfish and Bacon Brochettes

. . . .

SERVES 4

24 thin rashers of unsmoked bacon, rind
  removed
450 g (1 lb) monkfish, cut into 24 chunks
2 teaspoons fresh marjoram, chopped

freshly ground black pepper
50 g (2 oz) butter
juice of 1 lemon

Roll up the bacon rashers and thread on to 8 skewers, alternating each bacon roll with a piece of fish. Sprinkle with marjoram and pepper.

Put a drip tray to catch the juices under a preheated hot grill and grill the brochettes for about 6–8 minutes, turning frequently, until the bacon is crisp and the monkfish is cooked.

Drain off the juices from the drip tray and whisk them together with the butter and lemon juice. Pour over the brochettes and serve with rice.

Floyd's Tasmania on a Plate

Photograph on pages 154–5

. . . .

Here's a little one that I knocked up with the tuna I caught, and cooked at Mures Restaurant in Hobart.

THIS RECIPE FEEDS 4 PEOPLE

take one 60 lb tuna caught early that morning at the Hippolyte Rocks. Fillet out one 150 g (6 oz) steak for each person, about 1 cm (½ inch) thick
olive oil

FOR THE ANCHOVY BUTTER:

100 g (4 oz) butter, softened
6 anchovy fillets
squeeze of lemon juice
1 teaspoon fresh dill, finely chopped
freshly ground black pepper

FOR THE TOMATO CONCASSE:

4 ripe tomatoes, skinned and finely chopped
1 small onion, finely chopped
½ red pepper, seeded and finely chopped
1 clove of garlic, crushed
1 tablespoon olive oil
freshly ground black pepper

Rinse the tuna steaks really well to remove any traces of blood. Drain on kitchen paper.

Beat together all the ingredients for the anchovy butter until smooth and well blended, or whizz in a blender. Form into a roll on a piece of greaseproof paper or foil and chill until firm, about 15 minutes.

Make the tomato concasse by cooking together the tomatoes, onion, red pepper, garlic and olive oil in a pan over a gentle heat for 20 minutes. Season to taste with black pepper and keep warm.

To cook the fish, brush a large, heavy-based frying pan with olive oil, heat for a moment until really hot, then seal the tuna steaks on each side over a high heat. Cook for about 2 minutes on each side, reducing the heat. Be careful not to overcook the fish – they should be cooked as medium-rare steaks, but sauté for longer if you really do prefer them cooked through.

Put a good spoonful of the hot tomato concasse on to warmed serving plates. Lay the tuna on top and then put a good dollop of anchovy butter on to each fillet. Serve immediately with steaming saffron rice.

Alligator Camp Pickled Fish

. . . .

While I was fishing for the elusive barramundi on the Drysdale River I managed to catch a barracuda and Craig, our pilot, suggested this delightful snack made from some thin slices of raw barracuda. But you could use monkfish, you could use tuna, you could use any damned thing for this dish.

All you have to do is find a clean glass jar or jam jar with a screw top and chuck in a handful of thinly sliced, skinned and boned white fish. Just add onion, garlic, red chillies – all chopped and fresh, of course. Then another layer of fish and so on until the jar is full. Next, you put a generous teaspoonful of salt into it, a good few dashes of soy sauce and, finally, you fill up the bottle with vinegar – white wine vinegar is best.

Put the bottle or whatever the receptacle is in the fridge for about two hours, then strain off the liquid, tip the lot on to a plate and eat the little bits of fish while you have your evening apéritif.

Darne of Blue Fin Tuna with Lemon Butter Sauce

. . . .

This is one of those absolutely perfect recipes created by an expert, my chum Urs, who is head chef at the Hyatt Regency in Adelaide. This will really please the editor of this book because the ingredients are very precisely listed and correctly proportioned. It even tells you how many it will serve.

SERVES 4

1 lemon
1 shallot, finely chopped
2 teaspoons double cream
175 g (7 oz) butter, chilled and cut into pieces
sea salt
freshly ground black pepper
1 tablespoon sunflower oil

100 g (4 oz) beansprouts, washed
2 teaspoons olive oil
2 teaspoons butter
450 g (1 lb) Blue Fin tuna fillet, cut into 4 pieces or 4 fresh tuna steaks
grated zest and juice of 1 lime

Pare the zest from the lemon, cut into fine strips and put to one side. Squeeze the juice from the lemon and cook the shallot in this until all the liquid has evaporated. Add the cream and whisk in the butter. Season with sea salt and black pepper, adding the reserved lemon zest just before serving. Set to one side and keep warm.

Heat the sunflower oil in a frying pan and briskly stir-fry the bean-sprouts for a few seconds. Season with sea salt and place on a warmed serving plate. Keep warm.

To cook the fish, heat together the olive oil and butter and sear the tuna quickly on both sides for about 4–5 minutes, until cooked. Season with lime zest, juice and sea salt. Transfer to the serving dish and pour over the sauce. Serve immediately.

Scallops and Tuna with Red Butter

· ·

When I climbed on to *The Ghan* for my famous journey to Alice Springs, I was delighted to find a superb private kitchen attached to my Prince of Wales coach. I thought it would be fun to do some cooking so, of course, I made the couscous, see page 72, for the train drivers, but then I also had to cook for my chums. And I wanted to do something simple, so I decided to make some red butter. I then had to think of something, anything, to go with the red butter. So the main part of this recipe is, appropriately, for red butter.

SERVES 4

FOR THE RED BUTTER:

2 red peppers, halved and seeded	6 capers
salt	3 tablespoons white wine vinegar
freshly ground black pepper	175 g (6 oz) butter, softened
3 shallots, finely chopped	

Put the peppers on to a baking sheet, skin-side uppermost, and roast them in a preheated oven, 190°C/375°F (gas mark 5), for 5–6 minutes. When the peppers have cooled a little, peel off any blackened or blistered skin, then chop them finely. Pop them in a pan with a little salt and some pepper and all of the other ingredients except the butter. Heat and bubble gently for 4 or 5 minutes, until the vinegar has disappeared. Transfer to your favourite food processor, blender or Magimix and whizz together for a few seconds.

Allow to cool completely, then beat into the softened butter until well amalgamated. Form into a roll, wrap in the paper from whence you took the butter or in some foil and chill until firm. You can store it in your refrigerator and cut into roundels as and when you need it. This red butter can be melted over grilled chicken or fish, over absolutely anything you like.

The dishes that I chose to go with the red butter were some firm scallops and little steaks or fillets of fresh tuna too:

2 tablespoons vegetable oil
4 × 175 g (6 oz) tuna steaks or fillets,
 well rinsed
4–6 scallops, shells and crescent-like
 muscles removed, and cleaned

juice of 1 lime
large knob of butter
lemon wedges and fresh coriander
 leaves, to serve

Heat the oil in a large frying pan and brown the tuna on both sides for about 2 minutes. Reduce the heat and cook the fish gently for 8 minutes or so, turning once, until it flakes easily. Meanwhile, marinate the scallops in the lime juice for a few minutes and then sear on both sides in a little butter in a hot frying pan – about 3 minutes. Served with wedges of lemon, the red butter melted over the steaks, and strewn with coriander, this is a delightful dish.

Tuna Steaks with Anchovy and Fennel Butter

. . . .

This is exactly the same sort of thing as the preceding recipe, only a bit quicker as you whack all the butter ingredients into your Magimix straightaway. For a dry fish like tuna, it is nice to have a little tomato sauce with it as well, so first make the recipe on page 128.

SERVES 4

4 × 150–175 g (6–7 oz) tuna steaks
150 g (6 oz) butter, softened
3 anchovy fillets (sold canned or bottled,
 in oil), drained

2 teaspoons fennel seeds or a small
 handful of fresh fennel fronds
freshly ground black pepper
2 tablespoons vegetable oil

Wash the tuna steaks well, and pat dry with kitchen paper. Make the flavoured butter by beating together the butter, anchovy fillets and fennel seeds or fronds with a little black pepper or whizz in a food processor or blender. Form the butter into a roll on a piece of greaseproof paper and refrigerate until firm – about 15 minutes.

Heat the oil in a large frying pan and brown the tuna steaks on both sides for about 2 minutes. Reduce the heat and cook the fish gently for 8 minutes or so, turning once, until it flakes easily.

To serve, pour little lakes of tomato sauce on to your white plates and pop the tuna steaks on top with a roundel of anchovy butter melted over each one.

Seafood Chowder

. . . .

This is the delicious little recipe I made standing waist-deep (well, almost) in water at Watsons Bay, outside Doyle's Restaurant, in Sydney. Serve it on its own.

SERVES 8

50 g (2 oz) butter
2 onions, finely chopped
2 large carrots, finely diced
2 sticks of celery, finely chopped
salt
freshly ground black pepper
2 × 400 g (14 oz) cans tomatoes, and their juice
2 tablespoons tomato purée
2.5 litres (4 pints) hot fish stock, see page 126
2 bay leaves
dash of Tabasco sauce
3 tablespoons dry white wine

1.5–2 kg (3¹/₂–4 lb) mixture of seafood, to include any of the following:
lobster tails
few bits of squid – 'hoods' or tentacles, chopped, see page 176
mussels, scrubbed
fillets of red snapper or any white, firm-fleshed fish
some cubes of tuna
prawns, peeled and back vein removed
crab, cleaned and chopped into, say, 8 pieces, depending on size
scallops, shells and crescent-shaped muscles removed
crayfish, gutted, washed and central tail piece removed, then cut in half

Melt the butter in a very large deep pan and fry together the onions, carrots and celery, seasoned with a bit of salt and pepper, for about 2–3 minutes, or until they start to go golden-brown. Add the tomatoes and their juice, tomato purée, hot fish stock and bay leaves. Bring to the boil. The liquid should have a wonderful orangey hue; it shouldn't be as thick as custard, but not thin. Tip in the Tabasco sauce, wine and all the seafood. Stir and allow to simmer gently for 20 minutes. Fish out and discard the bay leaves before serving.

Yabbies – Freshwater Crayfish

. . . .

Every Australian's first fishing experience is to tie little bits of meat on to a string on the end of a stick and chuck it into the local pond to catch these delicious little yabbies – which in England we call freshwater crayfish or in France they call *écrevisses*.

SERVES 4

3 tablespoons olive oil
1 kg (2¼ lb) yabbies (freshwater
    crayfish) – about 24–32
1 blade of lemon grass, bruised and
    chopped
2.5 cm (1 inch) piece of fresh root ginger,
    chopped
6 shallots, finely chopped
2 cloves of garlic, finely chopped

2 medium red chilli peppers, seeded and
    thinly sliced
dollop of brandy (about 2 tablespoons)
1 wineglass of dry white wine
300 ml (10 fl oz) fresh tomato sauce, see
    page 128
salt
freshly ground black pepper

Heat the oil in a large frying pan or wok. Add the yabbies and let them sizzle for 3–4 minutes. Add the lemon grass, ginger, shallots, garlic and chillies and cook for 2 minutes, then pour in the brandy and white wine. Bring to the boil and bubble for a few seconds. Add the fresh tomato sauce, return to the boil, then reduce the heat and simmer for 10 minutes. Season to taste with salt and black pepper. Serve immediately.

P.S. The Americans call them crawfish a mud bng!

Crawfish Baked in a Salt Crust

. . . .

Most of the dishes we had in Tasmania were pretty alfresco affairs, uncomplicated and delicious. But I thought it would be a good idea to include a rather sophisticated dish cooked by a pal of mine, John T. Bailey, who is Head Chef at the Sheraton in Hobart.

SERVES 2

2 × 450 g (1 lb) crawfish (otherwise
   known as spiny lobster and,
   confusingly, crayfish, but these are not
   the same as the delicate freshwater
   crayfish)
1 kg (2¼ lb) rock salt
1 clove of garlic, crushed
1 cm (½ inch) piece of fresh root ginger,
   finely grated

few sprigs of fresh herbs (for example,
   oregano, basil, marjoram, parsley or
   thyme), chopped
4–5 tablespoons light soy sauce
egg noodles, cooked
selection of fresh vegetables, cut into
   julienne strips (for example, carrots,
   peppers, leeks, courgettes, parsnips)

First, kill your crawfish. Better still, get someone to do it for you. The most humane way to do it yourself is to boil up about 4 litres (8 pints) water. Keep it boiling fiercely and plunge in the crawfish, one at a time, for about 20 seconds.

Transfer the crawfish to a large roasting pan and cover completely with rock salt. Bake in a preheated oven, 200°C/400°F (gas mark 6), for 25 minutes, until cooked. Allow to cool for a few minutes, then remove the meat from the shell, cutting the tail meat into thin slices. Mix together the garlic, ginger, chopped fresh herbs and soy sauce, stirring well.

Put the cooked egg noodles on to a warmed serving plate and arrange the crawfish alongside. Blanch the vegetables in boiling water for a few seconds and serve with the noodles. Pour the soy sauce dressing over the crawfish and serve immediately.

Stir-fried Seafood with Oregano

· ·

SERVES 4 FISH LOVERS

700 g (1½ lb) mixed seafood (for
  example, cod, sea trout, squid,
  prawns, scallops, mussels, crab). The
  wider the selection, the better the dish
2 cloves of garlic, crushed
2 large green chilli peppers, seeded and
  chopped
1 tablespoon coriander root, chopped,
  see page 235

3 tablespoons vegetable oil
2 tablespoons oyster sauce
3 tablespoons fish sauce, see page 235
½ red and ½ yellow pepper, seeded and
  finely chopped
4–5 spring onions, trimmed and chopped
handful of fresh oregano, basil or mint,
  chopped
freshly ground black pepper

Persuade your fishmonger to clean and prepare the seafood for you. Cut any fish fillets into 5 cm (2 inch) pieces. Cut the squid into rings and chop the tentacles. Break up the crab into 8 pieces. Rinse all the seafood and put to one side.

Whizz together the garlic, chillies and coriander root in a food processor or blender to make a rough paste, or use a mortar and pestle and pound them instead.

Heat the oil in a large frying pan or wok and fry the blended paste for a minute or so. Tip in the seafood and stir-fry carefully for 2 minutes to avoid breaking up the fish. Add the oyster and fish sauces, then cover and simmer for 3–4 minutes. Add the pepper and spring onions and cook, stirring gently, for 2–3 minutes, then stir through the fresh herbs. Season to taste with black pepper.

Arrange in a large shallow bowl, garnish with more fresh herbs and serve with lots of plain, boiled rice – sprinkle a few herbs on this too.

· ·

Stir-frying
Stir-frying, as everybody knows, really is a quick way of cooking and there are a couple of simple rules. Your wok or your frying pan must be very hot and the ingredients that you are going to cook in it need to be cut into small pieces so that they can benefit from their quick cooking.

· ·

Stir-fried Seafood with Oregano

Marrons or Crayfish and Citrus Sauce

. . . .

Marrons are a freshwater crustacean that are unique, I believe, to Western Australia. They resemble the English freshwater crayfish, but differ in that they grow much larger – maybe up to eight inches long – and weigh well over half a pound. They have a sweet, lobster-like flesh so this little recipe can therefore be adapted to use any shellfish that you like.

SERVES 4

3 litres (5 pints) cold water
2 tablespoons salt
1 kg (2–2¼ lb) live marrons or crayfish
(this allows about 1–2 marrons or 6–8
crayfish per person)
the juice of:
1 lime
1 lemon
2 mandarin oranges or clementines
6–8 kumquats
1 grapefruit

150 g (6 oz) butter, chilled and cut into
small pieces
mandarin segments or thinly-sliced
kumquats

Bring the water and salt to the boil in a large pan, plunge in the marrons or crayfish and bring back to the boil. Bubble for 4 minutes for small beasts and for 8 minutes for large, then remove them and drain well.

While the marrons or crayfish are cooking, make the sauce by gently heating the fruit juices. Simmer until the liquid has reduced by about one-third, then whisk in the butter, a little at a time until you have a glossy, thickened sauce. Stir in the mandarin segments or sliced kumquats and serve with the cooked shellfish.

Serve with simple rice a a crunchy green salad.

Mussel Kebabs

. . . .

If you get bored with eating mussels cooked with shallots, garlic and white wine, here's a pleasant alternative.

SERVES 4

48 mussels, in their shells
150 ml (5 fl oz) Australian dry white
   wine
1 small onion, finely chopped
1 teaspoon fresh thyme, chopped
1 tablespoon fresh parsley, chopped
1 bay leaf
salt

freshly ground black pepper
8 rashers of bacon, rinds removed and
   cut into thirds
100 g (4 oz) plain flour
2 eggs, beaten
fresh white breadcrumbs
vegetable oil, for deep-frying

Scrape the mussels thoroughly, removing their beards, then wash them in several changes of water. Discard any with broken shells or those that do not shut when tapped. Put the mussels into a pan with the wine, onion, herbs, salt and pepper. Bring to the boil, reduce the heat and simmer gently for 4–5 minutes, until the shells are open. Remove from the pan and allow to cool, then take the mussels out of their shells.

Thread the mussels on to 8 skewers, 6 on each, interspersed with bacon rolls. Coat each kebab in seasoned flour, dip in beaten egg and roll in breadcrumbs. Heat the oil in a deep-fat fryer (pop in a cube of bread to test the temperature – it should turn golden in 1 minute) and fry the kebabs for 3–5 minutes, until golden-brown. Drain on kitchen paper and serve with my brilliant recipe for Hollandaise Sauce, see below.

Hollandaise Sauce – The Quick and Easy Floyd Way

What a fuss some people make about Hollandaise Sauce. Don't panic.

MAKES 450 ML (¾ pint)

700 g (1½ lb) unsalted butter
6 eggs

juice of 1 lemon
freshly ground black pepper

Melt the butter in a pan with a pouring lip. Break the eggs into a food processor, add the lemon juice and pepper and switch on. Pour the hot melted butter in an even stream into the whisking eggs until the sauce has thickened. To keep warm, place over a pan of recently boiled water until ready to serve.

F
I
S
H

.

S
H
E
L
L
F
I
S
H

Butterfly Prawns

. . . .

This delightful dish has its origins in Japanese cooking. And this method of quickly frying delicate pieces of fish or vegetables in a light batter is known as Tempura. It can be quite fiddly to prepare, but it does look extremely attractive (see the photograph opposite). If you want to simplify it slightly, leave out the broccoli.

SERVES 2

4 tablespoons plain flour
½ teaspoon salt
1 egg, beaten
4 tablespoons lager or water
12 uncooked (green) king prawns
12 pieces of bacon – each about 1 × 5 cm
  (½ × 2 inches)

24 small broccoli florets, blanched
2 tablespoons seasoned cornflour
vegetable oil, for deep-frying – you will
  need about 250 ml (9 fl oz)
lemon wedges, to serve
hoisin sauce, to serve

Sift the flour and salt into a bowl, add the egg and lager or water and whisk together to make a batter.

Shell the prawns and cut them through the centre lengthways, being careful to keep the tail intact. Remove the back vein from the prawns (see the note on page 175), then wrap one strip of bacon round the tail end, using a cocktail stick to secure it. Taking two broccoli florets for each 'butterfly', place one on each side of the cocktail stick, then wrap each half of the prawn round the broccoli and fasten on to each end of the stick. Dust the prawns with seasoned cornflour and coat with batter, avoiding the tail.

Heat the oil in a deep-fat fryer or wok (pop in a cube of bread to test the temperature – it should turn golden in 1 minute) and fry the prawns one at a time for about 2–3 minutes, until the tail turns pink. Lift out with a slotted spoon and drain on kitchen paper. Serve immediately with lemon wedges and hoisin sauce.

Above Butterfly
Prawns; **Below**
Chilli-hot Squid
with Vegetables
(page 176)

Prawns and Spinach

. . . .

I absolutely adore Indian food and this is an interesting combination of prawns and spinach that should satisfy those of you who are sick to death of meat, barbecues and heavy, over-cholesterised food. You could equally well use mussels or scallops instead of prawns.

SERVES 4

50 g (2 oz) ghee, see page 236 – ghee
(clarified butter) gives the most
authentic flavour, but if you don't
have the time, or if you're just feeling
lazy, use 2 tablespoons vegetable oil
1 large onion, sliced
2 cloves of garlic, sliced
1 tablespoon tomato purée
½ teaspoon **garam masala,** *see page 129*

1½ teaspoons ground coriander
½ teaspoon ground turmeric
½ teaspoon chilli powder
½ teaspoon ground ginger
1 teaspoon salt
450 g (1 lb) fresh spinach, trimmed
450 g (1 lb) peeled prawns

Heat the ghee or oil in a heavy-based frying pan and fry the onion and garlic gently for about 5 minutes, until soft. Stir in the tomato purée and fry, stirring, for 1 minute. Throw in the spices and salt and fry for 5 more minutes, stirring constantly.

While that's sizzling away, wash the spinach well until no trace of grit remains, then drain it. Pack the spinach into a large pan, add 1 cm (½ inch) cold water, cover and cook for 1–2 minutes over a high heat. Drain and squeeze out the excess moisture, then add to the frying pan with the prawns. Cook for 2 minutes, stirring gently, to heat through. Serve immediately with some chapatis.

The Australians are so lucky to have a large variety of fresh prawns – and they are very cheap.

Prawns Down Under

. . . .

When you are away from the cities it is pretty difficult to get much in the way of ingredients. So whenever I was stuck for a dish to do in a cooking sketch – this I did on a survey vessel off the Great Barrier Reef – I reverted to my trusty wok and a stir-fry dish. It is the sort of thing that is quick and easy to do. It is tasty, tangy and spicy and you can vary the ingredients to suit yourself.

SERVES 4

450 g (1 lb) uncooked (green) prawns
1 tablespoon vegetable oil
1 tablespoon sesame oil
1 clove of garlic, finely chopped
1 cm (½ inch) piece of fresh root ginger,
*   finely chopped*
1 red chilli pepper, seeded and finely
*   chopped*
1 bunch of spring onions, trimmed and
*   sliced*

1 large carrot, cut into matchsticks
2 tablespoons coriander root, see
*   page 235, finely chopped (optional)*
salt
freshly ground black pepper
2 tablespoons black bean sauce, see page
*   234*
fresh coriander leaves or parsley, to
*   garnish*

Shell the prawns, leaving the tails intact, and remove the black intestinal vein that runs down the back. In a large frying pan or wok, heat together the oils and sizzle the prawns for about 30 seconds, stirring constantly. Add the garlic, ginger and chilli and stir-fry for another 30 seconds or so.

Throw in the spring onions and carrot, stir for about 1 minute, then add the chopped coriander root, if using. Season with a little salt and some black pepper and stir through the black bean sauce. Dish out on to warmed serving plates. Drizzle over a little more black bean sauce and garnish with coriander leaves or parsley. You can't beat plain, boiled rice to accompany this.

Doyle's Stuffed Green King Prawns

. . . .

This was one of the best dishes I had in Australia, at Doyle's Restaurant in Sydney. I enjoyed it so much that I now have it on the menu at my pub, The Maltsters Arms.

Here is the recipe that Peter Doyle gave me, and it comes from *Doyle's Fish Cookbook* by Alice Doyle. As is so often the case with my 'recipisms', though, there are no terribly specific quantities.

MAKES ENOUGH FOR ABOUT 4 – 6

24 large uncooked (green) king prawns
beer batter, see page opposite
oil, for frying

FOR THE FILLING:

butter
1 onion, chopped
1 clove of garlic, crushed
6 thick rashers of bacon, rinds removed
 and finely chopped
225 g (8 oz) cooked fresh spinach, well-
 drained and squeezed
1 large egg
fresh parsley

pinch of salt
handful of sultanas, soaked in wine and
 drained
fresh breadcrumbs

FOR THE SAUCE:

1 small jar of good-quality fruit chutney
1 tablespoon curry powder
6 shallots, chopped
1 small jar of ready-made mayonnaise
1 egg white, beaten

Shell the prawns, keeping their tails intact, then remove the back vein. 'Butterfly' them by cutting a channel lengthways down each one to the start of the tail and gently flattening out both sides.

Melt the butter in a pan and lightly fry the onion and the garlic. Mix together the filling ingredients, using enough breadcrumbs to bind. Fill the cut section of the butterfly prawn with the mixture, then press the sides firmly together again and set aside in the refrigerator for a while to firm.

Prepare the sauce by mixing together all the ingredients carefully, adding the egg white last. Serve in one large bowl or in individual dishes.

When you are ready to cook the prawns, dip the stuffed prawns gently in the batter, and fry in your favourite cooking oil (mine is olive oil) in a deep pan for 5 minutes. Remember to have the oil hot, but not at boiling point or the prawns will cook on the outside first. Serve with the delicious fruity curry sauce.

Beer Batter

. . . .

100 g (4 oz) plain flour
1 teaspoon salt

300 ml (10 fl oz) lager
2 egg whites, lightly beaten

Sift the flour into a large bowl and add the salt. Pour in the lager slowly, stirring constantly to make a smooth, thin batter. Finally, whisk in the egg whites. The batter should be quite thin – about the consistency of single cream.

Prawn Stir-Fry

. . . .

You could serve this as a yummy starter or with rice and/or salad as a main course – lunch or dinner.

SERVES 4

450 g (1 lb) large peeled prawns
2 tablespoons sesame oil
1 bunch of spring onions, trimmed and
  chopped
1 small handful of fresh coriander
  leaves, finely chopped
2 cloves of garlic, finely chopped
grated zest and juice of 1 lemon

5 cm (2 inch) piece of fresh root ginger,
  grated
juice of 2 limes
1 tablespoon soy sauce
salt
freshly ground black pepper
fresh coriander leaves, to garnish

Remove the back vein from the prawns by making a shallow incision along the top of each prawn and removing the white or black intestinal vein with the point of a knife.

Heat the oil in a large frying pan or wok and stir-fry the prawns for about 20 seconds, then add the spring onions, coriander, garlic, lemon zest and juice, and ginger. Stir-fry for 2–3 minutes, then squeeze over the lime juice and add the soy sauce. Season to taste with salt and pepper and serve immediately, garnished with the coriander leaves.

Squid, often called calamari or ink-fish, are usually sold whole by weight, though you can sometimes buy squid 'rings' – the sliced body pouch. If your fishmonger isn't too busy, you may be able to charm him or her into doing the messy bits for you.

Right, line up your squid. Cut off their tentacles and set aside – yes, you do eat these. Gently pull their heads off and discard, along with the eyes, innards and ink sac. Take out the quill from inside the body pouch – it looks like a piece of transparent plastic – and wash away all the white fluid. You should now be left with the body pouch or 'hood', which has two triangular fins, and the tentacles. At the base of the tentacles is the 'beak' or mouth – take it out and chuck out.

The hood or pouch can be stuffed or sliced into rings, or it can be cut into squares and scored with a diamond pattern to tenderise it. The tentacles are usually sliced and cooked. Sometimes the ink is reserved from the ink sac and used in recipes.

Chilli-hot Squid with Vegetables   Photograph on page 171

What makes Korean food subtly different is its sweetness, together with its use of boiled grains, chilli-hot sauces, near-raw vegetables and thinly-sliced meat as well as quick cooking. The preparation – that chopping, slicing, marinating – takes much longer. Nothing's wasted, always recycled.

SERVES 4

450 g (1 lb) squid – if your fishmonger is
  friendly, ask him to clean and prepare
  the squid for you, otherwise read the
  notes above
2 tablespoons vegetable oil
1 small green pepper, seeded and finely
  sliced into rings

1 small red pepper, seeded and finely
  sliced into rings
1 onion, finely chopped
2 cloves of garlic, crushed
2 teaspoons caster sugar
salt
freshly ground black pepper

Cut the squid into 2.5 cm (1 inch) pieces, scoring the flesh in a diamond pattern to tenderise it. Heat the oil in a large frying pan or wok and fry together the peppers and onion for 2 minutes. Pop in the squid, garlic and sugar and stir-fry for 2–3 more minutes, stirring constantly. Season and serve immediately with rice.

Squid with Chilli Sauce

. . . .

SERVES 4 GENEROUSLY

1 kg (2 lb) squid – ask your fishmonger to clean and prepare the squid for you, otherwise read the notes opposite
1 tablespoon white wine vinegar
5 cashew nuts, chopped
6 fresh red chilli peppers, seeded and chopped
6 shallots, chopped
2 teaspoons ground ginger
pinch of ground cumin

pinch of ground turmeric
pinch of lemon grass powder, see page 236
2 tablespoons vegetable oil
3 tablespoons tamarind water, see page 237
1 teaspoon brown sugar
salt

Cut the squid hood into small squares and the tentacles into 1 cm (½ inch) lengths. Rinse these in the vinegar, mixed with 600 ml (1 pint) cold water, then drain.

Using a mortar and pestle, pound the cashew nuts, chillies and shallots to a smooth paste, or whizz in a blender. Stir in the spices. Heat the oil in a large frying pan or wok and fry the paste for 1 minute, stirring constantly. Tip in the squid and tamarind water and cook, stirring, for 3–4 minutes. Add the sugar, salt and 150 ml (¼ pint) cold water and simmer for about 5–6 minutes, stirring often. Serve immediately with plain, boiled rice.

Sizzling Scallops

. . . .

SERVES 6

450 g (1 lb) scallops, removed from shells and washed
1 tablespoon light soy sauce
1 tablespoon dry sherry
2 tablespoons vegetable oil
1 large onion, sliced
1 teaspoon chopped fresh root ginger

FOR THE SAUCE:

2 teaspoons red curry paste, see page 237
2 teaspoons hoisin sauce
1 teaspoon sesame oil
½ teaspoon five spice powder
1 teaspoon sugar
3 teaspoons peanut butter
3 tablespoons fish stock, see page 126

Trim away the crescent-shaped muscle from each scallop, then put the scallops in a bowl (not aluminium) and add the soy sauce and sherry.

Leave to marinate for 30 minutes or so, stirring from time to time. Meanwhile, mix together the sauce ingredients.

Heat the oil in a large frying pan or wok and stir-fry the onion for about 1 minute. Tip in the ginger, scallops and marinade and stir-fry for 2–3 minutes. Stir in the sauce mixture and heat until boiling. Serve immediately with some boiled rice.

Red-hot Scallops

· ·

Elsewhere in this remarkable tome I have categorically stated that the crayfish, the saltwater variety that is, is absolutely my favourite shellfish. I have now decided that scallops are my most favouritist crustacean, arthroped, call them what you will, in the entire world. And here is a superb recipe.

SERVES 4

12–16 scallops, depending on size, removed from shells and washed
4 tablespoons red curry paste, see page 237
2 tablespoons vegetable oil
2 cloves of garlic, finely chopped

2 red chilli peppers, seeded and finely sliced
2 tablespoons fish sauce, see page 235
1 tablespoon caster sugar
1 large handful of fresh basil

Discard the crescent-shaped muscle from each scallop, then mix together the scallops and the curry paste in a bowl (not aluminium) and leave to marinate for at least 15 minutes. Heat the oil in a frying pan or wok and stir-fry the garlic until golden. Tip in the scallops with the curry paste and the chillies and stir-fry for 2 minutes. Add the fish sauce and sugar and cook, stirring, for 1 more minute. Taste and adjust seasonings – add more fish sauce, sugar or chilli if necessary.

When the scallops are tender and have just whitened (about 1 minute more – do not overcook scallops or they will be tough), stir in most of the basil, then remove from the heat. Serve on a bed of stir-fried *pak choy*, garnish with the remaining basil and accompany with a bowl of plain, boiled rice.

Above Whole Baked Snapper with Pine Nut Stuffing (page 141);
Below Red-hot Scallops

Abalone Stir-fry

. . . .

Fresh abalones are very difficult to find in the UK, but if you can ever get any this is a dish that will certainly bring the house down – or, in my case, bring the hotel down. Because while we were filming in my hotel room in Tasmania the smoke from the overheated wok set off the fire alarms and my suite was suddenly invaded by the Hobart fire brigade.

SERVES 4

2 tablespoons sesame oil
225 g (8 oz) pak choy (Chinese cabbage), shredded
2 spring onions, chopped
1 cm (½ inch) piece of fresh root ginger, chopped
1 clove of garlic, chopped

325 g (12 oz) fresh abalone, cut into thin slices, see page 234
2 tablespoons black bean sauce, see page 234
1 tablespoon oyster sauce
salt
freshly ground black pepper

Heat a large frying pan or wok and add 1 tablespoon of the oil. Tip in the *pak choy* and spring onions and stir-fry for about 30 seconds. Lift out the vegetables on to a warm plate.

Add the remaining oil to the pan, then whack in the ginger, garlic and abalone. Stir-fry for 2–3 minutes. Add the black bean sauce and stir through, then stir in the *pak choy* and spring onions. Season to taste with the oyster sauce, salt and pepper. Serve immediately on a bed of Chinese noodles.

Crab and Cucumber in Rice Vinegar Dressing

. . . .

A Japanese dish that is ideal for a buffet as it will keep well in the fridge. The scoring of the cucumber is for cosmetic reasons only. Of course, you could use prawns instead of crab.

SERVES 4

1 × 20 cm (8 inch) piece of cucumber
salt
100 g (4 oz) fresh crabmeat, flaked (or use canned)
5 teaspoons rice vinegar – or white wine vinegar will do

3 tablespoons caster sugar
freshly ground black pepper
toasted sesame seeds and pared lemon zest, to garnish

Score the length of the cucumber with a fork or cannelle knife, then slice it very finely. Sprinkle with salt and leave for 20 minutes or so. (This keeps the cucumber slices crisp.) Rinse the cucumber in cold water and drain well. Put on a serving dish with the crab. Mix the vinegar with the sugar and stir until dissolved. Season with salt and black pepper, pour over the cucumber and sprinkle with the sesame seeds. Garnish with lemon zest.

Chilli Mud Crabs

. . . .

Don't be put off by the name of this beast, which is, in fact, a smooth-shelled native Australian crab. You can use any fresh live crab.

What made this a particularly interesting dish for me was that I cooked it for a troupe of Aboriginal dancers, who were painted in their traditional manner, high up in a rainforest in the mountains above Cairns.

SERVES 4

4 live mud crabs or buy one large crab	*6 spring onions, trimmed and sliced*
weighing about 1.5 kg (3 lb)	*100 g (4 oz) broccoli, broken into florets*
1 tablespoon vegetable oil	*150 ml (5 fl oz) chicken stock, see page*
1 tablespoon sesame oil	*125*
2 cloves of garlic, finely chopped	*4 pak choy or Chinese leaves, shredded*
2.5 cm (1 inch) piece of fresh root ginger,	*1 tablespoon cornflour, mixed with a*
finely chopped	*little water*
2 small red chilli peppers, finely chopped	*salt*
1 large red pepper, cut into thin strips	*freshly ground black pepper*
4 shallots, thinly sliced	

First, and I appreciate this might be distasteful, drown the crabs in fresh water. Then detach the claws from the crabs and crack the nippers with a nut cracker or mallet. Cut the body into 2 or 4 pieces, depending on the size.

Heat the oils in a large frying pan or wok that has a lid. Add the garlic, ginger and chillies and stir-fry for about 2 minutes, until the garlic is golden, then add the crab, pepper, shallots, spring onions and broccoli. Mix well, then cover and cook for 3 minutes. Tip in the chicken stock and *pak choy* or Chinese leaves, cover and cook for 3 more minutes. Stir in the blended cornflour and heat until the mixture boils and thickens, stirring constantly. Taste and adjust the seasoning, if necessary. Serve with mounds of plain, boiled rice.

Couscous with Roast Chicken

. . . .

Traditional couscous is a wonderfully spicy, aromatic sauté of chicken and lamb merguez simmered with chickpeas, carrots, peppers and courgettes. It is served on a mountain of the steamed semolina known as couscous and downed with jugs of coarse Algerian wine.

But this is a refined, modernised version that my friend Tony Papas of the Bayswater Brasserie showed me. The only difference is that he serves it in an elegant restaurant and I actually cooked this in my splendid Prince of Wales coach on the mighty *Ghan*, then stopped the train and served it to the engine drivers on a table set up on the track in front of the train.

SERVES 4

4 × 175–225 g (7–8 oz) chicken breasts
25 g (1 oz) seasoned flour
2 tablespoons olive oil
2 red peppers, cored and halved
50 g (2 oz) ghee, see page 236, or use 2
  tablespoons vegetable oil
2 large leeks, sliced
2 tablespoons red curry paste, see page
  237

225 g (8 oz) dried couscous, soaked in
  hot water until it is swollen into tender
  little grains, then drained
4–5 tablespoons good chicken stock, see
  page 125
plenty of chopped fresh parsley

Wash the chicken breasts and pat dry, then roll in seasoned flour. Heat the oil in a frying pan and sauté the chicken breasts for 2–3 minutes, until golden, then transfer to an ovenproof dish and roast for 20–30 minutes, until cooked but still juicy.

Grill the red peppers until the skin is charred and blistered, about 6–8 minutes. Remove from the heat and cover with a damp cloth – the steam will help to loosen their skins. Peel with a paring knife and slice them thinly.

Heat the ghee or oil in a large frying pan or wok and fry the leeks for a minute or so. Stir in the curry paste and fry for 1 more minute, then stir in the drained couscous. Heat thoroughly, stirring constantly, then add the stock and most of the chopped red pepper and parsley. Reheat, taste and season, then tip out on to warm serving plates, alongside the roast chicken. Garnish with the remaining red peppers and sprinkle with chopped parsley. Simple – but brilliant.

Warm Minced Chicken Salad with Fresh Herbs

Photograph on pages 142–3

. . . .

This is a dish that has a delicate combination of spicy warm meat and crunchy fresh herbs. Do be really liberal with the fresh herbs, but remember to pluck the leaves off the stalks.

SERVES 4

1 tablespoon vegetable oil
4 tablespoons long-grain rice
225 g (8 oz) chicken breasts, finely chopped
1 tablespoon fish sauce, see page 235
1 tablespoon finely chopped lemon grass
3 tablespoons chicken Thai soup stock, see page 127, or water
1½ tablespoons lemon juice
1 onion, finely sliced

1 tablespoon chopped spring onions
1 tablespoon finely chopped fresh coriander leaves
1 tablespoon fresh mint, finely chopped
1 teaspoon chilli powder
cos or crunchy lettuce leaves, fresh mint and coriander leaves, chilli flowers, see below, and sliced spring onions, to garnish

Heat the oil in a frying pan and fry the rice over a low heat, stirring frequently, until golden-brown. Allow to cool slightly, then whizz to a powder in an electric coffee grinder, blender or food processor. Cook the finely chopped chicken with the fish sauce, lemon grass and stock or water in a pan over a medium heat. Stir constantly to keep the chicken pieces separate. Cook for about 5 minutes, adding a little extra water to the pan if needed. The chicken should be cooked through yet still moist. Transfer to a large bowl.

Mix together the lemon juice, onion, spring onions, coriander and mint leaves and add to the chicken. Stir through gently. Add the rice and chilli powder. Check the seasoning, adding a little more fish sauce or lemon juice if necessary.

Serve on a bed of lettuce leaves, garnished, if you like, with fresh mint and coriander leaves, chilli flowers and sliced spring onions.

. . . .

Chilli flowers

To make these for a garnish, you need some firm chilli peppers, about 5–7.5 cm (2–3 inches) long. Using a sharp knife, cut each chilli from tip to stem – but without cutting through the stem – at equal distances all the way round. Make light incisions only so as to leave the seeds intact. Carefully pull apart the strips and drop the 'flowers' into a bowl of iced water so that they open fully.

Hot Chicken Salad

Photograph on page 186

. . . .

This is a super Sunday brunch dish, particularly good for using up any leftover cold roast chicken or turkey, though in the original version I did at the Botanical Hotel in Melbourne, I prepared the chicken expressly for this dish.

But it is fun to cook and I made it for my chums Harold and Madge of *Neighbours*, in between rehearsals. And it must have been okay because they are still in work.

SERVES 4

*4 × 150 g (6 oz) boneless chicken
    breasts, skinned*
2 tablespoons plain flour
4 tablespoons sesame seeds
2 tablespoons olive oil
*2 tablespoons fresh shiitake or button
    mushrooms, wiped*
4 spring onions, trimmed and chopped
1 clove of garlic, crushed
*2.5 cm (1 inch) piece of fresh root ginger,
    fried in deep fat, then chopped*

1 teaspoon coriander seeds, crushed
4 tomatoes, skinned and quartered
2 tablespoons balsamic vinegar
salt
freshly ground black pepper
*variety of lettuce leaves, for example cos,
    lollo rosso, oak leaf, Chinese leaves, to
    serve*

Cut each chicken breast into 4–6 pieces. Dust with the flour and roll in the sesame seeds. Pop into a roasting tin and roast in a preheated oven, 200°C/400°F (gas mark 6), for 15–20 minutes, until tender.

Heat the oil in a large frying pan or wok and tip in the cooked chicken, mushrooms, spring onions, garlic, ginger, coriander and tomatoes. Cook for 2–3 minutes, then add the vinegar and season to taste with salt and pepper. Stir through and serve immediately on a bed of lettuce leaves.

Sweet and Sour Fried Chicken

. . . .

This is a Vietnamese-inspired dish that I have recalled to the best of my memory after my visit to Cabramatta, which no doubt you have read about earlier in the book.

You could use a whole chicken and joint it yourself or, equally, for an economical dish you could buy a bag of chicken wings and use them instead.

SERVES 4

3 tablespoons vegetable oil
pinch of salt
1 large onion, roughly chopped
4 cloves of garlic, finely chopped
50 g (2 oz) lemon grass, finely minced
1 teaspoon ground dried chillies or 1
  small red chilli pepper, minced
  (optional)

1.5 kg (3 lb) chicken, jointed
4 tablespoons fish sauce, see page 235
1 tablespoon caster sugar
1 tablespoon caramel sauce, see below
250 ml (9 fl oz) cold water

Heat the oil in a large frying pan or wok over a medium heat. Add the salt, then the onion and garlic and fry for about 5 minutes, until transparent. Pop in the lemon grass and chilli, if using. Fry for 1–2 minutes more, then add the chicken. Stir well for about 5 minutes or so. Next add the fish sauce, sugar and caramel sauce, mixing well.

Add the water, cover and cook over a moderate heat for 45 minutes, or until the chicken is tender. Stir from time to time, adding more water if needed to prevent the pan from boiling dry. Serve with lots of plain, boiled rice.

Caramel Sauce

100 g (4 oz) granulated sugar

Mix the sugar with 4 tablespoons cold water in a heavy-based pan. Bring to the boil over a medium heat. Do not stir. Allow the mixture to boil until it changes colour. When it is golden-brown, add 100 ml (4 fl oz) cold water to dissolve the caramelised sugar. Be careful – the mixture has a tendency to spit. Stir for about 10 minutes, until the sugar has dissolved. Remove from the heat, allow to cool and store in a jar with a screw-topped lid.

Turmeric Chicken

. . . .

This is another of those lovely, creamy, nutty Vietnamese-style curries that you can make as hot and as spicy as you wish merely by adding a little chopped chilli pepper. Or, if you wish, leave the chilli out. And the gentle flavours of turmeric and coconut milk make it a dish to drool over.

SERVES 4

2 tablespoons vegetable oil
1 large onion, chopped
3 cloves of garlic, finely chopped
1 small green chilli pepper, seeded and finely chopped (optional)
450 g (1 lb) boned chicken meat, cut into bite-sized pieces
1½ tablespoons ground turmeric

generous pinch of salt
1 tablespoon lemon grass, finely minced
1 teaspoon ground bean sauce
500 ml (18 fl oz) coconut milk, see page 234 – or use canned coconut milk if you can get it
roasted peanuts and fresh coriander leaves, chopped, to garnish

Heat the oil in a large frying pan or wok, add the onion, garlic and chilli, if using, and then the chicken. Stir-fry for about 3–4 minutes, until the meat changes colour. Pop in the remaining ingredients, apart from 3 table-spoons coconut milk. Cook over a moderate heat for 30 minutes or until the chicken is tender. Stir from time to time adding extra water if necessary to prevent burning.

Remove from the heat when the chicken is cooked and the sauce has reduced and thickened. Stir through the reserved coconut milk. Sprinkle with the chopped roasted peanuts and coriander and serve with mounds of plain, boiled rice or cellophane noodles.

*Above Turmeric Chicken; **Below** Hot Chicken Salad (page 184)*

Bishop's Chicken Curry

· · · · · · · · · · · · · · · · · ·

What do you cook for a Bishop? I was sitting in my luxurious Indonesian suite at the Cable Beach Club in Broome, gazing at the coconut trees, pondering a meal for the Bishop of Western Australia. And I thought, since they go round preaching hell and damnation to the godless, something to set fire to his palate would be appropriate. But the quality of mercy should not be strained, so to tone down this fiery concoction I plucked some coconuts from a tree and strained in the juice to mellow this dish.

SERVES 4

50 g (2 oz) ghee, see page 236
2 onions, finely sliced
1 clove of garlic, crushed
1 cm (½ inch) piece of fresh root ginger,
   finely chopped
1 red chilli pepper, seeded and finely
   chopped
2 tablespoons red or green curry paste,
   see page 237

1 tablespoon ground coriander
½ teaspoon ground turmeric
450 g (1 lb) lean chicken, cut into cubes
1 lemon, sliced into little, thin slivers
4 tomatoes, skinned and chopped
450 ml (15 fl oz) coconut milk, see page
   234
salt
freshly ground black pepper

Heat the ghee in a large pan and fry the onions and garlic for about 2–3 minutes, until transparent. Stir in the ginger and chilli, then add the curry paste, coriander and turmeric and cook gently for 2 minutes. Add the chicken and cook for 2 more minutes, stirring constantly, until the meat is well coated with the spices. Now add the lemon slivers, tomatoes and coconut milk, reheat gently until just bubbling, then cover and simmer for about 1 hour. Taste and season with salt and black pepper, if needed. Delicious served with Coconut Rice, see page 222, poppadoms, chutney, Cucumber Raita and Banana Coconut, see below.

Cucumber Raita

½ cucumber, peeled and thinly sliced
1 teaspoon salt
150 ml (5 fl oz) natural yoghurt

fresh coriander leaves or parsley, to
   garnish

Spread out the cucumber slices and sprinkle with the salt, then leave for 20 minutes or so. Rinse in a colander and drain well, then pat dry with kitchen paper. Put into a serving dish and stir in the yoghurt. Garnish with coriander leaves or parsley.

Banana Coconut

2 large bananas, thickly sliced
juice of ½ lemon
juice of ½ lime
2 tablespoons desiccated coconut or fresh
*   coconut, coarsely grated*

3 tablespoons thick coconut cream, see
*   page 234*

Put the bananas into a shallow serving dish and sprinkle with the lemon and lime juices, tossing well. Scatter the coconut over the top and spoon over the thick coconut cream.

A Burmese Chicken Curry

. . . .

This is the sort of curry where East meets East. The delight of Burmese food is the subtle blend of influences from the Indian subcontinent and the great People's Republic of China. A tasty little number, this.

S E R V E S   4

4 × 175 g (6 oz) chicken pieces
3 tablespoons light soy sauce
½ teaspoon ground turmeric
salt
freshly ground black pepper
2 large onions, sliced
4 cloves of garlic, crushed
2.5 cm (1 inch) piece of fresh root ginger

1 teaspoon chilli powder, or 2 if you like
*   it hot*
3 tablespoons vegetable oil
2 bay leaves
5 cm (2 inch) piece of cinnamon stick
600 ml (1 pint) cold water or chicken
*   stock, see page 125*

Put the chicken into a shallow dish. Mix the soy sauce with the turmeric and season with salt and pepper. Pour over the chicken. Using a blender or food processor, whizz together 1 of the onions, 3 cloves of garlic, the ginger and chilli powder. Tip over the chicken and rub it into the flesh.

Heat the oil in a large frying pan and fry the remaining onion and garlic for 3–4 minutes, until transparent. Add the chicken and chilli mixture and fry for 10 minutes, stirring and turning the chicken pieces occasionally until they are brown.

Pop in the bay leaves and cinnamon, then stir in the water or chicken stock. Bring to the boil, then reduce the heat, cover and simmer for 40 minutes, until the chicken is tender. If there is too much liquid, increase the heat and bubble, uncovered, so that the sauce thickens. Discard the bay leaves and cinnamon stick. Serve with Coconut Rice, page 222.

Thai Chicken Curry

. . . .

On a sunny autumnal day at a cricket ground in Romsey, Victoria, I had the dubious distinction of playing cricket with Frank Tyson. Or, rather, he played cricket, I just got bowled out.

However, I was able to restore some of my dented sporting pride by hitting them for six – ho ho! – with this frightfully simple, terribly delicious little curry.

SERVES 4

2 tablespoons vegetable oil
4 × 150 g (6 oz) boneless chicken
   breasts, skinned and cut into small
   strips
450 ml (15 fl oz) thick coconut milk, see
   page 234
2 medium green chilli peppers, seeded
   and chopped
2 tablespoons green curry paste, see page
   237

2 blades of lemon grass, bruised and
   finely chopped
2 tablespoons fresh coriander leaves,
   chopped
1 tablespoon fresh basil or mint, chopped
1 tablespoon fish sauce, see page 235
salt
freshly ground black pepper
fresh coriander leaves, to garnish

Heat the oil in a large pan and fry the chicken pieces for 3–4 minutes, until sealed. Pour in most of the coconut milk and add the fresh chillies, green curry paste and lemon grass. Bring to the boil, then reduce the heat and simmer gently for 15–20 minutes.

Tip in the coriander, basil or mint and fish sauce. Stir in the remaining coconut milk and bubble for 5 more minutes. Check the seasoning and add a little salt and pepper if necessary. Serve with plain, boiled rice and garnish with some fresh coriander leaves.

Chilled Australian lager in elegant cold glasses goes really well with this dish 🙂

Curried Peanut Chicken

. . . .

This is a fairly dry curry and the peanuts combined with the coconut milk gives a nice cloying texture, so you will need lots of glasses of iced lager to swill down with it.

SERVES 4

3 tablespoons vegetable oil
3 tablespoons red curry paste, see page 237
500 ml (18 fl oz) coconut milk, see page 234
450 g (1 lb) boneless chicken breasts, cut into 2.5 cm (1 inch) pieces

2 tablespoons caster sugar
2 tablespoons fish sauce, see page 235
100 g (4 oz) roasted peanuts, ground to a paste with 3 tablespoons coconut milk
pinch of ground cumin, ground coriander or salt
small handful of fresh basil leaves

Heat the oil in a large frying pan or wok and add the curry paste. Cook over a medium heat for about 2 minutes, then pour in 125 ml (4 fl oz) of the coconut milk. Reduce the heat and stir in the chicken. Cook gently for 5 minutes, stirring constantly. Add a further 250 ml (9 fl oz) of coconut milk, then the sugar and fish sauce. Bring to the boil, then add the ground peanut and coconut milk paste and remaining coconut milk.

Simmer gently for 10 minutes, then taste and season with a little more sugar, ground cumin, coriander or salt. Serve, scattered with some basil leaves, accompanied by boiled rice.

Barbecued Chicken

. . . .

This one needs no real introduction. It is just I feel that in keeping with the great Aussie tradition, I ought to put in the odd barbecue dish.

SERVES 4

1.4 kg (3 lb) chicken, jointed

FOR THE MARINADE:

1 clove of garlic, crushed
$\frac{1}{2}$ teaspoon cayenne pepper
$\frac{1}{2}$ teaspoon ground coriander

$\frac{1}{2}$ teaspoon ground cumin
1 tablespoon lemon juice
$\frac{1}{2}$ teaspoon tomato purée
5 tablespoons extra virgin olive oil
salt
freshly ground black pepper

Wash and pat dry the chicken pieces. Mix together the marinade ingredients in a large bowl (not aluminium) and add the chicken, making sure that all the pieces are nicely coated. Leave to marinate for about 2 hours.

Lift out the chicken and barbecue or grill for about 15–20 minutes, turning regularly. Serve with plain, boiled rice, a salad, and warm pitta bread, if you like.

Chicken Korma

. . . .

For me Chicken Korma embodies the mild, mystical flavours of the East.

SERVES 4

175 ml (6 fl oz) natural yoghurt
2 teaspoons ground turmeric
3 cloves of garlic, sliced
1.5 kg (3 lb) chicken, skinned and jointed
100 g (4 oz) ghee, see page 236, or 4
   tablespoons vegetable oil
1 large onion, sliced
1 teaspoon ground ginger
5 cm (2 inch) piece of cinnamon stick

5 whole cloves
5 whole cardamon pods
1 tablespoon crushed coriander seeds
1 teaspoon ground cumin
1/2 teaspoon chilli powder
1 teaspoon salt
1 1/2 tablespoons desiccated coconut
2 teaspoons roasted almonds

Mix together the yoghurt, turmeric and 1 of the cloves of garlic. Put the chicken pieces in a shallow dish (not aluminium) and pour over the yoghurt mixture. Cover and leave to marinate in a cool place, preferably overnight.

Heat the ghee or oil in a heavy-based pan and fry the remaining garlic and onion for about 3–4 minutes, until soft. Throw in all the spices and salt and cook for 3 more minutes, stirring constantly.

Add the chicken pieces with the marinade and coconut, cover and simmer for 40–50 minutes, or until the chicken is tender. Serve the chicken, sprinkled with the almonds, with basmati rice.

PS Do you think that this recipe's introduction will get me into Pseud's Corner?

Yes, I know there are lots of curry dishes – but I really like curry, so there. KF

Sweet and Sour Sesame Chicken Photograph on pages 194–5

. . . .

SERVES 4 GENEROUSLY

1.5 kg (3½ lb) chicken, jointed
3 tablespoons plum sauce, available from
*   oriental food suppliers*
1 tablespoon rice or white wine vinegar
500 ml (18 fl oz) chicken stock, see page
*   125*
80 ml (3 fl oz) dry sherry
1 tablespoon fresh root ginger, finely
*   chopped*
1 onion, quartered
150 g (6 oz) canned straw mushrooms,
*   drained, see page 236*

2 sticks of celery, sliced
225 g (8 oz) canned water chestnuts,
*   drained – but use 8 fresh ones if you*
*   can get them from Chinese stores, see*
*   page 237*
225 g (8 oz) canned bamboo shoots,
*   drained and sliced*
2 tablespoons cornflour mixed with a
*   little cold water*
1 tablespoon sesame seeds

Put the chicken pieces into a flameproof casserole. Mix together the plum sauce, vinegar, stock, sherry and ginger and pour over the chicken. Cover and bake in a preheated oven, 180°C/350°F (gas mark 4), for 40 minutes. Tip in the vegetables, return the casserole to the oven and cook for 15 minutes more. Lift out the chicken and vegetables on to a warmed serving plate.

Stir the cornflour mixture into the remaining liquid in the casserole, bring to the boil over a direct heat and bubble away for about 2 minutes, until the sauce has thickened. Pour over the chicken and vegetables. Scatter over the sesame seeds and serve immediately with plenty of plain, boiled rice.

Next page, from ▷
left to right: Duck
in Green Chilli
Sauce (page 205);
Sweet and Sour
Sesame Chicken

Chicken Pepper Stir-Fry

. . . .

This simple dish, quick and fun to make, is a sort of Chinese chilli con carne. Serve it in your best porcelain Chinese bowls with a dish of plain, boiled rice or Chinese egg noodles on the side.

SERVES 4

*225 g (8 oz) chicken breasts, skinned and
  finely sliced*
1 tablespoon light soy sauce
1 egg white, lightly beaten
1 tablespoon cornflour
salt
freshly ground black pepper
4 tablespoons vegetable oil
*1 cm (½ inch) piece of fresh root ginger,
  finely chopped*

4 spring onions, trimmed and sliced
*1 red chilli pepper, seeded and finely
  sliced*
*1 green pepper, seeded and cut into thin
  strips*
*1 red pepper, seeded and cut into thin
  strips*
3 sticks of celery, finely sliced
*2 tablespoons black bean sauce, see page
  234*

Put the chicken into a large bowl. Mix together the soy sauce, egg white, cornflour, salt and pepper. Pour over the chicken and mix well to coat.

Heat 2 tablespoons of the vegetable oil in a large frying pan or wok and stir-fry the chicken briskly for 3–4 minutes. Lift out the chicken from the pan with a slotted spoon and put to one side. Wipe out the pan and heat the remaining oil until almost smoking, then stir-fry the ginger, spring onions, chilli, peppers and celery for 2 minutes. Stir in the black bean sauce, then return the chicken to the pan, stir-frying for about 1 more minute. Serve immediately.

Chicken Kebabs with Lemon Sauce

. . . .

SERVES 4

*4 large chicken breasts, skinned, boned
  and cut into chunks*

FOR THE MARINADE:

150 ml (5 fl oz) natural yoghurt
4 tablespoons double cream
3 onions, finely chopped
2 cloves of garlic, finely crushed

salt
freshly ground black pepper

FOR THE SAUCE:

1 onion, grated
juice of 1 lemon
150 ml (5 fl oz) extra virgin olive oil

Mix together the ingredients for the marinade in a large bowl (not aluminium). Stir in the cubes of chicken, coating well, then leave to marinate for at least 2 hours.

Lift out the chicken cubes and thread them on to skewers. Barbecue or grill for 10 minutes, turning the skewers regularly. Whisk together the sauce ingredients until they are well mixed, pour over the chicken and serve with plain, boiled rice.

Chicken Fried with Honey and Ginger

The delight of this dish comes from the combination of textures and flavours that you get from mixing cooked and raw ingredients.

It is typical of many Thai and Vietnamese dishes. Garnish them liberally with uncooked herbs and spring onions.

SERVES 4

2 tablespoons vegetable oil
450 g (1 lb) boneless chicken breasts,
   skinned and very thinly sliced
1 onion, finely sliced
2 cloves of garlic, finely chopped
100 g (4 oz) field or wild mushrooms –
   chantrelles, ceps, something like that –
   chopped
2 tablespoons soy sauce
good dollop of clear honey – about
   1 tablespoon

100 g (4 oz) fresh root ginger, coarsely
   grated and soaked in a little cold
   water
1 bunch of crunchy spring onions,
   trimmed and chopped
salt
freshly ground black pepper
more chopped spring onions, to serve

Heat the oil in a large frying pan or wok, if you prefer to use a wok, and fry the sliced chicken briskly for 5 minutes. Lift out from the pan with a slotted spoon and set aside.

Now fry together the onion and garlic in the pan for 2–3 minutes, then add the mushrooms and stir-fry the lot for 1 more minute. Return the chicken to the pan or wok. Add the soy sauce and honey and mix in well with the chicken.

Squeeze out the soaked ginger and rinse under cold running water – this reduces its hot taste. Drain well and toss into the pan with the spring onions. Stir-fry for another couple of minutes or so. Season to taste with salt and pepper.

Pour into serving bowls and chuck spring onions over each serving.

Gumnut or Chicken and Leek Pies

. . . .

When I went walking in Ku-ring-gai Chase National Park with my botanist chum Libby Buhrich, she prepared a picnic that we hungrily ate after walking for miles looking at flora and fauna and the Aboriginal carvings. And one of the delicious aspects of that day were these little Gumnut Pies, shaped rather like English pork pies.

I am sorry to confess I forgot to ask her why they are called Gumnut Pies – something to do with the pastry decorations shaped like gumnut leaves. Anyway, they tasted damned good.

MAKES 6 LITTLE PIES

FOR THE PASTRY:

300 g (11 oz) plain flour
pinch of salt
175 g (7 oz) butter
2 eggs, beaten
2–3 tablespoons cold water
2 egg whites, to glaze

FOR THE FILLING:

25 g (1 oz) butter
3 leeks, trimmed and shredded finely
600 ml (20 fl oz) single cream
2 eggs
6 egg yolks
3 × 150 g (6 oz) chicken breast fillets
freshly ground black pepper

Make the pastry first. Sift the flour and salt into a bowl and rub in the butter, using your fingertips, a food processor or pastry blender, until the mixture resembles fine breadcrumbs. Add the eggs and mix well. Stir in sufficient of the cold water to make a soft dough. Roll into a ball, place in a plastic bag and refrigerate for at least 1 hour.

Divide the pastry into 6 portions. Roll each one thinly out on a lightly floured surface and use to line six 10 cm (4 inch) soufflé dishes, bringing the pastry well over the sides. Trim away the excess, roll into 6 balls, and reserve to make the lids. Put to one side while you get on with the next bit.

Melt the butter in a pan and sauté the leeks for a few minutes. Beat together the cream, eggs and egg yolks in a bowl. Put the chicken fillets in a steamer or steaming basket over a pan of boiling water and cover. Steam lightly for 10–15 minutes. Allow the chicken to cool, then slice and fill the pastry-lined dishes with alternate layers of leek and chicken. Pour in the cream and egg mixture, keeping a little back for the glaze. Sprinkle with pepper. Roll out the remaining pastry to rounds large enough to cover the pies and cut some pastry leaf decorations – so that they look like eucalyptus or oak leaves. Beat together the reserved cream and egg with the egg whites. Brush the pies liberally with the mixture and put the decorations on top. Brush again to glaze. Prick 3 holes in each of the pie tops. Bake in the centre of a preheated oven, 180°C/350°F (gas mark 4), for 15 minutes. Reduce the heat to 150°C/300°F (gas mark 2) and cook for a further 10 minutes.

Chicken Fillet Parcels

. . . .

This is a version of the old favourite of the 1960s – Chicken Cordon Bleu.

I have included it here because when I was on the Ross River Station (see page 76 and you will know what I am talking about), I had to cook a simple meal for a precocious ten-year-old and her pet camel. And I can assure you the old adage 'never work with children and animals' is absolutely correct.

SERVES 4

4 × 175–225 g (7–8 oz) chicken fillets, *skinned*	*2 tablespoons milk*
	25 g (1 oz) seasoned flour
4 thin slices of good roast ham	*100 g (4 oz) fresh white breadcrumbs*
4 slices of Gruyère cheese	*6 tablespoons vegetable oil*
2 eggs, separated	*lemon wedges and parsley, to garnish*

Put the chicken fillets between sheets of greaseproof paper or Clingfilm. Using a meat mallet or rolling pin, bash them out, gently but firmly, to flatten and tenderise them.

Lay one slice of ham on each chicken fillet and top with a slice of cheese. Fold over the chicken to make a parcel and secure with cocktail sticks. Beat together the egg yolks and milk, and brush all over the chicken parcels, then roll them in seasoned flour. Dip these parcels into the lightly beaten egg whites, then roll in breadcrumbs. Heat the oil in a large frying pan and fry the chicken parcels for 3–4 mintes on each side, until cooked and golden-brown.

Serve immediately with lemon wedges and parsley, accompanied by a fresh, crisp salad.

Road Train Chicken

· ·

Katherine in the Northern Territory has superb Mediterranean vegetables, courgettes, peppers and so on. So I cooked this little sort of
Chicken Provençale dish for my two chums 'The Padre' and 'Strawberry',
a pair of tough road train drivers. I must say it is more a dish for a
summer Sunday lunch with gallons of iced rosé than it is for a pair of
rough diamonds who would rather have had half a roast steer any day.

SERVES 4

4 × 175 g (7 oz) boneless chicken breasts
salt
freshly ground black pepper
2 tablespoons vegetable oil
2 cloves of garlic, crushed
2 small green chilli peppers, seeded and
*   chopped*
4 large tomatoes
75 g (3 oz) butter, softened

1 clove of garlic, crushed
2–3 anchovies, drained and mashed
2 tablespoons fresh white breadcrumbs
1 large red pepper, chopped
1 medium green pepper, chopped
1 small aubergine, chopped into 1 cm
*   (1/2 inch) pieces*
1 onion, chopped
1 tablespoon fresh oregano, chopped

Rinse the chicken breasts and pat dry on kitchen paper, then season with
some salt and black pepper. Heat a little oil in a flameproof casserole dish
and fry the chicken pieces for about 5–6 minutes, until brown on all sides.
Stir through the garlic and chillies, then transfer to a preheated oven,
190°C/375°F (gas mark 5), and roast for 20–25 minutes, until tender.

Cut the tops off the tomatoes and remove the seeds from inside,
because you are going to stuff them with garlic and anchovy butter. To
make this, beat the softened butter for a moment or two, add the crushed
garlic and mashed anchovies and beat really well until smooth and
blended. Season with a twist of freshly ground black pepper – you don't
need salt as the anchovies are salty enough. Divide this flavoured butter
between the tomatoes and top with the breadcrumbs. Pop under a
preheated hot grill 5 minutes before the chicken is cooked, until they are
brown.

Add the remaining oil to a frying pan or wok and heat it, then tip in all
the chopped vegetables at once and stir-fry for about 2–3 minutes.
Flavour with the oregano and season with salt and pepper.

Serve the chicken with the stir-fried vegetables and stuffed tomatoes,
accompanied by a big bowl of steaming, buttery pasta. Delicious!

Roast Duck with Plum Sauce

There are two important tips that will enable you to get a really authentic Chinese flavour into this simple dish. The first one is, if possible, use a fresh and not a frozen duck that is plump and heavy. And what you must do is drop the duck into a saucepan of boiling water for 5 minutes. Remove it from the water and dry it very carefully. This tightens the skin round the meat of the duck and you get a really superb, crispy skin as a result. The second very important thing is that during the roasting of the dish, as you will see, you must baste it about every 20 minutes.

SERVES 6–8 – OR A FEAST FOR 4

2.5 kg (5½ lb) duck
3 tablespoons plum sauce – you can buy
this from your local Asian store

FOR THE MARINADE:
(you need about 300 ml/½ pint of this):

3 tablespoons chicken stock, see page 125
1 tablespoon soft brown sugar
2 tablespoons soy sauce
1½ tablespoons clear honey
1 teaspoon five spice powder

Right, first put your duck into the marinade that you have mixed together. Leave the duck in the marinade for a couple of hours, turning it from time to time to make sure that all sides get impregnated with the juices.

Drain the duck well and pop it on to a rack with a tray filled with 1 cm (½ inch) water underneath it, so that the fat and the juice dripping from the duck will combine with the water, which makes the liquid necessary to baste the beast with. Cook the duck in a preheated oven, 180°C/350°F (gas mark 4), for about 2 hours, depending on its size, of course, and how hot your particular oven is. Baste every 20 minutes or so.

When it is cooked, chop it into bite-sized pieces, that is, big enough to pick up with your chopsticks, quickly heat through the plum sauce and pour it over the duck.

Autumn Barossa Pheasant

Needless to say at the Pheasant Farm restaurant in the Barossa Valley, chef-patron Maggie Beer specialises in pheasants. And so, using what I could find in her kitchen, I came up with this fun dish for one of the cooking sketches.

SERVES 4

100 g (4 oz) butter
1 pheasant
450 g (1 lb) fresh baby beetroot, peeled
    and par-boiled for 10 minutes, then
    halved or quartered depending on size
6 shallots, finely chopped
25 g (1 oz) plain flour
12 juniper berries, crushed

3–4 tablespoons strong red wine
2 tablespoons chicken stock, see page 125
salt
freshly ground black pepper
325 g (12 oz) ceps (wild mushrooms, also
    known as boletus) – or use field
    mushrooms
fresh noodles or pasta, to serve

Rub half the butter over the pheasant and roast the bird, breast-side down, in a roasting tin in a preheated oven, 200°C/400°F (gas mark 6), for about half an hour. Remove from the oven, put the par-boiled beets round the bird so that they can roast like little potatoes and then roast for a further 30–40 minutes, until tender.

Strain about 150 ml (5 fl oz) pheasant stock from the roasting pan and return the pheasant, with the beets, to a low oven to keep warm. Melt half the remaining butter in a pan and fry the shallots for 4–5 minutes, until golden. Remove from the heat, stir in the flour, and then cook over a low heat for 1 minute. Add the pheasant stock, crushed juniper berries, red wine and chicken stock and bring to the boil, stirring constantly. Boil away until the gravy has reduced by half: you should now have a thick, rich gravy. Season to taste with salt and pepper and strain into a sauceboat.

Melt the remaining butter in a frying pan and sauté the ceps or mushrooms for 3–4 minutes. Carve or joint the pheasant and serve with the roast beets, ceps and rich gravy, with a bowl of buttered noodles or pasta of your choice.

Autumn Barossa Pheasant

Lake Leek Rabbits

. . . .

There is a brilliant brewery in Tasmania that makes a beer called Cascade. The brewery is in a beautiful old sandstone building, probably built round 1890, where they have a wonderful hospitality suite. During a break from filming they invited us for lunch and because I'd had so many refined, extravagant meals I requested a humble stew that was cooked for me by Michael Carnes and Robin Cooney.

SERVES 4

2 rabbits, skinned and jointed
50 g (2 oz) seasoned flour
2 tablespoons vegetable oil
25 g (1oz) butter
6 rashers of streaky bacon, chopped
2 large onions, sliced
3 carrots, sliced

1 litre (1¾ pints) beef stock, see page
  125
1 large wineglass decent Australian red
  wine
100 g (4 oz) dried apricots, halved
few sprigs of fresh rosemary

Dust the rabbit pieces with seasoned flour, reserving any flour left over. Heat together the oil and butter in a large frying pan and fry the rabbit pieces for about 5–6 minutes, until golden brown. Transfer to a large casserole dish. Add the bacon to the frying pan and cook for a couple of minutes, then throw in the onions and carrots and sauté for 2 or 3 more minutes. Add to the casserole pot.

Remove the frying pan from the heat and stir in any remaining seasoned flour to make a *roux*. Cook gently over a low heat for 1 minute, then stir in the beef stock gradually. Heat until the sauce boils and thickens, then pour into the pot with the wine, apricots and some of the rosemary. Cover and cook in a preheated oven, 190°C/375°F (gas mark 5), for about an hour or so. Garnish with a few more rosemary sprigs. Delicious served with jacket potatoes and butter.

I thought there were thousands of rabbits in Oz but this was the only time I ate one.

Duck in Green Chilli Sauce   Photograph on pages 194–5

. . . .

SERVES 4

10 green chilli peppers or 3 green
 peppers, seeded and chopped (the
 chilli peppers give a hotter, spicier
 flavour)
8 macadamia or cashew nuts
3 tablespoons vegetable oil
10 shallots, finely sliced
4 cloves of garlic, finely sliced
2 teaspoons ground ginger
$\frac{1}{2}$ teaspoon ground turmeric
pinch of galingale powder, see page 235
1 blade of lemon grass, bruised, or $\frac{1}{2}$
 teaspoon lemon grass powder, see
 page 236

1.75 kg (4–4$\frac{1}{2}$ lb) duck, skinned and cut
 into 8 pieces
3 tablespoons tamarind water, see page
 237
1 bay leaf
salt
freshly ground black pepper
300 ml ($\frac{1}{2}$ pint) cold water
2 tablespoons snipped chives

Using a mortar and pestle, pound the chillies or peppers and macadamia or cashew nuts to a smooth paste. Alternatively, if you're busy, whizz in a blender. Heat the oil in a large frying pan or wok and fry the shallots and garlic for about 3–4 minutes, until golden. Add the chilli paste and fry for 1 minute, then throw in the spices and lemon grass. Stir in the remaining ingredients, apart from the water and chives. Cover and bubble gently for about 45 minutes.

Pour in the water and add the snipped chives. Bring to the boil, then reduce the heat and simmer for 15 minutes, stirring occasionally. Fish out and discard the lemon grass and bay leaf. Check and adjust the seasoning. Allow to cool, then chill in the refrigerator, preferably overnight. This gives the flavours the chance to develop brilliantly and means that the fat can be skimmed off.

Skim off the fat from the surface – it is important to do this meticulously as the duck tends to be rather greasy – then reheat the dish thoroughly. Serve piping hot with plain, boiled rice.

Barbecued Beef Kebabs

The Australians are so obsessed with barbecues that dotted around in the gardens of the Fitzroy Crossing Motel are about fifteen of them just so that people using the swimming pool or the recreational facilities can cook their own meal.

Again, this is the type of barbecue with a solid sheet-steel top with shelving underneath to pile the logs on. You don't find many charcoal brickettes in Australia, I am happy to say; it is much more the tradition of gathering up old wood.

It was here that I cooked these simple kebabs, just minced beef – one lot mixed with Type A and the other with Type B – rolled into sausages and stuck on a skewer for my two Aboriginal chums, Mitch and Butcher.

olive or vegetable oil, for basting
you will also need some satay sauce for accompanying the kebabs. (Be lazy and buy a bottle, or be virtuous and make it yourself – see the recipe on page 210.)

Type A:

450 g (1 lb) minced beef
2 tablespoons curry powder
1 tablespoon fresh oregano, finely chopped
3 tablespoons olive oil
¼ teaspoon salt

Mix together well all the ingredients in a bowl and then, with floured hands, shape into little sausages and thread on to skewers. Next, prepare:

Type B:

450 g (1 lb) lean minced beef
2 onions, finely chopped
1 large red pepper, seeded and finely chopped

1 large green pepper, seeded and finely chopped
salt
freshly ground black pepper

Mix the beef with all the remaining ingredients and put the whole lot through a mincer or pound in a food processor. With floured hands, shape into small sausages and thread on to skewers.

Make sure your barbecue is going well, or preheat your grill, then cook both kebab versions for a few minutes, until the meat is done to your liking, brushing with oil and turning from time to time.

Serve with piles of plain, boiled rice or jacket potatoes and salad, and some satay sauce.

Warm Spiced Beef Salad

Photograph on page 211

. . . .

This dish is based on a Thai recipe and will make a spicy, light lunch for three to four people.

SERVES 3 – 4

*700 g (1½ lb) rump steak, about 2.5 cm
    (1 inch) thick*
4 tablespoons soy sauce
4 tablespoons sesame oil
2 tablespoons ground coriander
1 tablespoon freshly ground black pepper
1 tablespoon soft brown sugar

1 tablespoon vegetable oil
150 ml (5 fl oz) cold water
1 medium cucumber, finely sliced
*1 cm (½ inch) piece of fresh root ginger,
    bruised*
salt

Put the piece of beef into a shallow dish (not aluminium). Whizz together the soy sauce, sesame oil, ground coriander, black pepper and sugar in a food processor or blender. Tip it out and smear it all over the steak. Leave to marinate for at least 1 hour.

Heat the oil in a large frying pan or wok and sear the steak on both sides to brown, about 30 seconds for each side. Pour in the water and simmer for about 3–5 minutes, until the meat is medium-rare. Remove from the pan. Add the piece of ginger to the liquid left in the pan, adding more soy sauce and water if necessary, and simmer for a few minutes while you slice the beef into wafer-thin slices.

Arrange the cucumber on serving plates or one large platter, then the sliced beef. Remove the ginger from the sauce and either pour it over the meat or hand it round separately. Serve with plain, boiled rice or noodles.

Minute Steaks with Anchovies

There is no real mystery to cooking on a barbecue, but there is a golden rule that if you are cooking over charcoal or wood on a grill-type barbecue, make sure there are no flames and that the hot ashes are covered with a fine white dust before you start to cook. If you are using the Australian type with a solid top make sure it is well and truly hot before you place your food on it.

Another useful tip is to divide the coals or the embers under your plate or grill into two piles, one stacked right up to give you the highest temperature, and one raked out in a shell where you have a lower temperature.

So after you have sealed your kebab or steak all the way round on the hot bit you can transfer it to the slightly cooler side to continue cooking.

So, armed with these tips, you could try your hand at this recipe.

SERVES 4

*4 large, thin slices of sirloin steak –
    weighing about 175 g (7 oz) each*
4 tablespoons olive oil

freshly ground black pepper
8 salted anchovies
100 g (4 oz) green olives, stoned

These are called minute steaks because they cook quickly – so they have to be very thin.

Brush the steaks with oil, season with pepper (you don't need salt because the anchovies are salty), and barbecue or grill for 2 minutes on each side. Then whack two anchovy fillets on top of each one and garnish with the olives and the remaining olive oil. Serve with watercress sprigs and matchstick chips.

Camp Oven Beef Stew

The Australians make terrific use of empty oil drums and when we arrived late one night at a remote cattle station only to discover we had run out of gas, I was able to cook the crew's supper using half an oil drum that had been cut to form a rudimentary stove fired by wood – and cooked this necessarily simple beef stew.

SERVES 4 HUNGRY CAMPERS

4 tablespoons vegetable oil
2 onions, chopped
700 g (1½ lb) stewing steak, cut into
   large chunks
2 large carrots, sliced
3 sticks of celery, chopped

1 small swede, chopped
1 medium parsnip, chopped
1 tablespoon fresh parsley, chopped
salt
freshly ground black pepper
700 g (1½ lb) potatoes, boiled

Take two frying pans and put half the oil in each. Heat it and fry the onions in one pan and the stewing steak in the other, until both are browned, about 4–6 minutes. Add the carrots to the onions, stir and cook for a couple of minutes, then add the celery, swede, parsnip and parsley. Stir and season with salt and black pepper. Add the browned steak to the vegetables and pour in about 150 ml (5 fl oz) water.

Cover and cook over a low heat for about 1–1½ hours, until the meat is tender, adding more water if necessary. Tip in the boiled potatoes and cook for 5 more minutes to heat them through. Taste and adjust the seasoning. Serve in large bowls, with hunks of bread.

Carpet Bag Steak à la Toyota

· · · · · · · · · · · · · · · · · · · ·

This has to be the daftest thing that I cooked on the entire trip. But it does prove the point that the determined cook can produce some kind of meal under any circumstances.

1 sirloin steak
1 onion, thinly sliced
some mushrooms, thinly sliced
salt
freshly ground black pepper

a little butter
aluminium foil
1 tin can
a little wire

Slice the steak through the middle to form a pocket, then stuff the onion and mushrooms into the said pocket. Sprinkle with a little salt and pepper, pop a knob of butter on top and wrap the steak in foil. Then put it into a tin can, open the bonnet of your Land Rover or jeep, wire it to your exhaust pipe and leave for a couple of hours.

This is a sort of a joke but it could work if you are daft enough to try).

Spicy Beef Satay

. . . .

The bamboo satay sticks needed for this recipe can be bought from good cookshops. Soaking them in water first prevents them from burning.

SERVES 4

450 g (1 lb) rump steak, cut into very thin strips
1 tablespoon soy sauce
1 teaspoon sesame oil
2 teaspoons red curry paste, see page 237

2 tablespoons peanut butter or sesame (tahini) paste
2 tablespoons dry sherry
2 tablespoons vegetable oil

Mix together the steak, soy sauce and sesame oil in a large bowl (not aluminium) and leave to marinate for 15 minutes or so. Soak about a dozen bamboo satay sticks in water.

Thread 3 or 4 slices of beef on to each satay stick. Leave 2 cm (1 inch) at the pointed end of each stick without meat.

Stir together the curry paste, peanut butter or sesame paste, and sherry in a bowl and use to baste the beef. Brush well with the oil and pop under a preheated hot grill. Cook for 1–2 minutes on each side. Serve with plain, boiled rice and some satay sauce, see below.

PS If you like, beat the steak out thinly between sheets of greaseproof paper with a meat mallet or rolling pin before cutting it up. This will tenderise it.

Satay Sauce

6 tablespoons crunchy peanut butter
1 tablespoon dark soy sauce
1 tablespoon fish sauce, see page 235
1 small onion, roughly chopped
1 tablespoon soft brown sugar

150 ml (5 fl oz) coconut milk, see page 234
½ teaspoon cayenne pepper
pinch of salt

Chuck all the ingredients into a food processor or blender and whizz together until smooth. Pour into a small pan and heat gently until just boiling. Pour into a bowl to serve with the satays.

***Above** Warm Spiced Beef Salad (page 207); **Below** Spicy Beef Satay*

Quick Cantonese Beef

. . . .

If your butcher is a good sort, he will sell you the tails of fillet steaks at a much cheaper rate than the nice plump bits from the middle, and this is a perfect recipe to take advantage of such favours. The dish is really a sort of Chinese Beef Stroganoff – ho, ho!

SERVES 6

4 tablespoons vegetable oil
2 onions, finely shredded
4 large tomatoes, skinned and cut into
* eighths*
1 teaspoon sugar
generous pinch of salt
1 tablespoon black beans, chopped, see
* page 234 (optional)*
1 teaspoon chopped fresh root ginger

1 teaspoon chopped garlic
450 g (1 lb) rump steak, cut into very
* thin strips*
2 tablespoons soy sauce
250 ml (9 fl oz) beef stock, see page 125
1 tablespoon cornflour mixed with 2
* tablespoons beef stock or water*
few spring onions, trimmed and sliced, to
* garnish*

Heat 2 tablespoons of the oil in a frying pan or wok and stir-fry the onions for 2 minutes. Add the tomatoes, sugar and salt and stir-fry for 1 minute. Cover and cook for about 3–4 minutes, or until the tomatoes are just tender and still retain their shape. Transfer the tomato mixture to a bowl.

Clean the pan, then heat the remaining oil and stir-fry the black beans, if using, ginger and garlic for 1 minute. Tip in the beef and cook over a high heat for about 2–3 minutes, until brown. Add the soy sauce, tomato mixture and beef stock.

Reheat gently, then carefully stir in the cornflour mixture to thicken. Cook for 2 minutes and serve, scattered with spring onions.

Spicy Beef in Yoghurt

. . . .

When I was a little boy I was ill for a long period of time and Dr Kerwin prescribed me a diet that seemed to consist of foul- and evil-tasting natural goats' yoghurt. And I hated it. When in the 1960s it was fashionable to eat small tubs of fruit yoghurt I hated that too.

But one day an Indian friend introduced me to a yoghurt drink called Lassi (see page 233) and I thought, hold on a minute, this is good – and years of prejudice were wiped out in a single sip of this delicious drink. And so I began to look at yoghurt in a different light and discovered that it combines brilliantly with the sort of spicy food I adore. Hence this little recipe.

SERVES 4

450 g (1 lb) rump steak, thinly sliced
1 teaspoon salt
300 ml (10 fl oz) natural yoghurt
100 g (4 oz) ghee, see page 236, or 4
*   tablespoons vegetable oil*
1 large onion, sliced
3 cloves of garlic, sliced

1½ teaspoons ground ginger
2 teaspoons chilli powder
½ teaspoon ground cumin
1½ teaspoons ground turmeric
2 teaspoons ground coriander
1 teaspoon **garam masala**, *see page 129*

Put the beef into a bowl (not aluminium), sprinkle with the salt and pour over the yoghurt. Cover and leave to marinate in a cool place, preferably overnight.

Heat the ghee or vegetable oil in a large, heavy-based pan and fry the onion and garlic for about 3–4 minutes, until soft. Whack in all the spices, apart from the *garam masala*, and cook for 3 more minutes, stirring constantly. Stir in the beef and marinade, then cover and cook gently for about 1 hour, until the meat is nice and tender. Mix in the *garam masala*, then serve with plain, boiled or basmati rice.

Kidney Brochettes with Orange and Oregano

· ·

SERVES 4

8 lambs' kidneys, skin removed and
*   cored*
finely grated zest and juice of 1 orange
4 tablespoons olive oil
1 tablespoon fresh oregano, finely
*   chopped*

225 g (8 oz) button mushrooms, wiped
salt
freshly ground black pepper

Cut each kidney into eight pieces. Mix together the orange juice and zest, oil and oregano in a large bowl (not aluminium) and add the kidneys. Leave to marinate for at least 2 hours.

Lift out the kidneys, reserving the marinade, and thread them on to the skewers with the mushrooms. Season to taste with salt and pepper. Barbecue or pop under a preheated hot grill for 5–8 minutes, turning frequently and brushing from time to time with the marinade.

Ground Lamb Kebabs

. . . .

In homage to the strong Greek influences present in Australian cooking, I suggest you serve this dish with a Greek salad. As you all know, this is made from firm, ripe tomatoes cut into wedges, thinly-sliced cucumber and a little sweet onion cut into rings, all tossed with some good quality olive oil and salt and pepper. This is then garnished with black olives (preferably Kalamata), cubes of crumbly white Feta cheese and some coarsely-chopped fresh flat-leaved Continental parsley, plus a sprinkling of dried oregano or marjoram. A colourful, delicious salad.

SERVES 4

550 g (1¼ lb) ground lamb
16 green olives, stoned and chopped
1 hard-boiled egg, chopped
75 g (3 oz) grated Parmesan cheese
1 small lemon, finely minced – take out the pips first

salt
freshly ground black pepper
freshly grated nutmeg
2 tablespoons olive oil, for basting
lemon wedges, to garnish

Put the lamb, olives, egg, cheese, minced lemon and seasonings in a bowl. With your fingers mix together the ingredients well, then divide and shape into walnut-sized balls. Thread on to skewers and barbecue or grill for about 10 minutes, basting with the oil from time to time. Serve with the lemon wedges and plain, boiled rice as well.

Fried Pork Spareribs

. . . .

A deliciously simple snack that you can pan-fry. Alternatively, you could just as well grill it over charcoal.

SERVES 4

1 kg (2–2¼ lb) pork spareribs
2 tablespoons fish sauce, see page 235
1 tablespoon brown sugar
3 cloves of garlic, crushed

freshly ground black pepper
3 tablespoons vegetable oil
fresh coriander leaves or parsley, to garnish

Put the spareribs into a shallow bowl. Mix together the fish sauce, sugar and garlic and brush over the ribs. Season with black pepper and leave the ribs to soak for 30 minutes or so.

Heat the oil in a large frying pan and fry the ribs for about 20–30 minutes, until cooked and tender, turning from time to time. Drain on kitchen paper and serve with rice, garnished with coriander or parsley.

PS Don't forget the fingerbowls!

Spiced Red Pork

. . . .

At my favourite Chinese restaurant they serve a dish called Pork *Su Mai*, which is a bit of loin of pork that has been roasted. It is red on the outside, it is thinly sliced and it is invariably served cold on a bed of *pak choy* (which is that leafy, Chinese, green, spinach-like vegetable).

In Burma, which, after all, isn't so far away from Australia though it is a long way away from my favourite Chinese restaurant, there is a version of this self-same dish, Spiced Red Pork. I include it here because I like it.

By the way, I also include this recipe in fond memory of my father Syd, who served in the Signals Regiment in the Second World War. He always had a fondness for Burmese food and, I think, Burmese ladies.

FEEDS 4 HUNGRY PEOPLE

1 kg (2–2¼ lb) lean pork, cut into 2.5 cm (1 inch) cubes	*3 cloves of garlic*
3 tablespoons soy sauce	*200 ml (7 fl oz) boiling water*
1 teaspoon freshly ground black pepper	*3 tablespoons vegetable oil*
5 cm (2 inch) piece of fresh root ginger	*1 teaspoon chilli powder*
3 onions, roughly chopped	*salt*

Put the pork in a large bowl with 2 tablespoons of the soy sauce and the black pepper. Stir it and leave while you get on with the next bit.

In a blender, whizz together half the root ginger, the onions and the garlic. Add the boiling water, then strain it all, reserving both the liquid and the onion mixture. Cut the remaining ginger into thin shreds. Heat the oil in a large frying pan and sizzle the ginger for 1 minute, then add the pork and stir-fry for 3–4 minutes, until browned.

Pour in the reserved liquid, cover and simmer for 8–10 minutes, then pop in the remaining soy sauce, onion mixture and chilli powder. Cover and cook for 20–30 minutes, or until the pork is tender, stirring from time to time. Season to taste and serve with stir-fried *pak choy*, or noodles.

Hot and Spicy Barbecued Pork

. . . .

In the continuing saga of the great Australian barbie, mixed with my love of Asian food, herewith a recipe that you can cook either in the luxury of your fitted kitchen or, more enjoyably, on your barbecue on one of those fine summer days, which I am sure we shall be having plenty of now there is the Greenhouse Effect.

SERVES 4

4 red chilli peppers, chopped
2 dried red chilli peppers, chopped
2 small onions, chopped
small piece of fresh root ginger
1 tablespoon soft brown sugar
pinch of ground saffron

350 ml (12 fl oz) coconut milk, see page 234
700 g (1½ lb) pork, cut into 10 cm (4 inch) pieces
salt

Using a mortar and pestle, crush the fresh and dried chillies, onions and ginger to a paste, or whizz in a blender. Add the sugar, saffron and coconut milk.

Season the pork with salt and put in a bowl (not aluminium). Pour over the spice and coconut mixture and leave to marinate for 2 hours or so, turning frequently.

Lift out the pork pieces and barbecue or grill for 3–4 minutes on each side, basting regularly with the marinade. Heat the remaining marinade in a small pan and pour over the cooked meat.

Peking Pork

. . . .

Ah, the gentle art of stir-frying in a wok. Such fun, so quick, and as with many of these stir-fried pork or chicken dishes, for me the pleasure is being able to have loads of Chinese spinach – otherwise known as *pak choy.*

SERVES 4

450 g (1 lb) pork fillet, thinly sliced
1 tablespoon soy sauce
1 teaspoon cornflour
1 tablespoon dry sherry
1 tablespoon chicken or vegetable stock, see page 125 or 127

350 g (12 oz) pak choy
2 tablespoons vegetable oil
2 tablespoons hoisin sauce
½ teaspoon sesame oil or seeds

Put the pork in a bowl (not aluminium) with the soy sauce, cornflour, sherry and stock. Leave to marinate for at least 15 minutes. Blanch the *pak choy* in boiling water for 1 minute, drain well, then purée in a food processor or blender. Arrange on a serving plate and keep warm.

Heat the oil in a large frying pan or wok and stir-fry the pork for about 3–4 minutes, until cooked. Add the hoisin sauce and stir through until reheated. Pop in the sesame oil or sesame seeds and serve immediately on the bed of spinach.

Roast Red Pork   Photograph on pages 142–3

. . . .

SERVES 4

1 kg (2¹/₂ lb) pork fillet or boneless pork
    loin, trimmed
fresh coriander leaves, to garnish

FOR THE MARINADE:

¹/₂ teaspoon red food colouring, mixed
    with 3 tablespoons cold water
1 tablespoon fish sauce, see page 235
1 tablespoon soy sauce

2 tablespoons hoisin sauce
1 tablespoon dry sherry
1 tablespoon caster sugar
2.5 cm (1 inch) piece of fresh root ginger,
    grated
3 cloves of garlic, chopped
1 tablespoon sesame oil
¹/₂ teaspoon ground fennel or fennel
    seeds, or 3 star anise, crushed

Pop all the ingredients for the marinade into a food processor or blender and whizz to a smooth paste. Put the pork and marinade into a large plastic bag, tie securely and leave the meat to marinate for at least a couple of hours, but preferably overnight. Turn the bag occasionally to make sure that the meat is well covered with the marinade.

Remove the pork from the plastic bag and put it on a rack over a roasting tin, reserving the marinade for basting. Cook the pork in a preheated oven, 230°C/450°F (gas mark 8), for 10 minutes. Reduce the heat to 180°C/350°F (gas mark 4), and continue to roast for 45 minutes, basting from time to time. Allow the meat to rest in a warm place for 10–15 minutes or so before carving.

The pork can be served warm, sliced thinly and arranged on a flat serving dish, garnished with coriander leaves and served with rice. Alternatively, it can be used in many soups and stir-fries.

Afghan Curry

. . . .

I arrived in one of the remotest spots of Australia near the Ross River in the Northern Territory to do a cooking sketch, only to find that a bunch of long-limbed lovelies from Melbourne had chosen the same spot to photograph the spring collection for some Aussie magazine.

I bounced up in my four-wheel drive with a lot of pots and pans and cardboard boxes filled with a large assortment of ingredients and my beloved director said, 'Just make something for the girls.'

You can vary the ingredients quite a bit in this recipe, and it is just the sort of thing you can make in the bush if you find you have the following goodies.

S E R V E S 4

1 teaspoon coriander seeds
1 teaspoon mustard seeds
1 teaspoon fennel seeds
2 cloves of garlic, crushed
2.5 cm (1 inch) piece of fresh root ginger,
  chopped
2 medium green chilli peppers, seeded
  and chopped
2 tablespoons red curry paste, see page
  237
1 tablespoon sesame oil
2 tablespoons olive oil
1 onion, sliced
2 carrots, sliced

100 g (4 oz) cauliflower florets
2 small leeks, sliced
1 eating apple, cored and chopped
1 pear, cored and chopped
75 g (3 oz) dwarf green beans, sliced
50 g (2 oz) dried apricots
600 ml (20 fl oz) coconut milk, see page
  234
2 tablespoons fish sauce, see page 235
juice of 2 limes
chopped fresh coriander leaves, to
  garnish

Using a mortar and pestle, crush the coriander, mustard and fennel seeds. Mix with the garlic, ginger, chillies and red curry paste.

Heat the sesame and olive oils in a very large pan and fry the spice mixture for 2 minutes, stirring constantly. Pop in the onion and fry for 2 minutes more, then add all the remaining ingredients. Bring to the boil, reduce the heat and simmer gently, covered, for about 30–40 minutes, until cooked. Garnish with the chopped coriander and serve with mounds of plain, boiled rice.

Top *Thai Fried Rice*
(page 221);
Centre *Cellophane Noodles*
with Vegetables (page 223);
Bottom *Afghan Curry*

A Malaysian Vegetable Stew

. . . .

One for you vegetarians here, with this Malaysian stew. Delicious on its own, or with rice or noodles.

SERVES 4

3 shallots, thinly sliced
1 clove of garlic, thinly sliced
1 green chilli pepper, seeded and thinly
*   sliced*
7 tablespoons cold water
1 teaspoon ground turmeric
1 teaspoon ground ginger
1 blade of lemon grass, bashed with a
*   knife handle to release the flavours*
salt

2 potatoes, peeled and quartered
450 ml (³/4 pint) beef or chicken stock, see
*   page 125*
100 g (4 oz) white cabbage, coarsely
*   shredded*
¹/2 small marrow, peeled, seeded and cut
*   into chunks*
50 g (2 oz) creamed coconut, chopped,
*   see page 235*

Put the shallots, garlic, chilli, water, turmeric, ginger and lemon grass into a large pan. Add a little salt and bring to the boil. Bubble for 2 minutes, then whack in the potatoes and half the stock. Bring to the boil, cover and simmer for 5 minutes. Tip in the cabbage, marrow and remaining stock, return to the boil and simmer, covered, for 5–6 minutes, or until the vegetables are just tender. Add the creamed coconut and stir until dissolved. Check the seasoning, fish out and discard the lemon grass and serve with noodles.

Spicy Aubergines and Tomatoes

. . . .

A popular vegetable in Indian cooking, the purple aubergine should always be shiny and firm. Chuck out any that are soft and past their best.

This concoction is ideal as a side dish with any curry and rice or tandoori recipe – or served with rice alone for you veggies.

SERVES 4

175 g (6 oz) ghee, see page 236, or
*   6 tablespoons vegetable oil*
1 large onion, sliced
2 cloves of garlic, sliced
1 teaspoon ground coriander
1 teaspoon chilli powder
2.5 cm (1 inch) piece of cinnamon stick

1 teaspoon salt
1 teaspoon freshly ground black pepper
450 g (1 lb) aubergines, chopped into
*   2.5 cm (1 inch) pieces*
450 g (1 lb) tomatoes, chopped into
*   2.5 cm (1 inch) pieces*
3 tablespoons tomato purée

Heat the ghee or oil in a heavy-based pan and fry the onion and garlic for about 3–4 minutes, until soft. Throw in the spices and salt and pepper and fry for 3 more minutes, stirring constantly.

Stir in the aubergines, tomatoes and tomato purée, coating well with the spice mixture. Add 200 ml (7 fl oz) cold water and bring to the boil. Reduce the heat and bubble for 25–30 minutes, uncovered, until the aubergines are tender and the sauce fairly thick. If necessary, increase the heat to boil off any excess liquid.

Thai Fried Rice

Photograph on page 219

. . . .

A colourful and appetising dish with bite-sized pieces of meat. Make the garnish as simple or elaborate as you like.

SERVES 4

3 tablespoons vegetable oil
2 large onions, finely chopped
2 cloves of garlic, crushed
1 teaspoon caster sugar
1 tablespoon red curry paste, see page 237, or 1 tablespoon Tabasco sauce
450 g (1 lb) mixture of peeled prawns, sliced pork, beef, chicken or ham
3 eggs, beaten
1 kg (2–2¼ lb) cooked long-grain rice

2 tablespoons fish sauce, see page 235
1 red or green pepper, seeded and finely chopped
50 g (2 oz) dwarf green beans, sliced
2 tomatoes, skinned and chopped
3–4 spring onions, trimmed and chopped, or 2 shallots, chopped
coriander leaves, spring onion curls, cucumber slices or chilli flowers, see page 183, to garnish

Heat the oil in a large frying pan or wok and stir-fry the onions and garlic for 3–4 minutes, until golden. Stir in the caster sugar and red curry paste. (If using Tabasco, add this later.) Tip in the prawns and sliced meat, stir through and cook for 30 seconds or so. Push to one side of the pan, add a few more drops of oil, then pour in the eggs. Allow to set for a few seconds, then scramble them. Add the rice and stir-fry the lot until thoroughly heated, about 2–3 minutes. Add the Tabasco now, if using, and the fish sauce, pepper, beans, tomatoes and spring onions or shallots. Cook for a couple of minutes, then serve with the garnishes.

Coconut Rice

. . . .

Who wants plain rice all the time – not me! This is scrumptious with A Burmese Chicken Curry, see page 189.

SERVES 4

450 g (1 lb) long-grain rice, thoroughly rinsed
1 onion, chopped
75 g (3 oz) creamed coconut, roughly chopped, see page 235

½ teaspoon salt
few drops vegetable oil or a knob of butter

Measure the rice in cups and transfer to a large pan. For each cup of rice, add 2 cups of water to the pan. Stir in the onion, coconut, salt and a few drops of oil or a good knob of butter. Bring to the boil, then reduce the heat to low. Cover and cook for about 20 minutes, or until all the liquid has been absorbed and the rice is tender and fluffy. Serve hot with curry.

PS For a delicious, spicy change, why not add a piece of cinnamon stick, a couple of cloves and cardamon pods and a bay leaf. Remember to fish out and discard them before serving.

Pilau Rice

. . . .

This is a real pilau, with the rice well sautéed in ghee with onion and garlic before boiling (not just boiled in stock instead of water). Perfect pilau should be dry, each grain separate.

SERVES 4

225 g (8 oz) ghee, see page 236
50 g (2 oz) blanched almonds
1 onion, sliced
2 cloves of garlic, sliced
450 g (1 lb) long-grain or basmati rice, well rinsed

10 whole cloves
10 whole cardamon pods
5 cm (2 inch) piece of cinnamon stick
1 teaspoon salt
1.2 litres (2 pints) boiling water

Melt the ghee in a heavy-based pan, add the almonds and sizzle until lightly coloured, stirring constantly. Using a slotted spoon, lift out the almonds and drain on kitchen paper. Put to one side. Add the onion and garlic to the pan and fry for about 5 minutes, until soft.

Add the rice to the pan with the spices and salt. Fry for 3 minutes, stirring constantly until each grain of rice is nicely coated. Pour in the water and bring back to the boil, then reduce the heat, cover and simmer for 20–25 minutes, or until all the liquid has been absorbed. Whack in the almonds and serve piping hot.

Cellophane Noodles with Vegetables

Photograph on page 219

. . . .

A pretty dish with slightly crunchy vegetables.

SERVES 4 AS A SIDE DISH OR 2 AS A MEAL

175 g (6 oz) dried cellophane noodles, see
  page 236
3 tablespoons vegetable oil
1 clove of garlic, finely chopped
1 carrot, cut into matchsticks
1 courgette or ½ stick of celery, thinly
  sliced
3 tablespoons cold water or vegetable
  stock, see page 127

50 g (2 oz) Chinese leaves, shredded
handful of beansprouts
1 tablespoon fish sauce, see page 235
1 tablespoon oyster sauce
1 teaspoon caster sugar
freshly ground black pepper

Put the noodles into a large bowl, cover with hot water and leave to soak for 5 minutes. Drain them thoroughly and put to one side.

Heat the oil in a large frying pan or wok and fry the garlic for a couple of minutes, until golden. Add the carrot and courgette or celery and stir-fry for about 1 minute. Tip in the water or stock, Chinese leaves, beansprouts, fish and oyster sauces and cook for 2 more minutes. Stir in the sugar and season with a little pepper. (You don't need salt because the fish sauce is salty.) Add the noodles and heat them thoroughly for about 2 minutes, tossing them to mix all the ingredients.

Noodles are not naughty, they're nutritious. And I like them very much.

Granny Smith's Macadamia Nut Cake

. . . .

Now here's some useless but interesting information. Macadamia nuts were originally discovered by an Australian chemist, one J. Macadam (get it?), in 1865. A couple of entrepreneurial Americans took a bunch of small trees back to Hawaii, invented a commercial nut-cracking machine, and made a fortune. If you don't have any of these hard-shelled miniature cannon balls (actually, you can buy them ready-shelled) in your larder, use brazils, almonds or walnuts instead.

MAKES ENOUGH FOR 4 GREEDY GASTRONAUTS

225 g (8 oz) self-raising flour
150 g (6 oz) caster sugar
2 eggs
5 tablespoons soya oil
100 g (4 oz) Granny Smith's apples, peeled and grated
225 g (8 oz) fresh pineapple, peeled and finely chopped (or use well-drained canned pineapple)

100 g (4 oz) macadamia or brazil nuts, or almonds or walnuts, finely chopped

FOR THE TOPPING:

225 g (8 oz) cream cheese
macadamia or brazil nuts

Sift the flour into a large bowl and stir in the sugar. Make a well in the centre and gradually beat in the eggs and oil. Add the grated apple, chopped pineapple and nuts and mix well.

Turn the mixture into a greased and lined 18 cm (7 inch) cake tin and bake in a preheated oven, 180°C/350°F (gas mark 4), for 35–40 minutes. Test with a skewer to make sure it is cooked and the skewer comes out clean. Allow to cool in the tin for 10 minutes, then turn out on to a rack and cool completely.

To make the topping, beat the cream cheese until soft and smooth, and use it to cover the top of the cake. Decorate with macadamias or brazils.

Chinese Gooseberries and Lime in Red Wine

. . . .

Chinese gooseberries are just another name for the familiar kiwi fruit.

SERVES 4

250 ml (9 fl oz) red wine
250 ml (9 fl oz) cold water
100 g (4 oz) caster sugar
2 whole cloves

7.5 cm (3 inch) stick of cinnamon
4 large kiwi fruit (Chinese gooseberries),
  peeled and thickly sliced
1 lime, cut into 8 thin slices

Put the wine, water, sugar and spices in a pan. Bring to the boil, then simmer gently for 15 minutes. Allow to cool, then pop in the fruit. Chill before serving.

Baked Apple and Pear Pancake

. . . .

Although I absolutely adore eating puddings, I am really bad at making them. So I asked one of Tasmania's well-known cooks and writers for a couple of suggestions. Judith Sweet gave me these from her delicious little booklet, *Taste of Tasmania*. For this pancake, you could use quinces as well as the apple and pears if you can find any.

SERVES 4 OR 2 PUDDING FANATICS

1 teaspoon sunflower oil
325 g (12 oz) cooking apples, peeled and
  thinly sliced
325 g (12 oz) ripe pears, peeled and
  thinly sliced
125 g (5 oz) caster sugar
few drops of vanilla essence

100 ml (4 fl oz) sunflower oil
3 eggs, beaten
150 g (6 oz) plain flour
250 ml (9 fl oz) milk
icing or caster sugar and ground
  cinnamon, for sprinkling

Grease a 26–28 cm (10–11 inch) tart tin, at least 2.5 cm (1 inch) deep, with a little sunflower oil. Arrange the sliced apples and pears evenly over the base.

In a large bowl, beat together the caster sugar, vanilla essence, sunflower oil, eggs and flour. Mix well, then gradually add the milk and beat until smooth. The mixture should have the same consistency as pancake batter. Pour this batter over the sliced fruit and bake in a preheated oven, 220°C/245°F (gas mark 7), for about 45 minutes, until cooked in the centre. Serve immediately, sprinkled with a little icing or caster sugar and cinnamon, with lashings of softly-whipped cream or vanilla ice cream. Yum yum.

Lavender Honey Ice Cream

. . . .

Something from Judith again is this delicately-flavoured ice cream.

SERVES 4 OR 1, FOUR TIMES!

375 ml (13 fl oz) double cream
4 tablespoons natural yoghurt
175 g (6 oz) lavender honey (or use any clear honey with a good flavour) – the honey should be quite liquid, so if it has candied, melt over a bowl of hot water

1 teaspoon fresh lavender flowers, if you can find some!
fresh lavender flowers or a drizzle of honey, to decorate

Whip together the cream and yoghurt, using a balloon whisk in preference to an electric beater so that you get more air into the cream. When the mixture holds its shape, fold in the lavender honey and flowers (if you found some). Pour into a well-chilled ice cream tray, cover with foil or freezer-wrap and freeze until set, about 2–4 hours. Serve, scooped into pretty glasses, sprinkled with a few lavender flowers or drizzled with a little extra honey.

Coconut Custard

. . . .

SERVES 4

250 ml (9 fl oz) thick coconut milk, see page 234

4 eggs, beaten
100 g (4 oz) caster sugar

Whisk together in a bowl the coconut milk, eggs and sugar until the sugar has dissolved and the mixture is well blended. Pour through a fine sieve so the mixture is smooth, place in an ovenproof dish inside a steamer and steam for about 30–40 minutes, until firm. (Don't forget to top up the water level in the pan with boiling water as necessary.)

Alternatively, you can bake the custard in the oven, placed in a *bain-marie* (use a roasting tin half-filled with warm water). Bake in a preheated oven, 180°C/350°F (gas mark 4), for about 40 minutes, until set.

Meringue Berry Roll with Raspberry Sauce

For a really visually stimulating dish at the height of summer, try this.

MAKES 1 LARGE ROLL

5 egg whites
pinch of cream of tartar
5 rounded tablespoons caster sugar
2 tablespoons caster sugar
3 tablespoons roasted hazelnuts, finely
*   chopped*

FOR THE FILLING:

325 g (12 oz) mixed summer berries, for
*   example, strawberries, raspberries,*
*   tayberries, redcurrants*
425 ml (15 fl oz) double cream, whipped
1 tablespoon cassis (blackcurrant
*   liqueur) or framboise (raspberry liqueur)*
2 level teaspoons powdered gelatine,
*   dissolved in 1 tablespoon raspberry juice*

Grease and line a Swiss roll tin with silicon or non-stick baking paper. Beat together the egg whites and cream of tartar until stiff, then whisk in the 5 tablespoons sugar until the mixture has formed stiff peaks. Spread this meringue into the Swiss roll tin and bake in a preheated oven, 200°C/400°F (gas mark 6), for about 8 minutes, until light brown, but not overcooked. Please note, you are not trying to dry out the meringue – this will have a soft, marshmallow consistency.

Cut a piece of silicon paper slightly bigger than the size of the baking tin. Sprinkle this evenly with the 2 tablespoons caster sugar and the hazelnuts. Turn the cooked meringue on to this prepared paper, then carefully remove and discard the lining paper. Roll up the meringue lengthways, with the new paper inside, and allow it to cool completely, about 30 minutes.

Slice any large berries, then fold all the fruit into the whipped cream, with the cassis or framboise. Melt the gelatine over a pan of hot water, cool slightly, then pour into the fruit and cream mixture, stirring constantly. Unroll the meringue and spread the fruit mixture over the surface, then roll up again. Serve chilled, with lots of raspberry sauce, see below, poured over.

Raspberry Sauce

325 g (12 oz) raspberries   *2 tablespoons icing or caster sugar*

Purée the raspberries in a food processor or blender with the sugar, then strain through a sieve to remove the seeds. Taste and add a little more sugar, if necessary.

Mangoes with Sticky Rice
Photograph on pages 230–1

. . . .

A snack or a dessert, this dish is a favourite in Thailand where, wrapped in banana leaves, it is sold in lidded baskets – also made from leaves – from street stalls. But they don't have those in Australia. The rice is tacky to the touch – just pick it out with your fingers, roll it into a ball, coat it with sesame seeds and eat it with the fruit. Or you could serve it wrapped in banana leaves, which you can buy from some oriental stores.

SERVES 4 GENEROUSLY

250 ml (9 fl oz) thick coconut milk, see page 234
100 g (4 oz) granulated sugar
½ teaspoon salt
400 g (14 oz) freshly-cooked sticky rice, see below

roasted sesame seeds
4–6 large ripe mangoes, peeled, halved and stoned
pared lime zest, to decorate
4 tablespoons coconut cream, skimmed from the top of the coconut milk

Put the coconut milk, sugar and salt in a pan and bring to the boil over a medium heat. Turn down the heat and simmer for about 4–5 minutes, until the milk has reduced and thickened.

Put the already prepared sticky rice into a bowl and carefully pour over the coconut milk. Using a fork to fluff up the rice, allow the milk to trickle through but not drown the rice.

Leave the rice mixture to stand for 10 minutes, then roll dessertspoons of rice in the sesame seeds, coating well. Wrap in banana leaves if you have any. Slice the mangoes and arrange on a serving plate with the rice balls. Decorate the mangoes with the pared lime zest and serve with the thick coconut cream.

Sticky Rice

Sticky rice – pearly white and aromatic – is always steamed. But you can steam it in your microwave if you prefer: check it out in your particular microwave book. But don't forget to rinse the slightly greasy grains several times, to remove the starch.

SERVES 4

225 g (8 oz) short-grain rice

Rinse the rice several times until the water runs clear. Cover with cold water and soak for 12 hours or overnight, then drain.

Line a saucepan steamer or bamboo basket with muslin and put in the rice. Steam for 45 minutes, until the rice is tender and translucent (remembering to top up the water level in the pan with boiling water as necessary). Remove from the heat and fluff up the rice with a fork.

Floating Diamonds   Photograph on pages 230–1

. . . .

Basically, this is just a glorified fruit salad with almond-flavoured jelly wedges on top. Softer fruits like bananas, grapes, orange or pomelo segments are more suitable than hard fruits such as apple.

SERVES 4

600 ml (1 pint) milk
50 g (2 oz) caster sugar
1 teaspoon almond essence
1½ tablespoons powdered gelatine
4 tablespoons cold water

mixture of fresh fruits – for example,
clementine and pink grapefruit
segments, black grapes, sliced
starfruit and kiwi fruit
fresh lychees

Heat the milk in a pan until it is almost boiling. Remove from the heat and add the sugar, stirring until it has dissolved. Allow the mixture to cool slightly, then stir in the almond essence. Leave to cool again for about 10–15 minutes.

While the almond milk is cooling, sprinkle the gelatine into the water in a small bowl. When the water has been absorbed, dissolve the gelatine over a pan of hot water and leave to cool for about 5 minutes. Gradually pour the cooled gelatine into the milk mixture, stirring constantly. Pour into a shallow dish and allow to set in the refrigerator, about 2–3 hours.

Meanwhile, prepare a fresh fruit salad with a selection of your chosen fruit and the lychees. Cut the set almond jelly into diamond shapes and arrange them on top just before serving.

*Next page, from left ▷
to right: Floating Diamonds
(page 229);
Sydney Sunrise (page 233);
Mangoes with Sticky Rice
(page 228)*

Ginger Lychee Mousse

. . . .

One for the sweet-toothed – but the ginger prevents it from being too sweet. The dish looks rather like a light lemon soufflé.

SERVES 4 – 6

400 g (14 oz) canned lychees, drained –
but reserve 2 tablespoons juice
1 tablespoon stem ginger in syrup,
drained and chopped – reserve 1
tablespoon syrup

2 teaspoons powdered gelatine
300 ml (10 fl oz) double cream,
whipped
2 egg whites, stiffly beaten
whipped cream, to decorate

Chop most of the lychees with the ginger. Put the gelatine in a small bowl, add the lychee juice and dissolve over hot water. Lightly fold the cream into the stiffly beaten egg whites. Add the lychee mixture, reserved ginger syrup and dissolved gelatine, stirring well.

Pour into four or six glasses and chill for 2–3 hours, until set. Decorate with the remaining lychees and whipped cream.

Rice Fritters

. . . .

Serve these as a snack, rather than a pudding.

MAKES ABOUT 20

50 g (2 oz) plain flour
1 teaspoon baking powder
pinch of salt
2 eggs, beaten
½ teaspoon vanilla essence
3 tablespoons caster sugar

4 tablespoons desiccated coconut
150 g (6 oz) short-grain (pudding) rice,
cooked
vegetable oil, for deep-frying
icing sugar, for dusting

Sift together the flour, baking powder and salt into a large bowl, then whisk in the eggs and vanilla essence. Stir in the sugar, coconut and cooked rice to make a thick batter.

Heat the oil in a deep-fat fryer to 180°C/350°F – test by popping in a cube of bread to see if it sizzles. Deep-fry tablespoonfuls of the mixture in the hot fat, one at a time, until nicely golden-brown. Drain on kitchen paper, then dust with icing sugar. Serve immediately.

Sydney Sunrise

Photograph on pages 230–1

. . . .

SERVES 2

2 tablespoons Australian runny honey –
    try eucalyptus blossom flavour
juice of 4 oranges
2 eggs

juice of 2 limes
¼ teaspoon cinnamon (optional)
2 slices of blood orange or lime, to
    decorate

Whisk together the honey, oranges, eggs and lime juice or whizz briefly in
a blender. Pour into glasses and sprinkle with cinnamon, if using. Pop the
slices of blood orange or lime on top. Drink and wake up!

*I know its alcohol-free
but it is full of sunshine.*

Lassi

Here is a recipe for Lassi (see page 212).

Whizz 350 ml (12 fl oz) rich, creamy (but not sweet) yoghurt, 3 tablespoons double cream, 1 tablespoon rosewater and either 75 g (3 oz) sugar
or some salt to taste, depending on whether you like it salty or sweet, until
the sugar or salt has dissolved.

  Then add several ice cubes and whizz for 30 seconds more, until the
mixture is thick and frothy, but with some ice crystals. Pour into chilled
glasses. This should make enough for 2 or 3 servings.

The last Aussie shopping list

ABALONE This is a type of mollusc with a delicate flavour, similar to the clam. Once extracted from the shell, the abalone should be cleaned to leave the white 'meat'. This should then be tenderised with a mallet. Cook quickly in stir-fries for 3–4 minutes. As a substitute, use either clams or scallops.

BAMBOO SHOOTS As their name suggests, these are the young edible shoots of bamboo. Sold fresh in Far Eastern markets, they are sold canned everywhere else. Drain and use in stir-fries and salads.

BEAN SAUCE Known as yellow bean and brown or black bean sauce as well, bean sauce is made from crushed yellow soya beans, mixed to a paste with flour, vinegar, spices and salt. It tastes quite salty, but has a spicy, aromatic flavour. Sold in jars and cans and available in large supermarkets under popular brand names – look in the oriental foods section.

BLACK BEANS These are whole soy beans preserved in salt and ginger. When combined with other ingredients, black beans give a delicious, slightly salty flavour to a dish. The dried ones are best and they can be stored for months in a cool, dry place. It is also possible to buy black beans canned in brine – rinse them before use. Transfer any unused canned beans and liquid to a screw-topped jar and keep in the refrigerator – they will keep for ages in this way.

CELLOPHANE NOODLES See Noodles.

COCONUT MILK Coconut milk is one of the most important ingredients in Thai cooking, featuring in all types of dishes. You can buy coconut milk in cans, from oriental stores and this is by far the easiest to use. Make sure it is unsweetened. Otherwise, coconut milk is made by soaking the flesh of fresh coconut in boiling water or milk, then extracting the liquid. It is also possible to use dried, unsweetened (desiccated) coconut available from health food shops. Use ordinary silver-top milk to make the coconut milk rather than water – it will produce a much richer, creamier result. It will also produce the heavier coconut cream that will rise to the surface and can be skimmed off to use in various recipes.

To make about 250 ml (9 fl oz) coconut milk, heat 500 ml (18 fl oz) milk until almost boiling. Remove from the heat and stir in 225 g (8 oz) unsweetened desiccated coconut. Allow to cool to room temperature, stirring from time to time. Pour through a sieve, using the back of a spoon to extract as much liquid as possible. If you need coconut cream, allow to stand so that this rises to the surface, then skim.

You can use the leftover coconut again for further extractions, but these really will be thinner and less flavoursome. Treat coconut milk as you would fresh milk – keep in the refrigerator and use within a couple of days.

CHILLI PEPPERS Fresh chilli peppers come in a variety of colours, from yellow to purplish-black, as well as different degrees of hotness. Their flavour mellows when cooked, but if you've added too many, there is, I'm afraid, little you can do to rescue a dish.

The general rule is the smaller the chilli, the hotter it is. The seeds and ribs are the hottest bits so these are often discarded. But the heat and flavour of all chillies vary enormously, so it is a good idea to taste some to see and adjust the amount you're using accordingly. The smallest chillies are usually found in specialist stores whereas supermarkets tend to stock the larger, milder types. Do not do what I did when cooking yabbies on Kangaroo Island, rub your eye while chopping one up. So remember, wash your hands!

When a recipe calls for dried chillies, you should either leave them whole or cut them in half lengthways, and leave the seeds in. Dried chillies are quite small – only about 1 cm (½ inch) long – and add quite a bit of oomph to a dish. Take them out before serving if you don't like too hot a flavour. They can be bought from many supermarkets and specialist stores and they keep well.

CHINESE DRIED MUSHROOMS See Mushrooms, Chinese Dried.

CHINESE LEAVES Like an elongated white cabbage in appearance, Chinese leaves are refreshing and crisp. The tender leaves are great in stir-fries – cook, shredded, for 2–3 minutes, until just heated through.

CORIANDER, FRESH Did you know that coriander is the world's most popular herb? It is widely used in cooking all over South-east Asia, China, Japan, India, the Middle East etc. The leaves should be strewn over a dish just before serving or stirred in towards the end of cooking so their fresh, distinctive flavour is not lost. Although coriander is sometimes called Chinese parsley, English parsley is a very poor substitute for it. And many supermarkets as well as oriental stores do stock coriander nowadays. Look for deep-green and not tired or wilting leaves.

In Asia coriander is sold complete with root, but in the West they tend to cut the roots off. The roots and stems are also used in Asian cooking, either finely chopped or pounded, in marinades and curry pastes and so on. If you do get the chance to buy some coriander roots from a specialist shop, they will keep well in an airtight jar.

CREAMED COCONUT Sold in slabs or packets in many supermarkets, it is more concentrated than coconut milk.

To make coconut milk from it, cut up, say, 75 g (3 oz) and then heat gently with 175 ml (6 fl oz) water, stirring until dissolved. Use as coconut milk, see above.

CURRY PASTE, RED OR GREEN See Red Curry Paste.

FISH PASTE This is a thick paste made from fermented fish or shrimps and salt. It is used in small amounts as a relish and is available from Chinese and oriental stores. You could use anchovy essence or paste as an alternative.

FISH SAUCE This is a light, clear liquid with a similar consistency to soy sauce. It is salty and gives a very distinctive flavour – it is as fundamental a flavouring for Vietnamese and Thai cooking as salt is for Western. It is made from fresh anchovies and salt that are layered in wooden barrels and left to ferment. The liquid that is drained off first is considered to be the best quality; the later extractions are darker and poorer in quality. It is available, bottled, from oriental stores and some supermarkets.

FIVE SPICE POWDER A fragrant mixture of spices that usually includes cinnamon, cloves, fennel, Sichuan peppercorns and star anise. Available in most supermarkets in the spice section.

GALINGALE Called laos in Malay cooking, galingale is related to ginger, but has a more delicate flavour. It can be bought fresh from oriental stores, and needs to be peeled like ginger before slicing. It is also sold as a powder and dried – soak before using and fish out and discard before serving.

GINGER, FRESH ROOT The wonderfully refreshing, pungent, citrus-like aroma and flavour – as well as hotness – that fresh root ginger adds to all kinds of meat dishes, fish, shellfish, marinades and so on is only just beginning to be appreciated in Western cooking. It will transform even a dish of plainly-cooked vegetables and it is, of course, indispensable to many Asian cuisines.

The pale-brown, gnarled skin has to be peeled, like a potato, before it can be grated, chopped, sliced, whatever. Fresh root ginger will keep in the refrigerator for a couple of weeks, but make sure when you buy it that the skin is firm and isn't at all shrivelled-looking.

GHEE A type of clarified butter with a strong, sweet and nutty flavour, ghee is, of course, used extensively in Indian cooking. You can buy it ready-made from Asian grocers. If you want to make it yourself, then melt, say, 100–225 g (4–8 oz) unsalted butter in a pan over a low heat. Skim off any froth or impurities, then cook it very gently for 30–45 minutes, until the sediment at the bottom of the pan has become golden-brown. (This means the butter has caramelised and produces the sweetish flavour.) Strain through a sieve well-lined with muslin, then store in the refrigerator.

GREEN CURRY PASTE See Red Curry Paste.

HOISIN SAUCE Dark reddish-brown in colour, this thick sauce is sweet and spicy. It is made from soy beans, wheat flour, salt, sugar, vinegar, garlic, chilli and sesame oil. It is used as a dip for marinades and other recipes. Sold in jars and tins, it is available from Chinese grocers, delicatessens and some supermarkets. Once opened, it will keep in a screw-topped jar in the refrigerator for several months.

LEMON GRASS This looks a little like a hard-skinned, elongated spring onion, with fibrous, grey-green leaves. It adds an intense, but not sharp, lemon flavour and scent to cooking. You can buy it fairly easily from the greengrocer's sections in supermarkets and from specialist stores. When a recipe specifies chopped or sliced, then the bulky part is the bit to use. Trim the end and slice finely. One blade or stalk should give about 3 tablespoons finely-sliced lemon grass. Alternatively, the whole stalk can be bashed hard with a knife handle to release all the flavour and then added while cooking; don't forget to take it out before serving. Stalks will last for about 2–3 weeks in the refrigerator. You could use chopped lemon balm leaves or grated lemon zest instead, but you would not get an authentic flavour. Powdered lemon grass is also available; it is often called sereh powder.

LIME LEAVES The glossy, dark-green lime leaves (from the Keffir lime, which has a more knobbly skin than the familiar lime) give dishes a lovely lemony-lime flavour. You can find them, packed in plastic bags, in some specialist oriental shops – and it is well worth the effort looking for them – otherwise you can usually find dried lime leaves.

MUSHROOMS **Chinese Dried** Known as dried shiitake in Japan, these can be black or brown, are very fragrant and have a different flavour from the fresh varieties. Buy from Chinese grocers. To use, soak in warm water for 30 minutes or so, then squeeze out and cut away the tough stems.
Straw Popular in Chinese cookery, straw mushrooms are extremely tasty and have dark brown caps moulded against their stalks. They are available canned – look out for them in oriental stores and delicatessens. Some supermarkets may also stock them. Rinse and drain before use.

NOODLES, CELLOPHANE Very fine, transparent noodles, these are sometimes called 'glass' noodles or 'bean thread vermicelli' as they are made from ground mung beans. Available dried from Chinese grocers and some supermarkets, they need to be soaked for 5 minutes in warm water, then drained before use.

OYSTER SAUCE Dark brown in colour,

this thick sauce is made from a concentrate of oysters cooked with soy sauce, wheat flour, cornflour and rice. It has a rich flavour that is not fishy, despite its name. Often part of recipes for Chinese cookery, it can also be used as a condiment.

PAK CHOY Chinese dark-green cabbage or *pak choy* looks like spinach or Swiss chard and was originally grown in Shanghai where it was considered the king of vegetables for its crispness and light fresh taste. It cooks quickly and is ideal for stir-fries.

RED OR GREEN CURRY PASTE Used in Thai cooking, this aromatic paste can be bought in jars or foil packets from Asian food shops. You can make it yourself, though – see the recipe on page 129.

RICE VINEGAR Distilled from white rice, rice vinegar has a very sweet, aromatic quality and is much milder than cider vinegar. Most cider and white vinegars can be used instead, but do try and find the real thing from Chinese or other specialist shops.

SESAME SEEDS Sesame seeds are usually white, but they can be black, red or brown too. They have a delicious nutty flavour, particularly after roasting. To roast sesame seeds, dry fry them in a heavy, heated frying pan until they turn darker and give out a wonderful roasted aroma.

SESAME OIL A strongly-flavoured seasoning oil which, if you're buying the real thing, is made from roasted sesame seeds. Many European sesame oils are made from unroasted seeds and are a pale yellow in colour as well as less flavoursome. So it is worth tracking down authentic brands from specialist stores. Sesame oil is used for its fragrance and for the flavour it adds to foods, rather than as a cooking oil as it burns easily. It keeps well.

SHRIMP PASTE This is sometimes called terasi, and should be used fairly

sparingly. Some recipes call for it to be mixed with spices to make a paste that is then sautéed. Buy it from oriental stores. Anchovy paste could be used as an alternative.

SOY SAUCE Made from fermented soya beans, wheat flour, water and salt, soy sauce has a high salt content – not good for your blood pressure! There are two main types of soy sauce:
Light Obviously, light in colour but full of flavour, it is saltier than the dark variety and best used in cooking.
Dark This is aged much longer than light soy sauce, hence its darker colour. It is a little thicker and stronger too and is better for dipping sauces, and for adding colour to dishes as well as flavour.

Most soy sauces sold in supermarkets are the dark version, but Chinese stores sell both and usually the more authentic brands.

STAR ANISE Shaped like an eight-pointed star, this spice has a pungent liquorice taste that is used to add flavour to meat and poultry.

TAMARIND Now you will be interested to know that tamarind is the dried fruit of the tamarind tree, native to East Africa. It is sometimes called an Indian date because the tree is grown all over India and the fruit has a sticky appearance. It has a sharp, acidic taste.

To use, soak a small piece in water for 5 minutes or so, until pulpy, then rub through a sieve and use the water. The longer you soak the tamarind the stronger the flavour. If necessary, use double the amount of lemon juice that the recipe specifies for tamarind water.

WATER CHESTNUTS These, in fact, are not nuts at all, but tubers with a crisp texture. They are usually bought canned, but you can occasionally find them fresh. These are much tastier than the canned ones, though the latter have good texture. Peel fresh ones and drain and rinse canned ones before use.

Index